Vocational Education

Vocational education and training (VET) have a key role to play in raising skill levels and improving a society's productivity. In this important new book, a team of international experts argue that too often national VET policy has been formulated in ignorance of historical and political developments in other countries and without proper consideration of the social objectives that it might help achieve.

Examining a wide range of contrasting international approaches and development strategies, this book demonstrates the central role of the state in implementing an effective system of VET and assesses the extent to which different VET policies can promote equality in the labour market and social justice. Key themes include:

- The broader educational and social aims of VET
- The nature of learning in vocational contexts
- The historical development of VET in the UK, US, Australia, France, Germany, the Netherlands and elsewhere

Including a full range of case studies and practical examples, this book is essential reading for all students, researchers, practitioners and policy-makers with an interest in vocational education and training, industrial and labour relations or social policy.

Linda Clarke is Professor of European Industrial Relations at the Westminster Business School, University of Westminster, where she undertakes research on training, skills, wage and labour relations in Europe, particularly in the construction sector. Her publications include: *A Blueprint for Change: Construction Skills Training in Britain* (1998) and, as co-editor, *The Dynamics of Wage Relations in the New Europe* (2000).

Christopher Winch is Professor of Educational Philosophy and Policy at King's College, London. He has wide-ranging interests in the Philosophy of Education and in the aims, content and pedagogy of vocational education. His publications include *The Philosophy of Human Learning* (1998), *Education, Work and Social Capital* (2000) and *Education, Autonomy and Critical Thinking* (2005).

Vocational Education

International approaches, developments and systems

Edited by Linda Clarke and
Christopher Winch

Routledge
Taylor & Francis Group

LONDON AND NEW YORK

First published 2007
by Routledge
2 Park Square, Milton Park, Abingdon, Oxon OX14 4RN

Simultaneously published in the USA and Canada
by Routledge
270 Madison Avenue, New York, NY 10016

Routledge is an imprint of the Taylor & Francis Group, an informa business

Typeset in Perpetua and Bell Gothic by RefineCatch Limited, Bungay, Suffolk
Printed and bound in Great Britain by Antony Rowe Ltd, Chippenham, Wiltshire

British Library Cataloguing in Publication Data
A catalogue record for this book is available from the British Library

Library of Congress Cataloging in Publication Data
Vocational education : international approaches, developments and systems / edited by Linda Clarke
and Christopher Winch.
    p. cm
Includes bibliographical references and index.
1. Vocational education. I. Clarke, Linda, 1947– II. Winch, Christopher.
LC1043.V624 2007
370.11'3–dc22   2007001184

ISBN10: 0–415–38060–X (hbk)
ISBN10: 0–415–38061–8 (pbk)

ISBN13: 978–0–415–38060–7 (hbk)
ISBN13: 978–0–415–38061–4 (pbk)

July 28, 2008

Contents

Contributors

Linda Clarke is Professor of European Industrial Relations at the Westminster Business School, University of Westminster and has been responsible for research projects on training, employment, wages relations, skills, gender and ethnic segregation, and diversity in Europe. Originally a historian, she has a burning interest in social history and a particular expertise in the construction sector, being on the presidium of the European Institute for Construction Labour Research. Her publications include: *Building Capitalism* (Routledge 1992), *The Dynamics of Wages Relations in the New Europe* (co-editor, Kluwer 2000) and *Women in Construction* (co-editor, CLR Studies 2/Reed 2004).

Jean-Paul Géhin is Professor of Sociology at the University of Poitiers and the Head of the Research Laboratory, SACO (Savoir, cognition et rapports sociaux, UE 3815). His interests are divided between the sociology of education and the sociology of labour. He is the author of numerous books and articles on these subjects, and especially on vocational education, training and development and lifelong learning.

Wolf-Dietrich Greinert was Professor of Vocational Education and Research into Vocational Education at Hannover Technical University and Berlin Technical University. His main areas of research are: the social history of vocational education; analysis of vocational education systems; and comparative international research on vocational education. He has more than two hundred publications including numerous books and has been translated into the major European languages as well as into Japanese and Chinese.

Paul Hager has been involved in vocational education for over thirty years, with his major focus being the professional development of vocational teachers and trainers. Since the 1990s he has concentrated on contributing to Australia's expanding research programme in vocational education and training. He was a joint author of the 1992 report *No Small Change: Proposals for a Research and Development Strategy for Vocational Education and Training in Australia*. He is the author (with David Beckett) of *Life, Work and Learning* (Routledge 2002).

John Halliday is Professor of Education in the Department of Educational and Professional Studies, University of Strathclyde, Glasgow. He is a philosopher of education with wide-ranging intellectual interests and publications. His recent book, co-authored with Paul Hager, is published by Springer and titled *Recovering Informal Learning: Wisdom, Judgement and Community.*

Georg Hanf is head of the International Monitoring and Benchmarking/European VET Policy unit of the Federal Institute for Vocational Education and Training in Bonn, Germany. His main area of interest is comparative research into the development of VET systems in Europe. He is the author of numerous articles on the history of VET, the impact of EU policy on the German VET system, qualifications systems and frameworks.

John Holford is Professor of Political Education in the Department of Political, International and Policy Studies, University of Surrey. His interests are in adult education, citizenship and social movements. His book *Union Education in Britain* (Nottingham 1994) is a full-length history of the Trades Union Congress' (TUC) work in trade union education. He is joint editor of the *International Journal of Lifelong Education* (Routledge). His recent work has addressed informal adult learning of citizenship in Europe, adult citizenship education in Britain, as well as more general themes in lifelong education.

Ewart Keep is Professor in the Cardiff School of Social Sciences, Cardiff University, and Deputy Director of the ESRC Centre on Skills, Knowledge and Organisational Performance. His research interests include education and training policy, 14–19 education and training, lifelong learning and the relationship between skills and economic performance.

Theodore Lewis is Professor in the Department of Work and Human Resources, College of Education and Human Development, University of Minnesota. His interests include issues at the intersection of school and work, and technology and design as a school subject. He has published widely on these topics, including 'Tracking, Expectations, and the Transformation of Vocational Education' (with Cheng, S.-H.), *American Journal of Education* (2006), 113(1); 'At the Interface of School and Work', *Journal of Philosophy of Education* (2005), 39(3), and 'Design and Inquiry: Bases for an Accommodation between Science and Technology Education?', *Journal of Research in Science Teaching* (2006), 43(3).

Philippe Méhaut is an economist, and a senior researcher at the French national centre for scientific research. His main fields of research are human resources management and public policies concerning training and educational questions. He is the author of numerous articles and books, most of which are situated in an international perspective.

Richard Pring, Professor, is Lead Director of the Nuffield Review 14–19 Education and

Training, England and Wales, and formerly Director at the University of Oxford's Department of Educational Studies. His recent books include: *The Philosophy of Educational Research* (Continuum 2004, 2nd edition) and *Philosophy of Education: Aims, Values, Common Sense and Research* (Continuum 2004).

Anneke Westerhuis is team leader of the Expertise Centre for VET in The Netherlands. Her interests are in the multi-dimensional system developments in VET. She has published several books and articles in English, including *European Structures of Qualification Levels: Volumes 1–3* (Office for Official Publications of the European Communities 2001) and *Research and Innovation in Vocational Education and Training: A European Discussion* (CINOP 2005).

Christopher Winch is Professor of Educational Philosophy and Policy in the Department of Education and Professional Studies, King's College, London. His interests are in Philosophy of Education and Vocational Education. He is the author of numerous books and articles, including *Education, Work and Social Capital* (Routledge 2000) and *Education, Autonomy and Critical Thinking* (Routledge 2005).

Acknowledgements

This book has been a long while coming to fruition, though each passing year of frustration with the vocational education system in Britain has reinforced to us the need for a book showing that other approaches and developments are possible. In the meantime, thanks to support from the Economic and Social Research Council (ESRC), we were able to organize a seminar series entitled 'Vocational Education: Aims, Values and History' which ran from 2002 to 2003 and from which the book has greatly benefited. We would like to thank all the participants in and contributors (a number of whose contributions appear here) to this series, as well as the various institutions which hosted the seminars, for the valuable discussions, comments, ideas and suggestions that they made which have helped to make this volume far better than it would otherwise have been.

Much of the material in John Halliday's contribution 'Social Justice and Vocational Education' appeared earlier as 'Distributive Justice and Vocational Education' and is being used, with the kind permission of the publishers of the *British Journal of Educational Studies*, 22(4), 2004, pp. 151–165.

Thanks are also due to our respective departments and universities for the support given to this endeavour: the Westminster Business School of the University of Westminster and the Department of Education of King's College, London. We would also like to thank Janet Fraser for her translations of Chapters 4 and 13.

Finally, we would like to thank Jörn Janssen and Cathy Winch for their patience and valued advice.

Chapter 1

Introduction

Linda Clarke and Christopher Winch

If we regard vocational education broadly as concerned with the social development of labour, we can begin to see what a critical role it plays. As a guardian of entry into the labour market, it acts as a filter, dividing labour into different occupations, each with a distinct quality, skill and status. This filter may act as a means of inclusion or exclusion, giving certain groups access to particular occupations and denying others. Women, those from ethnic minority groups, and those with disabilities may be discouraged or prevented from entering particular labour market occupations, whether through their schooling, by the system of vocational education and training (VET) provision or by the fact that their group is seriously underrepresented. In this sense, VET is to do with the division of labour in society, whether on the basis of class, gender or ethnicity.

The ways in which particular qualities of labour are nurtured, advanced and reproduced through VET tells us a great deal too about the value accorded to labour in society. For the state, the aim of VET is to improve the productive capacity of society on the assumption that the greater the effort and investment put into this, the more productive the labour. In this respect, VET is critical to productivity, to producing value in production. For the individual, VET is about preparation for working life and about entering and progressing in the labour market, on the assumption that the greater the care and time given to this, the longer it will stand him or her in good stead. The employer, on the other hand, has more immediate concerns, regarding vocational education as a means of skilling labour to meet the immediate needs of the particular firm. These are conflicting interests and, as a result, the VET system represents a compromise and at the same time reflects the power attached to each of these different interests. The British employer-based system, for instance, is more directed to firm-specific skills than the state-dominated French system or the German system built on consensus between the social partners, that is the employers and the employees.

The approach to and the development of VET tends therefore to be specific to different societies. And when we examine these, we gain insights not only into our own society but into similarities and differences with other societies, thereby opening up alternative policy options. This is especially important at this moment in history when VET systems in the Anglo-Saxon world and in many European countries, on which this book is focussed, are in a process of profound transformation. The apprenticeship system in many countries is in crisis as employers increasingly abdicate responsibility for training. At the same time, VET has itself become increasingly school and college based, giving the state a potentially more extended regulatory role. And the trans-European and indeed trans-continental mobility of labour means that the different qualities and skills of labour increasingly confront each other, leading to ever-louder calls for international recognition of skills and qualifications. Our study is therefore apposite in informing both national and international VET policy and in highlighting the difficulties in establishing some form of equivalence between skills, qualifications and VET systems.

This volume is the product of a series of seminars, supported by the Economic and Social Research Council and held over a two-year period between 2003 and 2004. The series was intended to present a range of examples of developments in and approaches to VET and in this way to help set United Kingdom (UK) policy and practice in an international perspective. It integrated historical, conceptual and policy perspectives on VET thematically and provided an opportunity for academics, practitioners and policy makers from Britain and abroad to evaluate and discuss together policies on VET and their impact. It involved many a lively discussion and was a rare occasion for many of those attending from Britain to appreciate different VET systems, particularly those developed on mainland Europe.

This book shares with the seminar series the aim of helping to improve the knowledge and profile of VET through giving it a clearer historical and conceptual underpinning. It is an aim guided by a growing concern, if not alarm, with policy towards VET in the UK and especially in England. Through government encouragement, 42 per cent of school-leavers in England and Wales are today guided through the GCSE (General Certificate of Secondary Education) and 'A' (Advanced) level qualification route towards entry into higher university education. This route remains the 'sacred cow' of education policy for young people. But what of the remaining 58 per cent of young people? They are confronted with a myriad of alternative routes, whether staying on at school, going to Further Education (FE) College, apprenticeship or entering into employment. These do not constitute a 'system', though the diplomas soon to be introduced represent another attempt at least to systemise the qualifications which can be obtained through the school and college-based routes, just as the GNVQs (General National Vocational Qualifications) attempted to before them.

The school and college-based 'vocational route' thereby represents a second route, distinct both from the 'A' level/higher education and the work-based apprenticeship routes. Indeed, despite its 'vocational' label, this second route offers little work experience and is not an automatic route into employment. In FE Colleges the vocational route is often very much more 'vocational' than in the schools, covering such activities as carpentry, bricklaying and catering as opposed to the childcare, media and leisure-related options which tend to be offered in schools. In FE too, vocational education provided is regarded as preparation for work in a particular occupation, given the variable quality and paucity of apprentice places available, though it offers little possibility to obtain the necessary work experience.

A third route, apprenticeship, is underpinned by the employer-led NVQ (National Vocational Qualification) system, which provides a tool to assess workplace learning. It represents a route of variable quality in training terms, dependent for places on individual employers' goodwill and for skill formation on the nature of the activity undertaken and on day release once a week or block release to college. As a result, whilst there are some exemplary high quality apprenticeships available, these are becoming ever rarer and the apprenticeship route is in considerable danger. This is because of both a lack of places, as employers have little incentive and considerable risk and cost in taking on apprentices, and lack of diversity, as apprenticeships remain largely confined to traditional occupations and target groups. The newly launched Skills Academies represent an attempt to address these problems, whilst remaining firmly locked into the British employer-led tradition.

The book is focussed on the vocational routes, on the 'other' and larger half of the educational divide. It sprang out of a continual puzzlement and anger about the undervaluing of VET in England compared to much of continental Europe, an under-valuing which extends to the workforce itself where the skilled carpenter or engineer shares nothing like the same status in society as his or her equivalent in a country such as Scandinavia or Germany. We hope to show how and why VET can — and indeed must — be valued differently to the benefit of the individual, employers and society and the economy at large. Thus, though the focus is on VET in many different countries, it is always with the perspective of informing the British situation and those with considerable similarities to it, like the systems of the US and Australia. As a result, even our terminology — the use of terms such as 'skill' and 'training' — remains inevitably with an Anglo-Saxon bias, as does consideration of the literature in the area which follows.

THE DEVELOPMENT OF COMPARATIVE VET RESEARCH

This volume is distinctive in its intention to draw out different approaches to VET internationally, to explore their philosophical underpinnings and to trace their histor-ical developments. The international and comparative study of vocational education in English and emanating largely from Britain has proceeded apace since the 1980s, though it has been largely dominated by sociological and economic concerns. It includes some notable landmarks, beginning with the publication of a series of com-parative studies of the way in which qualifications and skills are configured and related both to the changing workplace and to productivity in different European countries

(Prais 1995). This series showed the quite different levels of skill and knowledge deployed in comparable sectors. The suggestion was that different forms of vocational education were responsible for such differences and that, therefore, the quantity and quality of labour deployed and its productivity are related in an important way to national vocational education systems. The work reflected the growing policy concerns with the low levels of productivity in the British economy compared to many other leading European countries and gave supporting evidence to attribute this to the level of skills and hence to the VET system.

Ashton and Green (1996) – another landmark – took up a distinction first made by Finegold (1991) between economies that develop and operate as 'high skill' and 'low skill' equilibria, applying this to a comparative study of a variety of national VET systems in economically developed countries, including not just the major ones in Europe, but also Japan, the United States and Singapore. A skills equilibrium is seen as a relatively stable state of affairs that satisfies the interests of the concerned parties – employers, employees and customers (Varoufakis and Hargraves-Heap 1995). In Ashton and Green's (1996) typology of skill equilibria, the UK is characterized as a low skill equilibrium country, whilst Japan and most of northern Europe exemplify a high skill equilibrium, and the United States a mixed high-low skill equilibrium. Different models of high skill equilibrium, some dependent on the active role of the state, others on social partnership of some form or another, were also identified. Thus this work too has served to highlight the distinct nature of the skill structure in Britain and the importance of raising the value of skills for any future development.

A third landmark in the literature on the subject available in English is Jobert, Marry, Tanguy and Rainbird (1997) which examined the interconnected relationships between education and work in Britain, Germany and Italy and was coordinated by a French team of researchers. This is noteworthy in its concern to scrutinize the questions, concepts and analytical approaches distinctive to particular countries, thereby representing a more theoretical approach, one which does not take for granted Anglo-Saxon usage of such terms as 'skills', 'qualifications' and 'vocational education'. Indeed, it sought to examine and extend the *effet sociale* approach developed by the Laboratoire d'Economie et de Sociologie du Travail (LEST) at the University of Aix-en-Provence, of which the most notable work is Maurice, Sellier and Silvestre's (1986) *Social Foundation of Industrial Power*. This latter compared wage labour relations, skill formation, occupational mobility, firm organization and industrial relations in France and Germany and challenged the view that societies converge towards similar industrial structures and relations.

In arguing that national specificities are maintained through relations in education, training and promotion, the work of Maurice *et al.* (1986) is especially important to this book. It showed the institutionally bound nature of the labour and productive systems in different countries and their dependence on education. The suspicion raised, that labour has distinct qualities which are related to its historical, institutional and social contexts, was reinforced at this time too by Biernacki's *The Fabrication of*

4

Labor (1995), a seminal work comparing the historical development of labour in Britain and Germany. This showed that divergent understandings of the essential character of labour as a commodity in the two countries influenced industrial development, affecting experiences of industrial work, methods of remuneration, disciplinary techniques and forms of collective action. In Germany, labour is formed and rewarded on the basis of *Arbeitskraft*, that is 'labour power' or the potential and inherent capacity of the labour itself. In Britain, in contrast, labour is – as Biernacki expresses it – 'concretized in products', or, in other words, appropriated for its output and not its intrinsic qualities (1995: 42–3). Though this was not Biernacki's subject, it nevertheless follows that such a distinction is fundamental to understanding the rationale of the VET systems in the two countries.

Subsequent literature has examined more closely and from a more Anglo-Saxon perspective the VET systems underlying different approaches to economic development. Finlay *et al.* (1998), for example, presented changes in, and long-term strategies for, VET systems in different countries, highlighting the ways in which these have benefited economies, been coordinated with economic and industrial policies, and achieved consensus amongst stakeholders. Green, Wolf and Leney (1999) looked at the ways in which different national VET systems in Europe are organized, noting school-based systems, such as in France, apprenticeship-based systems such as Germany and mixed ones, such as the UK, and arguing that these systems show no obvious convergence. The authors emphasized the deep historical roots and persistence of the different national systems and built upon the work of Green (1990), which had examined the role of the state in developing and, in some cases, building national education systems in general and VET systems in particular.

Subsequent work looked in more detail and in a comparative way at VET systems within different countries, trying to tease out how they operate, how they mesh with the economy and how they differ from each other. Notable among these studies were Crouch, Finegold and Sako's (1999) exploration of the difficulties presented by the institutional diversity of skill formations in advanced industrial countries and the relation between VET and employment policy. Brown, Green and Lauder (2001) developed this further in their comparison of national routes to and policies for a high skills economy in Britain, Germany, Japan, Singapore, South Korea and the USA. This stressed the necessity for a multi-disciplinary approach to the study of skill formation, a study seen to lie at the heart of the social sciences and becoming a central plank in national debates concerning globalization, economic competitiveness and social justice. Our more philosophical and historical approach well complements this, including its rejection of the evolutionary model of technology as the motor of social progress. The comparative theme was continued with the publication of Warhurst, Grugulis and Keep (2004), which concentrated on the concept of skill and noted its shifting usage but without, however, seeking to develop a critique of the way in which 'skill' – a concept peculiar to the Anglo-Saxon world – is used, or to compare 'skill' with cognate terms in different languages.

5

While these studies mostly argued for the importance of VET for skill formation and for economic and social development, there were others – more in tune with the prevailing political and economic climate in Britain – which adopted a more sceptical attitude to the need for systematic VET as a prerequisite for economic success. These took their cue from Adam Smith (1776), who argued that employers attend to their own skill needs in ways that they find fit, and that, more controversially, in many sectors and in certain strata, the fragmentation of the labour process – subsequently described as 'Taylorism' and 'Fordism' – makes universal extensive skill development superfluous, a thesis also familar in the popular idea of deskilling as a consequence of technical progress. Although not situating itself explicitly within this tradition, *Does Education Matter?* (Wolf 2002), for example, expresses considerable scepticism about the capability of education systems in general and state-sponsored VET to benefit economic development. The collection of contributions presented in this volume does not support this scepticism. It shows rather not only how important VET has been to the development of labour power and hence of society (e.g. Westerhuis, Chapter 2, and Hanf, Chapter 7), but also how approaches to it vary with the value accorded to labour (e.g. Clarke, Chapter 5).

WHAT ARE THE DIFFERENT APPROACHES TO VET?

Although this literature – and Green (1990) in particular – draws on social and cultural differences in the way in which VET is perceived, little comparative or analytical work has been carried out to examine either the ideas that animate different VET systems or their different historical developments.

Ideas animating VET can be approached in two broadly different, although not necessarily incompatible ways. The first of these is *hermeneutic*, whereby the evolution of central concepts within societies is examined with a view to interrogating their current meaning. The second is to analyse and explain the meaning of current terms in use. Neither of these approaches has been widely applied to VET, even within a national context. A notable exception would be, for example, Pring's *Closing the Gap* (1995) in relation to the English system. This volume breaks new ground in VET studies by paying particular attention to the origins of the central ideas that animate VET systems in different parts of the world and the ways in which those ideas came to be so dominant. By putting together a collection that does this for different countries (especially Britain, France, Germany, the Netherlands and the USA), we hope that readers will come to appreciate the importance of these ideas and how they differ from country to country.

Comparison of the ideas and concepts underlying different VET systems has considerable practical as well as academic importance, particularly within the European Union (EU). The Lisbon Agreement of 2000 set out an aspiration for the countries within the EU to improve the overall VET performance of Europe and to integrate and make more transparent the diverse VET systems across Europe. This is to be achieved through specific, highly ambitious projects. One of these is the European Credit (Transfer) System of Vocational Education and Training (ECVET), which aims to develop an EU-wide modular and credit accumulation scheme for VET. The other is the European Qualification Framework (EQF), launched in pilot form in 2006, which aims to provide a translation device for VET qualifications in different countries so that they can be compared with each other. With these projects, we can begin to see the difficulties in gaining mutual understanding of historically different VET systems and the central concepts and different realities associated with each. These difficulties are likely to have a direct impact on the transferability of vocational education and of qualifications. This collection aims, therefore, to help readers appreciate such difficulties and at the same time to lay the basis for developing transcendent categories and concepts that can be applied transnationally.

What are the potential problems entailed in transferring skills and qualifications? Well, they surface within the contributions to this book. Given the specificities of each VET system, terminology in one country cannot easily be translated from the language of that country into another language without losing the distinct meaning attached to it. The English verb 'to train' is a case in point. It is used in at least three distinct senses in English, while other languages, for example German, use a different word in each case: first, in the sense of to train an animal, where German uses the verb *abrichten* or, in familiar use, the word *trainieren;* second to train someone to carry out a specific job or activity, where German uses *anlernen;* and, finally, the sense of education for an occupation like medicine or carpentry, where German uses *ausbilden*. These distinctions are not mere terminological peculiarities but reflect conceptual distinctions. Gilbert Ryle (1949) attempted to distinguish the first two through a distinction between 'drilling' and 'training', but was uncomfortable with the presupposition of the term *Ausbildung* which in German implies learning to apply occupationally relevant theory to the practice of the occupation, together with a significant element of general and civic education. Again, the term 'occupation' if used as the translation of the German *Beruf* misses not only the social status and significance of that term within German society, but also the application of theoretical knowledge to practice and the responsibility which it implies. Another term widely used in English, 'skill' – defined in the *Oxford Dictionary of Etymology* as 'practical knowledge with ability' (Onions 1996) – has even more acute translation problems, having no equivalent in other languages. German, for instance, distinguishes between *Fertigkeit* (similar to a simple, usually manual skill like drilling or planing wood) and *Fähigkeit* which is more akin to a holistic occupational capacity such as being a carpenter.

Such distinctions are very evident from the approach to German VET outlined by Wolf-Dietrich Greinert (Chapter 4) and to British VET by Christopher Winch (Chapter 10). Greinert highlights the importance of notions of *Beruf* and *Bildung* to the German system, which succeed in incorporating a general and civic education. In contrast, Winch carefully dismantles the sharp opposition built into the British system

7

between liberal education, exclusively concerned with personal development and/or induction into the high culture of the society, and vocational education. These conceptual differences are vital to understanding the aims and nature of VET in different countries. The signs are, however, at the time of writing, that the translation of the key documents setting up the EQF ignores such important nuances. Thus, for example, the English term 'skill' which has quite a broad use, although it is rooted in the idea of a simple manual or coordinating ability, is translated in documentation setting out the EQF as *Fertigkeit* which begs questions about how broad the concept of skill is in current official usage. Another example concerns the term 'general education' whose German equivalent is given as *Allgemeinbildung*.[1] The German term, however, carries with it a hermeneutic significance, as evident from Wilhelm von Humboldt's discussion of the role of a broadly based education as the basis for a continuing and possibly never completed process of both developing one's unique individuality and fitting into a settled place in the economic life of the society (Benner 2003).

The different concepts reflect in turn differences in the nature and development of different VET systems, as well as in the nature of labour and the labour market. There can be no sharper contrasts than between the French, German and British systems, though these countries adjoin each other. As described by Jean-Paul Géhin (Chapter 3), the French system, though built on a divide between the vocational and academic, reflects the post-revolutionary attempt to establish through state intervention a more general system to which all were seen to be entitled as a preparation for the whole working life. The development of the British VET system, in contrast, described by Linda Clarke (Chapter 5), is characterized by narrowly conceived work-based skills and based largely on *laissez-faire* voluntarism and employer goodwill, with VET provision divided from academic and professional education. And the German system, as outlined by Wolf-Dietrich Greinert (Chapter 4), represents a very different adaptation to capitalism, being built originally on the protection of the petty bourgeoisie and then, as Georg Hanf (Chapter 7) shows, adapted to modern industrial capitalism at the beginning of the twentieth century. None of these systems exist in isolation from each other. Indeed, it is fascinating to learn from Hanf's account the close relation between the American system and the setting up of the German Dual System of VET, even though John Dewey, the inspiration for the American system (see Theodore Lewis, Chapter 6), rejected the German divide between general and vocational education and the emphasis on trades rather than citizens.

We cannot claim to deal with all the conceptual and developmental differences in this volume. We do, however, lay a claim to sensitizing our readership to the fact that different VET systems have different social, historical, institutional and political roots and that these are reflected in differences in conceptual and linguistic usage in different European languages and in different practices.

WHAT IS VOCATIONAL EDUCATION?

In the Anglo-Saxon world, vocational education is confined to preparing young people and adults for working life, a process often regarded as of a rather technical and practical nature. Indeed, it is contrasted with *liberal education*, concerned with individual development and fulfilment, and also with *civic education*, seen as concerned with preparation for citizenship. These are not, however, mutually exclusive aspects of education and in many countries are not regarded as even dissociable, with vocational education embracing elements of both civic and academic education. A key difference often revolves around how preparation for working life is perceived and valued, whether for a series of different and often short-term jobs each requiring relatively narrow skills or as lifelong, enriching and variable involvement in the labour market. This in turn can be an issue of whether VET furthers the interests of the individual, serves the needs of the economy and particular employers, or represents a compromise between the two – an issue very much to do with the power and rights of particular groups within a society.

One of the concerns of the book is to illustrate the often uneasy, but always unavoidable, relationship that vocational education enjoys with liberal and civic education. Paul Hager (Chapter 8), for example, explains how, where apprenticeship is viewed as an on-the-job activity, then formal off-the-job vocational education becomes morally uplifting knowledge, associated with the 'self-improvement of the labouring classes', as a background to work and not as learning to perform work itself. This division underlies the Australian system just as it does the English system, as is apparent from Linda Clarke's account of its development (Chapter 5) and from John Halliday's (Chapter 11), Richard Pring's (Chapter 9) and Christopher Winch's (Chapter 10) criticisms of the divide erected between vocational education – associated with outputs and competences, assessment-led learning and performance indicators – and liberal education, associated with judgement, management and critical enquiry. In contrast, the Dutch VET system described by Anneke Westerhuis (Chapter 2) is all about civic education and seen as a means for productive labour (workers, tradesmen, etc.) to become citizens. As a result, vocational education in the Netherlands was never about practical training alone but always about personal development, about rising above the narrow confines of a trade.

A contrast frequently made in the Anglo-Saxon world is between 'training' and 'education' (e.g. Dearden 1984), the idea being that training is inculcation into a set of usually rigid routines, while education develops the whole person. Sometimes these two terms are even used to distinguish skill formation associated with the status of different occupations, 'training' being applied to manual occupations and 'education' to professional. We have chosen the term 'vocational education' advisedly, as a term without such discriminatory class connotations, covering different kinds of learning and teaching processes and more readily describing the broader systems found in many other countries. Some of these processes involve, but are usually not exhausted

9

by, episodes of 'training'. But they also encompass instruction, simulation and pro-bationary practice. In any case, the perhaps peculiarly English idea that training is akin to getting a rat to run in a maze is itself a gross oversimplification of what are very often complex and demanding processes which involve making judgements using specialised knowledge. Vocational education in our sense can also take place in a variety of institutions and at different stages of life. Some of our contributions deal with school-based vocational education (e.g. Lewis, Chapter 6, Pring, Chapter 9, and Géhin, Chapter 3), others deal with initial vocational education at the outset of employment (e.g. Greinert, Chapter 4, Westerhuis, Chapter 2, Géhin, Chapter 3), while others again deal with learning that takes place in the course of a person's employment (e.g. Hager, Chapter 8, Méhaut, Chapter 13, Holford, Chapter 14).

Vocational education is both complex and varied. Like other forms of education it has aims which may be combined in different ways and vary from society to society. Perhaps the simplest and – in Anglo-Saxon countries – most influential way of seeing vocational education is as training for particular jobs in order to serve the needs of current employers. This perception of vocational education is most readily recognized in the United States and the United Kingdom, being associated with the approach of Adam Smith in the 'Wealth of Nations' in the first instance (see Winch, Chapter 10, and Keep, Chapter 12) and that of David Snedden in the United States (Lewis, Chapter 6). It fits too with Biernacki's product-oriented characterization of labour in Britain (Biernacki 1995). But there has long been an opposed and no less vigorous tradition that sees vocational education as concerned with personal emancipation as much as economic development, and in this sense more closely associated with the German *Arbeitskraft* or labour power. Notable figures in this tradition are Georg Kerschensteiner in Germany (Greinert, Chapter 4) and John Dewey in the United States (Lewis, Chapter 6, and Pring, Chapter 9). Although these traditions are opposed, the different aims that they espouse are not completely incompatible. Kerschensteiner, for example, thought that individual development was a key to economic success in a country where the mental as well as the physical powers of the population were released. The idea here is that, by developing high levels of skill, employers could capitalise on them and make high specification goods and services, giving them a particular niche in the market. This was seen to be possible not only in craft-based economies but even in those, like Germany, which were adapting them-selves to mass production techniques at the beginning of the twentieth century (Hanf, Chapter 7). The development of high skills is still an aspiration in the United Kingdom though the preferred means of achieving it are problematic (Pring, Chapter 9, and Keep, Chapter 12).

One aspect of vocational education that has come to prominence in recent years is that of 'lifelong learning'. Although this is often associated with continuing self-development during adulthood (an important theme of Holford's Chapter 14), it is also associated with the perceived need of societies to adapt to the increasing pace of social and economic change in the modern world. Different societies have made particular efforts to continue to develop skills and knowledge over a working life. There are complex questions here about finance and incentives (Méhaut, Chapter 13), the optimum kinds of learning appropriate to the workplace (Hager, Chapter 8) and the availability of opportunities for different groups in society (Clarke, Chapter 5 and Hanf, Chapter 7). The very British instrumental–liberal divide in vocational education appears at this point as well. Should workers develop a cultivated awareness or will such efforts 'muddle their minds' as far as getting the job done is concerned? (Holford, Chapter 14) At the other extreme is the current employer fad for 'just in time' learning, which is relatively geared to low-skill activities related to particular tasks. One of the themes of Keep's Chapter 12 is the difficulty of weaning British employers from such a conception, which is very much in the Smith–Snedden tradition of thinking about vocational education.

The volume illustrates some of the main conceptions of vocational education that continue to be influential, how they originated, how they differ from and relate to each other, and how far the development of different systems reflects them.

WHAT IS THE ROLE OF THE STATE IN VET?

Another theme running through the volume is the very different role played by the state in education generally, and in vocational education in particular. Political philosophy in Britain traditionally conceived of the state as the 'nightwatchman', concerned with internal and external defence. Marx is the great exception to this tradition but, despite his argument that the state has a critical role in sustaining a mode of production such as feudalism or capitalism and despite some references to technical education, he did not consider the role of the state in education. His model of capitalism, and the role of the state in promoting and sustaining it, was heavily influenced by the work of Adam Smith and in many respects describes a form of development that fits better with the British than with the continental experience. Adam Smith and John Stuart Mill are both interested in education as a means of promoting civil stability and both ascribe a significant role to the state in doing so. Neither, however, attaches much importance to vocational education in general and still less to the role of the state in promoting it. Like Marx, neither Smith nor Mill is especially interested in the role of the state as a promoter of national consciousness.

In this respect, many commentators from within the disciplines of both political economy and political philosophy appear to have missed something important. There is good evidence that, in the era of the nation state, the state itself has been an important agent in promoting a durable national identity, often associated with a national ideology. The extension of unified markets within national boundaries was facilitated through state activity, whether improvements in policing and law, transport and communications infrastructure, and customs and monetary union. This development of capitalism in turn strengthened the role of the state in terms of regulation and its scope of operation. But national development did not depend merely on the unification of markets; the governments of nascent nation states were concerned to develop a sense of national unity through extending a common form of linguistic, historical and social awareness. This is a particularly striking feature of, for example, France (Géhin, Chapter 3), the Netherlands (Westerhuis, Chapter 2), Prussia (Greinert, Chapter 4) and, to a certain extent, the United States at the beginning of the nineteenth century, all of which developed national systems of elementary education at around this time and some of which went on to develop forms of vocational and technical education as well (Green 1990; Westerhuis, Chapter 2). Indeed, Westerhuis implies that the identity of the Dutch state was formed through the system of education that was developed.

The United States was impelled by both territorial aggrandizement and immigration to rapidly forge a sense of national consciousness. However, the very fact of mass immigration helped to contribute to a pool of skilled labour that reduced the immediate need for vocational education, the more so as there continued to be great economic expansion in the agricultural sector due, in turn, to territorial expansion. At the same time, shortages of skilled labour also provided an incentive to American capitalists to find ways of overcoming the need for traditional skills among their workforce in manufacturing industry (Waks 2004; Hanf in this volume, Chapter 7). Such an apparent contradiction was expressed in the conflict described by Lewis (Chapter 6) between Dewey, emphasising social reconstruction with the individual as the focus, and Sneddon, emphasizing social efficiency and focussed on the state. The outcome of this was a triumph for 'vocationalism' in high schools, making for the system of tracking which reinforced the unequal position of black people in American society.

France, on the other hand, had a revolution that destroyed most mediaeval institutions, including the corporations and the apprenticeship system. The revolution's own ideological commitments and the belligerence of hostile neighbours impelled it, both during and after the revolution, towards a state-directed education system and to setting up an elite system of higher education. This state-sponsored system of education thus extended from the civic and individual into the vocational sphere and this continues to be a characteristic feature of French VET (Green et al. 1999; Géhin, Chapter 3).

The French state affected developments in the rest of Europe, including the post-Napoleonic Prussian state which, following defeat by France in 1807 and without its former feudal social structure, sought to build itself on Enlightenment principles. A system of elementary, secondary and higher education was developed that reflected social class conditions, created a common sense of identity as a basis for citizenship, and laid the groundwork for vocational education. Education reform thus proceeded apace under the influence of – amongst others – Wilhelm von Humboldt. Vocation was an important aspect of this, together with a general education (*Allgemeinbildung*) which continued into adult life and which represented a drawn-out and possibly incomplete educational process (Hafner 1985: 240–1; Green 1990; Benner 2003).

Germany as a whole did not become a nation state until 1871, largely under the influence of Prussia. Before then, at a time when such a policy was not popular with the rulers of the petty states in non-Prussian Germany, there were also powerful advocates for unification such as Friedrich List. List, identified a nation's economic strength, not merely with exchange values, but with productive powers, or the potential for the production of exchange values, which included knowledge and skill (List 1991). Thus vocational education was long thought to be associated with the development of national economic strength. Later, other thinkers, such as the Bavarian, Georg Kerschensteiner (Greinert, Chapter 4) made the connection between vocational and civic education explicit. The unified German state adapted previously existing apprenticeship forms of education, developed for craft-based industries, for the industrially based economy (Hanf, Chapter 7) and, subsequently, for service industries. The German pattern has been for the state to take a coordinating, regulatory and controlling role with respect to VET, leaving the regional governments (*Länder*), employers and trade unions with a substantial role in delivery (Streeck 1992; Greinert, Chapter 4). Germany is thus the clearest example of a fully fledged form of social partnership, with the state playing a central but not all-embracing role and the success of the VET model dependent on the strength of other institutions in civil society and particularly on the social partners whose collective agreements have statutory underpinning.

In terms of the development of VET, England is exceptional. Its revolution had occurred in the seventeenth century so that it did not go through the intensive period of national development witnessed in France at the turn of the eighteenth and nineteenth centuries.[2] Its *laissez-faire* approach to economic regulation was well expressed in Adam Smith's *Wealth of Nations*, published in 1776. Smith was hostile to the guilds and apprenticeship (what he called 'the Policy of Europe') and ascribed England's economic growth to its ever finer division of labour, or, more accurately, to the technique of fragmenting manufacturing processes so that, with strong managerial coordination, masses of unskilled workers could replace individual craftsmen (Smith 1776; Clarke, Chapter 5). Though Smith saw an important civic role for the elementary education of the 'common people', the state's part in this was supervisory rather than active, a position also adopted by Mill more than eighty years later. As Green (1990) points out, compulsory elementary education did not begin in England until much later than other major countries and largely as a result of their progress, which was attributed, in no small part, to their national education systems.

England represents the paradoxical situation of a society which has, since the eighteenth century, been dominated for long periods by a state which subscribes to a strongly *laissez faire* economic ideology. As Keep illustrates in Chapter 12, the British state constantly intervenes in the institutional arrangements, design, management and funding of VET without being willing to wrest power from or oblige employers. This

13

explains the apparently irreconcilable claim on the one hand by Keep (Chapter 12) of the British government's dominance in VET policy and, on the other, by Clarke (Chapter 5) of the state's weakness in regulating VET. In Britain, delivery is voluntary, left to employers who may be unwilling or unable to deliver what is required, unlike a country such as Germany where the social partners, the employers' federations and trade unions, play a statutory and leading role. Despite the lack of obligation on the part of employers and of rights to VET on the part of the individual in Britain, apprenticeship has survived in certain sectors and there have been attempts to revive it on a larger scale, including through the current 'modern apprenticeship' programme (e.g. Gospel and Fuller 1998).

The difference between the German and French systems, on the one hand, and the British, on the other, relates above all to the nature of the state's role in VET. In the former, this revolves around regulation, signifying a group of institutionalized rules, embedded in a structured institutional (local and national) framework, that determine, orchestrate or bind relations between capital and labour prevailing in a territory (Boyer and Saillard 2002). The state is, therefore, instrumental in setting a politically defined programme of VET, in the structuring of the labour market and in determining relations between capital and labour. In contrast in Britain, the state's role is one of governance or supervision, with introducing new sets of rules or laws, rather than in intervening in relations between capital and labour. As a result, the labour market and relations between labour and capital become or appear fragmented, often arbitrarily linked to state institutions and thus unresponsive or unpredictably responding to local or state policies. This very distance between the state and the labour market is highlighted by both Halliday (Chapter 11) and Clarke (Chapter 5). Indeed, Halliday decries the lack of social justice and truth in the British VET system, which appears to offer a 'just desert', a promissory exchange value, but, in the face of the deregulated labour market, in reality means that a student's position is fixed once it is established.

In Germany and France the state's interventionist role thus extends to what has come to be known as civil society, including also the social partners. The role of civil society in economic development has attracted some attention in recent years (e.g. Fukuyama 1995; Putnam 2001) and the concept of 'social capital' has been deployed in the study of educational success more generally. 'Civil Society', a term used by Hegel and popularized by Antonio Gramsci in his reflections on the failure of Bolshevism in Western Europe, refers to the level of society intermediate between the state and the individual. It is an area comparatively neglected by both political philosophers and economists, who have tended to polarize their units of analysis between the state on the one hand and the individual on the other, with the relationship between these two as the main focus of attention. 'Civil society' thus refers to a spectrum of institutions, from those closely related to the state such as political parties through to large-scale national institutions such as trade unions and employers' organizations and to individual businesses, charities, community and neighbourhood associations and cooperatives. Some commentators have referred to more or less spontaneous traditions of association within individual societies or to a 'public realm' in which individuals meet to contribute to a more or less clearly conceived public good (Fukuyama 1995; Marquand 2004).

The very notion of a social partnership in VET implies that there are sufficiently strong collective institutions within a society to negotiate and administer VET with the state which has a crucial co-ordinating role. There is, however, no simple correspondence between, on the one hand, state-organized VET and weak civil societies and, on the other, social partnership models of VET and a strong civil society. England, for example, is often regarded as a society with robust civil society institutions (political parties, trade unions, businesses, charities), but which has not developed appropriate forms of association for successful social partnership arrangements in VET. Keep (Chapter 12) draws attention to the weakness of employers' associations in the British economy, a situation which stands in contrast to, for example, Germany, where VET is built on social partnership between employers and trade unions at all levels (Clarke and Herrmann 2004). The United States, although considered by some to be a society with strong institutions of civil society, is also one that is deeply reluctant to construct a social partnership model of VET (Lewis, Chapter 6; Waks 2004). Civil society also reflects particular interests which may in turn impinge on VET. For example, Pring (Chapter 9) refers to the persistence and strength of the gentlemanly tradition in VET, Halliday (Chapter 11) to the role of class consciousness in the UK, Lewis (Chapter 6) to the role of race in the US and Clarke (Chapter 5) to traditional conceptions of the sexual division of labour.

CONCLUDING REMARKS

The different approaches to and development of VET in different countries therefore tell us a great deal about the different roles of the state and, in turn, the different social and class relations on which these are built and the different value accorded to labour. In Germany, for example, VET represents a system of 'qualification' to provide a given quality of labour, a system based on social partner consensus and integration into the state apparatus. 'Skills' and qualifications are socially constructed, collectively negotiated and recognized and are bound up with the value of labour under legal obligation, a value in turn reflected in the collectively agreed wage and associated with the potential as well as the responsibility to fulfil the particular tasks and activities agreed within a given *Beruf*. The result, though maintaining a divide between the academic and the vocational, is that VET has a higher status than it has in a country such as Britain and that the hairdresser, the carpenter or nurse are accorded more responsibility to plan, carry out, and control his or her own work.

In contrast, in Britain, skills remain individual attributes or properties required to fulfil particular outputs, and qualifications represent, not the end result of a process of VET, but certification of learning outcomes, whether achieved through training or practical experience. The result is a playing down of underpinning knowledge and a sharper and more impermeable divide between the academic and the vocational, a divide which might be regarded as helping to maintain traditional class relations.

Such contrasts appear to pose serious barriers to the establishment of a European qualifications framework. Certainly they imply that any comparator is almost bound to be unusable that fails to take account of the fact that 'qualifications', 'vocational education', 'skills' and even 'labour' itself have different meanings and are associated with different practices in different countries.

If, however, we focus not just on national differences but on emerging tendencies and similarities, the picture that emerges from this book is rather different. The transformation of the French VET system described by Philippe Méhaut, with the acceptance of accreditation of experiential learning (*validation des acquis de l'expérience*, known as VAE) and the development of individual training entitlements, has familiar echoes to those *au fait* with the British system. The increasing recognition in Britain of the need for a higher and wider range of skills, deeper underpinning knowledge, and a more systematic and comprehensive process of VET for different occupations supports a move in the German direction. And the German concern with standards is one shared by other European countries, suggesting – however superficial – a level of convergence. The greater the mobility of labour across borders, too, the weaker will be the imperative of VET to prop up national identities.

We hope that this book will contribute to an understanding of such similarities and differences, and – above all – to an appreciation of the value of vocational education to society.

NOTES

1 Thanks to Michaela Brockmann for drawing our attention to these translations.
2 It is arguable, however, that mass internal immigration both from within Great Britain and from Ireland helped to create what Marx called the 'reserve army of the unemployed' and thus a lack of a pressing need to develop a highly skilled workforce.

REFERENCES

Ashton, D. and Green, A. (1996) *Education, Training and the Global Economy*, Cheltenham: Edward Elgar.

Benner, D. (2003) *Wilhelm von Humboldt's Bildungstheorie*, Munich: Juventa.

Biernacki, R. (1995) *The Fabrication of Labor: Germany and Britain 1640–1914*, Berkeley: University of California Press.

Boyer, R. and Saillard, Y. (eds) (2002) *Régulation Theory: The State of the Art*, London: Routledge.

Brown, P., Green, A. and Lauder, H. (2001) *High Skills: Globalization, Competitiveness and Skill Formation*, Oxford: Oxford University Press.

Clarke, L. and Herrmann, G. (2004) 'The Institutionalisation of Skill in Britain and

Germany: Examples from the Construction Sector', in C. Warhurst, I. Grugilis and E. Keep (eds), *The Skills that Matter*, Basingstoke: Palgrave.

Crouch, C., Finegold, D. and Sako, M. (1999) *Are Skills the Answer? The Political Economy of Skill Creation in Advanced Industrial Countries*, Oxford: Oxford University Press.

Dearden, R. F. (1984) 'Education and Training', *Westminster Studies in Education*, 7, 57–66.

Finegold, D. (1991) 'Institutional Incentives and Skill Creation: Preconditions for a High-skill Equilibrium', in P. Ryan (ed.), *International Comparisons of Vocational Education and Training for Intermediate Skills*, Hove: Falmer Press.

Finlay, I., Niven, S. and Young, S. (eds) (1998) *Changing Vocational Education and Training: An International Comparative Perspective*, London: Routledge.

Fukuyama, F. (1995) *Trust*, London: Penguin.

Gospel, H. and Fuller, A. (1998) 'The Modern Apprenticeship: New Wine in Old Bottles?', *Human Resource Management Journal*, 8, 1, 5–22.

Green, A. (1990) *Education and State Formation*, London: Macmillan.

Green, A., Wolf, A. and Leney, T. (1999) *Convergence and Divergence in European Education and Training Systems*, London: Institute of Education.

Hafner, S. (1985) *Preussen ohne Legende*, Munich: Siedler.

Jobert, A., Marry, C., Tanguy, L. and Rainbird, H. (eds) (1997) *Education and Work in Great Britain, Germany and Italy*, London: Routledge.

List, F. [1841] (1991) *The National System of Political Economy*, New Jersey: Augustus Kelley.

Marquand, D. (2004) *Decline of the Public: The Hollowing Out of Citizenship*, Cambridge: Polity Press.

Maurice, M., Sellier, F. and Silvestre, J.-J. (1986) *The Social Foundations of Industrial Power*, Cambridge, Mass.: MIT Press.

Onions, C. T. (1996) *Oxford Dictionary of Etymology*, Oxford: Oxford University Press.

Prais, S. (1995) *Productivity, Education and Training: An International Perspective*, Cambridge: Cambridge University Press.

Pring, R. (1995) *Closing the Gap*, London: Hodder.

Putnam, Robert D. (2001) *Bowling Alone: The Collapse and Revival of American Community*, New York: Simon & Schuster.

Ryle, G. (1949) *The Concept of Mind*, London: Hutchinson.

Smith, A. [1776] (1981) *The Wealth of Nations*, Indianapolis: Liberty Press.

Streeck, W. (1992) *Social Institutions and Economic Performance*, London: Sage.

Varoufakis, Y. and Hargraves-Heap, S. (1995) *Game Theory: An Introduction*, London: Routledge.

Waks, L. (2004) 'Workplace Learning in America: Shifting Roles of Households, Firms and Schools', *Educational Philosophy and Theory*, 36, 5, 563–77.

Warhurst, C., Grugulis, I. and Keep, E. (eds) (2004) *The Skills that Matter*, London: Kogan Page.

Wolf, A. (2002) *Does Education Matter?*, London: Penguin.

Part One

Historical developments

Chapter 2

The role of the state in vocational education

A political analysis of the history of vocational education in the Netherlands

Anneke Westerhuis

INTRODUCTION

This chapter is about the evolution of Dutch vocational education as part of the formal education system. The concept of citizenship is critical to understanding the dynamics of the education system in the Netherlands. For the Dutch Enlightenment movement, for instance, education was the most appropriate instrument for nation building in eighteenth-century Europe, when the Dutch Republic had lost its role in the ranks of leading European states. The role of education was to define, if not redefine, the nation's character in overcoming the provincial demarcations characteristic of the seventeenth-century Dutch Republic. A national curriculum would mould young people from all provinces into Dutch citizens, into active members of the new Dutch nation. National history (an instrument for nation building in its own right!), Dutch language and religion were the core subjects of this curriculum apart from reading, writing and arithmetic. Vocational subjects were not seen as helpful for nation build-ing; the *homo economicus* was not included in this concept of citizenship. Preparation for a working life was considered to be the proper concern of the workplace with its tradition of apprenticeships, as it had always been.

The formal education system greatly expanded in the second half of the nineteenth century through new types of secondary education. Yet its students were still seen as young citizens, although the citizenship concept now also included manual workers. In their expansionist policies, Dutch national governments struggled with the question of the role of the state in relation to the growing need for professionals. There was far less of a problem in determining the role of the state in training for the workplace. While during the first industrial revolution there was a widely expressed need to formalize vocational preparation in the school system, it was still left to local industry to organize provision. It took more than 150 years before the position of vocational education in the educational system was substantially changed to achieve parity with the non-vocational under the influence of the second industrial revolution in the mid-twentieth century. One of the major arguments for including vocational education in a national education system was that vocational education is about personal development, as well as occupational mobility and social change.

The historical development of the Dutch education system can be seen as an ongoing dispute about the way education should contribute to citizenship and what role the state should take. This chapter will follow this dispute through four distinct periods: the seventeenth century, the French Revolutionary period, the second half of the nineteenth century and the post-war period. The chapter ends with a reflection on the current position of vocational education within the Dutch educational system, where it serves three aims simultaneously: economic growth and industrial innovation; social integration and cohesion; and as the individual's entrance ticket to a successful (lifelong) career. This plurality of aims is reflected in a plurality of stakeholders in vocational education whose roles are not limited to representation on the board of vocational institutes. Within the new concepts of a deregulating state these stakeholders take an active role in the governance of education. An interesting question for the future is whether or not the stakeholders will act as a consensus group defining a common local concept of citizenship as an overall aim of the school for vocational education. An alternative is for the struggle for power between local stakeholders, resulting in an Anglo-Saxon concept for vocational education serving local industrial needs.

UNDER THE DUTCH REPUBLIC

The Republic was characterized by provincial and municipal autonomy. The carefully guarded balances in provincial autonomy prevented the centralization of power in The Hague and hence the expansion of a central bureaucratic apparatus (Knevel 2001; Kuiper 2002). With economic prosperity developing under the Dutch Republic, which was ratified under the 1648 Treaty of Westphalia, the towns grew and hence also educational provision. For the municipal authorities education was an instrument for socio-economic policy-making. In the – utilitarian – view of the municipal councils literacy was necessary for self-survival, hence their willingness to support the provision financially; education was seen as a means of fighting poverty and investment in education would reduce councils' expenditure on benefits for the poor (de Booy 1987; Wolthuis 1999). The variety of this provision was regarded as a mark of a town's prosperity and a subject of rivalry, being ideally of three types:

- ■ *Elementary education* also called 'popular education', for those up to the age of 12. It has been estimated that roughly 65 per cent of all children between 4 and 8 years of age attended elementary education in the seventeenth century (van Deursen 1995);

- *the 'French school'*, from 12 years, offering a modern curriculum (French, business accounts and bookkeeping), extended in the eighteenth century to include German, English, natural sciences, mathematics, geography and history;
- *the 'Latin school'*, also from 12 years, with a classical curriculum (Israel 1995).

In the larger towns the Latin and French schools provided lectures in astronomy, mathematics and surveying for the general public. Thanks to these educational forms, there was a relatively open and lively world of learning in the Republic, with the Latin school as a particular centre of 'civilisation, inquisitiveness, and godliness' (Blom 2001).

Organized other than in institutes, vocational preparation took many forms, such as following the same occupation as one's father, joining a family member or family friend from one's own social circle in order to learn an occupation, or trying to make a career in a branch with an occupational hierarchy, such as the merchant navy or the civil service (Kooijmans 1997). In order to acquire new knowledge, merchants, sea-captains and practitioners of other higher occupations attended public lectures provided by universities and the French and Latin schools. Since there was no institutionalized structure that identified and selected knowledge relevant for occupations, however, it was generally necessary to find one's own way in what was on offer (Israel 1995; Blom 2001).

A kind of structuring of knowledge was to be found in the guild system, which enabled the training of vocational skills and the development and diffusion of new skills. Trades, the core of the local economy, were learned in the workplace, where arrangements were to hand for the transfer of vocational skills in and through practice. Until the emergence of national economies in the early nineteenth century, training for a trade was part of the guild system as the only economic structure providing for the training of new generations of tradesmen. Acquiring the skills of a trade was part of the process of socialization into an occupational community that took care of itself under the protection of the municipal authority. Guilds could manage their own economic and social policy – such as benefits in cases of sickness or death – in relative autonomy. Due to their monopoly in the production and selling of products, they were essentially protectionist in character. This was also expressed in the manner in which apprentices were admitted to a guild; a master tradesman could only take on an apprentice with the guild's permission. Having obtained this permission, the apprentice or his parents bought him a place with this guild member for a learning fee. Regulation of the speed at which someone could become a master – by distributing three practical examinations over a period of four to five years – was also a strategy for protecting the position of guild members (Schama 1977; Dodde 1995).

THE ERA OF THE FRENCH REVOLUTION

In the second half of the eighteenth century the political and economic decline of the Republic was undeniable, also for its inhabitants. Two political programmes developed, a Patriotic programme for the modernization of the state and the nation, inspired by the concepts and ideas of the Enlightenment, and the traditional Orangeist movement defending the existing political order and the orthodox Calvinistic character of the nation. Interpreting this decline and identifying remedies were subjects of the first political discourse in the Netherlands to recruit popular support and organize opinion-making in 'loyal' newspapers, bookshops, local discussion groups and action (van Sas 2004).

Following the fall of the old Republic in 1795, the new national convention decided just one year later to devise central regulation of national education. According to the new regime, the nation demanded another form of education that would educate its citizens. Many of the teachers appointed by the old municipal authorities were dismissed, to be replaced by personnel supporting the Revolution (Kuiper 2002). However, as reading and writing still formed the core of the curriculum, the state's interest in education was not so much in the real effects to be achieved as in its own institutional omnipresence. Following the Education Law of 1806, education was regulated for the first time at national level, although municipal authorities were allowed to retain some responsibilities. Nonetheless, the law aroused much resistance. Its passage owed much to Napoleon's threat to intervene in the constitutional order of the Netherlands if it was not approved by the General Assembly. As many delegates feared that such an intervention would result in a much more centrist French model, its passage was seen as the lesser of two evils (van Setten 1982).

In the 1806 law, education was divided into three levels: elementary, secondary and higher. The introduction of a centralized political system at the end of the eighteenth century involved first and foremost reform of elementary education, the form of education intended for all members of society. The elementary school should educate the younger generation to become citizens of the new state. Little progress was made in defining a national concept for secondary education as this form of education was not considered to be relevant for nation-building. The agenda was not to produce political-administrative elites but to organize and define the Dutch nation by means of a cultural and moral programme (van Setten 1982; van Sas 2004).

This lack of priority and consensus about the need for the state to interfere meant that it took another forty years before a national concept for secondary education was produced. There was absolutely no debate with regard to the position of vocational education in the education system. Although there was some discussion as to whether some form of formal vocational education was needed for commerce and manufacturing to replace the training activities of the guilds, which were dissolved in this period, the dominant opinion was that education in schools was intended to be a general education. An occupation, as distinct from the traditional professions of doctor, lawyer and church minister, should be taught through practice (Wolthuis 1999).

NEW CONCEPTS FOR EDUCATION AT THE END OF THE NINETEENTH CENTURY

The question of how to define secondary education returned to the political scene only in 1857, when Parliament first approved an extended form of elementary education and then later, in 1863, passed an integral law for secondary education. The Minister of Education proposed a tripartite definition of education: 'Elementary education is for everyone, secondary education is intended for a significant part of the population, the core of our society, and the smaller group is the learned class which shines out on the rest of society' (Idenburg 1963: 4).

Secondary education was to be subdivided into two types: the civic school (de Burger School in Dutch) for the lower orders and the higher civic school (de Hogere Burger School) intended for the upper citizenry. In the liberal view of the Minister of Education inherited from the Enlightenment movement, workers, tradesmen and small farmers were to be addressed as citizens: 'also the lowest classes belong to the citizenry and are to conduct themselves in working life in a worthy way' (Goudswaard, 1981: 244). The Minister set forth his view on education for the children of labourers in an address to the Society for Language and Literature in Ghent in 1830:

> Without good education the mass of the labourers is unable to act independently and will be reduced to unimportant numbers in the hands of the employers, living in servile dependency. Give the labourer appropriate secondary education, give them the opportunity to improve their position.
>
> (Goudswaard 1981: 237)

In this view, the ability to work was crucial and only productive labour gave entitlement to citizenship. In the words of the young liberal Member of Parliament Samuel van Houten, 'not ownership, but the productive contribution to the national wealth characterizes a full citizenship' (Stuurman 1992). It was in this capacity of capability for citizenship that secondary education would address its pupils, not in their capacity as a potential labour force. Both forms of secondary education inculcated general knowledge and civilization, vehicles for the intellectual emancipation of the population in *optimo civi* in the von Humboldt tradition of *Allgemeine Bildung* (Goudswaard 1981; van Hulst 1972). The concept was a compromise between a democratic and a meritocratic ideal intended to promote participation in education for a broad section of society but also preparing the social elite for its specific task (Blom 2001; Leune 1995).

25

Although the issue was raised in parliamentary debates, the government did not accept responsibility for the organization of education of a vocational nature. Education that was financed by the state should be general in nature. Indeed, the civic school was also intended for the children of manual workers but it was not the role of the school to prepare them for working life. Vocational preparation did not belong in the school but in the workplace; vocational qualifications were acquired through practice. Vocational education was not forbidden; the state simply did not see it as its task either to regulate or pay for it. The 1863 law offered every opportunity for employers and local groups to organize vocational education, while the provinces and municipalities could support private initiatives financially if they wished. It was only with the greatest reluctance and after much pressure from parliament that the Minister (Thorbecke) was willing to include arrangements in the law for polytechnic education for engineers and architects, following on the higher civic school. If polytechnic education had to be the subject of law making, it should be under the law on secondary education as, according to the Minister, the label 'higher education' should be reserved for academic education at universities (Goudswaard 1981).

This reluctance can also be illustrated from the history of the teacher training colleges. There was a growing demand for teachers as a consequence of the establishment of the new civic schools. It was clear from the beginning that the standard route to becoming a teacher in secondary education, the university, could not produce enough teachers to answer this growing need. Nevertheless, the Minister did not regard it as the state's role to organize professional training for teachers and limited state intervention to the creation of a set of teaching certificates. With the creation of these certificates in 1863, the teaching profession became accessible to people without a university degree, but it was left to the applicants, mostly primary education teachers, how best to prepare themselves for the examinations. It was not until 1912 that the first – privately funded – colleges opened their doors to prepare students for these examinations on a part-time basis (Vos and van der Linden 2004).

With the rather late industrialization of the Netherlands, initiatives to organize some sort of vocational education were taken in due course. Local organizations, such as associations for working people and associations of manufacturers and employers, established so-called trade schools where the emphasis was on learning technical-manual skills for the trades. The first, founded in Amsterdam in 1844 by an architect called Hanna, was not a great success. An initiative in 1861, also in Amsterdam, from a group of employers and patrons proved more successful (Goudswaard 1981). Ironically, the state concept of civic schools met with little support from its target group, which had little time available and did not see the additional value of attending this form of education. Civic evening schools were slightly more successful, but this form of secondary education made little more impact due to opposition from the employers and the practice of long working hours. The status of the schools also came under pressure because of high drop-out rates; for instance 49 per cent in 1880 (Dodde

1983). From five civic day schools in 1870 with 208 pupils, by 1900 there was only one with 37 pupils (Goodswaard 1981: 214).

Due to the success of the privately organized trade schools and the failure of the civic schools, attitudes towards vocational education changed at the end of the nineteenth century. In 1891 parliamentary pressure resulted in the granting of some small subsidies for vocational education schools. This was a beginning, but the state did not take the step of founding vocational schools itself. The possibility of subsidies was nonetheless important as it stimulated local initiatives in the development of this type of education. In contrast to Germany, where a combination of working and learning in an apprenticeship system became highly popular, employers and participants in the Netherlands demonstrated a preference for daytime education. Apprenticeships, as a combination of working and learning, were found in only a few firms and in less populated areas (Wolthuis 1999; Idenburg 1964).

The gradual expansion in the number of vocational trade schools, from only two in 1870 with 214 pupils to 69 by 1920 with 10,318 pupils, and government's growing financial involvement, led to legislation. A law of 1919 represented a compromise as it acknowledged that vocational education deserves the attention of the state, but respected the freedom of school authorities over the curriculum. With this 1919 law the Netherlands obtained a comprehensive educational system, in the sense that from that moment a great variety of forms of education were – however separately – regulated and subsidized by the state. The educational system became dual in character because the idea that the lower classes should have their own concept of general education was abandoned; 'their' curriculum addressed them as working people. However, the law clearly stated that vocational education should not be restricted to practical training, as occupational training should also contribute to personal development.

THE POST-WAR PERIOD: THE HEYDAY OF THE STATE IN EDUCATION

Following the Second World War, the government's influence on education, as in so many areas, increased significantly, including on vocational education. While formally the schools remained in private hands, the government defined priorities in education policy, turning schools into extensions of the state, not so much by intervening in their daily running as by defining the system and the role of its constituent segments. This policy met little resistance. Leune points to the broad consensus in educational ideas between political parties and the businesslike, pragmatic arguments that dominated political debate on education issues (Leune 2001). Many debates concentrated on the search for instruments that would enable education to best fulfil its main objectives: preparation for participation in society and the labour market. After 1945 the Trades School – now renamed 'Industry School' – was the most widely attended form of vocational education. The state saw in vocational education an important instrument for post-war economic reconstruction. Pippel, an influential advisor to the Ministry of Education, expressed this clearly in 1947:

> The serious losses that our country suffered as a result of the war and occupation, the major increase in the density of population, and the drying up of numerous sources of our national income are the causes of the serious impoverishment of our nation since 1940. All efforts must be undertaken to stop this process of impoverishment and increase the level of welfare. There can be no question that one of the means to this end is systematic expansion of our industry. This industrialisation implies that a great number of workers must be trained and that this training must have such a form and content that people are, so far as possible, able to meet the demands of firms and the trades.
>
> (Pippel, cited by Meijers 1983: 61)

More urgent than the question of whether the content of vocational education provided adequately for the needs of firms was that of how to attract enough (in terms of the capacities needed for expanding industry) young people to attend trade schools. Many government-appointed committees of psychologists, educational scientists and people from industry considered this issue. Government was directly involved, formulating their tasks and defining the concept and role of vocational education in the post-war education system. This involvement was a direct result of the active role that the government assumed in post-war economic reconstruction (Dercksen 1986). The advice by the Goote Committee not to reduce vocational education to practical training was very influential. The committee suggested that, by providing general education and a focus on preparation for skilled trades rather than by producing mere tradespeople, this form of education would not alienate itself from general education. In the event of a wrong choice of school, pupils would be able to transfer to a more suitable form of education with little delay (Meijers 1983). In order to play a distinct role in supporting post-war economic reconstruction, vocational education should be integrated into the wider education system.

The identity of this form of education within the broader education system was the subject of ongoing discussion, the point being to find a proper balance between the general and the vocational character of the curriculum. This can be deduced, for instance, from the change of nomenclature within a period of roughly forty years from 'Trades School', through 'Industry School', 'Lower Technical School', 'preparatory vocational education' to 'a practical strand within preparatory secondary vocational education'. Reluctance to deliver vocational education into the hands of the workplace also had another source of inspiration. Directly after the war many committees retained an ambivalent attitude towards the culture and habits of the workplace. Education, including vocational education, should protect young people from this culture by arming them with a proper education. An example was the government-appointed committee chaired by the social democrat Banning in the early 1950s, who stressed the importance of educating the personality in order to counter the temptation young people would face to 'run wild', especially in the workplace.

Industry did not oppose the more general character of vocational education, as this was seen to meet its needs:

> Pupils do not need to know so much but to understand things. The Lower Technical School will only fulfil its task of delivering capable young people when these have learned to think through a simple task and can then think of a solution that produces results. This will ensure that the often heard complaint that young people are unable to act independently will become a thing of the past.
>
> (Final Report of the Faber-Hennequin Committee 1956, cited by Meijers 1983: 86–7)

This opinion was not limited to the circles of government advisory committees but was also shared by employers, at least by their organizations. In 1958 the central organizations of employers and employees, meeting in the standing Social-Economic Council, the most important socio-economic advisory board to the Dutch government, produced a report emphasizing the need to concentrate on general technical thinking in vocational curricula. The report concluded that it would not be adequate in future merely to deliver trained specialists. The new generations of skilled workers and technicians must be able, both as skilled employees and as individuals, to rise above the narrow confines of their trade. Such a mentality was also seen to be needed for occupational mobility and social change. In future an increasing demand would be made not only upon the specialist knowledge of skilled workers but also upon their personal capacities. More than ever before vocational education would need to be concerned with general education (this in 1958!).

There was also agreement about extending the time that young people should be in the education system and about increasing participation in vocational education:

> It is clear that more education and training will be good for economic growth. Although more education and training means that youngsters will enter the labour market at a later stage, this will be compensated for, as a general rule, by the increased quality of their work, such that the longer duration of education will be economically profitable.
>
> (Eighth Industrialisation Report 1963, cited by Meijers 1983: 137–8)

Until the mid-1970s 80 per cent of the population of lower technical schools left school for work, but gradually the apprenticeship system was no longer seen as a dual alternative to but as an extension of the lower technical schools in offering practical preparation as a bridge between education and work (Meijers 1983). This system came under severe pressure, however, due to the dramatic reduction in the number of pupils attending vocational education. The lower technical school faced increasing difficulty in attracting students, given the growing level of participation in general secondary education. As a result lower technical education turned into a left-over category for youngsters that could not or did not want to follow general secondary education.

The government's response to these changing preferences was to build a three-layered education system for mass education: after primary education every youngster should acquire a form of general education and after that a form of vocational or higher education. Options in the third layer were still defined by a person's results in the second layer. Although the selectivity of the secondary phase of education was reduced, it was still highly selective in its streaming of young people either to vocational education (ISCED levels 3 and 4) or tertiary education (ISCED levels 5 and 6). Facilities for young people to move up through the system from a lower vocational level to a higher one were not envisaged, as these would encourage students to stay longer in the education system. Due to budgetary constraints and the priority given to the efficient structure of the system, such transfers were in fact discouraged until about 1998 (van der Mee 2002).

With the reconstruction of the economy from industry to service domination and the consequent growing need for more highly educated staff, this restrictive policy changed into one that acknowledged post-secondary vocational education as a route to higher professional education. A continuous vocational track was constructed from the vocational segments of general secondary education via vocational education to tertiary professional education (Ministerie van OCW 2004). However, budgetary restrictions are still there and these, together with the idea that the current system does not need major reconstruction, raise the question of what the state role in education should be in the near future?

CONCLUSION

Nowadays vocational education is rooted in a comprehensive education system and is unquestionably the gate that young people have to pass through in order to complete their route through the system. This situation may not as yet have come up to expectations, but the 'grand design' is at least in place.

We now live in an era where the state is gradually reducing its role in the public domain, including in education (de Waal 2001). Maybe this process is much more one of legitimizing multi-ownership in education: for industry, vocational education produces new generations of competent staff; for the public domain, now represented by the municipalities instead of the national state, it facilitates social integration and cohesion; and for the individual it is an entrance ticket to a successful career. Due to the new concept of a deregulating state, public demands in relation to education are no longer channelled through the state bureaucracy but directly expressed by the public itself, now defined as stakeholders in education; a plurality of aims is reflected in a plurality of stakeholders in vocational education. The national state will take a supervisory and moderating role, limiting its interventions and challenging institutions to think and act for themselves, under the condition of transparency in processes and outcomes (Mertens 2001; de Vijlder and Westerhuis 2002).

Von Mayntz points to the problem-solving bias in this dominant system-theoretical paradigm of governance (von Mayntz 2001). Policy development is basically concerned with the solution of societal, socio-economic problems, and new concepts in governance are developed because the old concepts have lost their effectiveness in problem solving. In the new concept of governance, vocational education institutes may turn into an arena where the conflicting expectations of many stakeholders come to the fore. It is not the point that institutes have to root themselves in local society, but that institutes have to define a *modus operandi* in order to deal with a variety of expectations (Ministerie van OCW 2004). In this, the shift from a public to an institutional rationale is imminent; surviving and channelling expectations in operational processes will become the *raison d'être* of many institutes, especially if the role of these stakeholders is not limited to representation on the board of vocational institutes but is extended to taking an active role in the education process.

Vocational education has a long tradition of public interest and of close relations with the world of work. For Waslander there is a parallel between the organization of work and the social organization of learning (Waslander 2004). Whereas in the guild system the organization of work implied the organization of learning, working and learning grew apart when mass production and mass learning were separated to optimize the linear organization of work and learning processes. The mass nature of education produced a system specializing in regulating streams of learners effectively. But this system no longer works when parents, participants and industry are allowed to express their own ideas about what comprises a good education, not only in terms of outcomes but also in the quality of the educational process. And can education respond to these greater expectations of being a means to all ends? Are premature school-leaving, aggression, absenteeism and bullying indeed signals of dissatisfaction with a system that prevents participants from developing themselves to the maximum (Coonen 2002)? Waslander's (2004) research reveals that for many schools the drive to innovate finds its roots in the need to raise students' motivation to attend lessons. As a result schools adopt modularization as the dominant principle in organizing the education process; differentiation and tailor-made arrangements are compromises between efficiency and the variety of demands. This principle is also adopted in digesting the demands of the remaining stakeholders, for instance in individualized, contract-based service relations (de Vijlder 2004). Taking this one step further, 'clients' will pay for education services and schools will face competition in obtaining lucrative new contracts.

However, more is needed for an education system that aims to respond to the dominant drivers of the knowledge society. It is also about new definitions of competences and knowledge that should be transmitted through education, about the organization of learning in open, corporate curricula and about the role of the learner who should interpret the learning process as a vehicle for self-realization (Geurts 2006). But who will take responsibility for this transformation of a vocational education that has to look for new relations between the production of knowledge, the organization of learning processes and the position of the learners?

REFERENCES

Blom, S. (2001) 'Onderwijs en wetenschappelijke vorming', in D. Fokkema and F. Grijzenhout, *Rekenschap 1650–2000*, The Hague: Sdu Uitgevers.

Booy, E.P., de (1987) 'Het onderwijs voor 1795', in P.Th. F.M. Boekolt and E.P. de Booy, *Geschiedenis van de school in Nederland*, Assen/Maastricht: van Gorcum.

Coonen, H.W.A.M. (2002) 'Laat leraren een nieuwe leeromgeving ontwerpen', in *Bouwen en breken, overheidssturing in de eenentwintigste eeuw*, Kompas, April, 33–6, BMC, Leusden.

Dercksen, W.J. (1986) *Industrialisatiepolitiek rondom de jaren vijftig*, Assen: van Gorcum.

Deursen, A.Th. van (1995) *Een dorp in de polder*, Amsterdam: Bert Bakker.

Dodde, N.L. (1983) *Het Nederlandse onderwijs verandert*, Muiderberg: Coutinho.

Dodde, N.L. (1995) 'Een lange onderwijsweg', in N.L. Dodde and J.M.G. Leune, *Het Nederlandse schoolsysteem*, Groningen: Wolters-Noordhoff.

Geurts, J. (2006) *ROC als Loopbaancentrum*, 's-Hertogenbosch: CINOP.

Goudswaard, N.B. (1981) *Vijfenzestig jaar nijverheidsonderwijs*, Assen: van Gorcum.

Hulst, J.W. van (1972) 'Thorbecke's betekenis voor het onderwijs', *Uitleg, weekblad van het departement van Onderwijs en Wetenschappen*, aflevering, 287, 18–23.

Idenburg, Ph.J. (1963) 'Thorbecke's Middelbaar Onderwijswet', in *Een eeuw middelbaar onderwijswet herdacht, 1863–1963* [Ten geleide van J.van 't Hul] Groningen: Wolters, 1–20.

Idenburg, Ph.J. (1964) *Schets van het Nederlandse schoolwezen*, Groningen: J.B. Wolters.

Israel, J.L. (1995) *The Dutch Republic: Its Rise, Greatness and Fall, 1477–1806*, Oxford: Oxford University Press.

Knevel, P. (2001) *Het Haagse Bureau, 17e eeuwse ambtenaren tussen staatsbelang en eigen belang*, Amsterdam: Prometheus/Bert Bakker.

Kooijmans, L. (1997) *Vriendschap en de kunst van het overleven in de zeventiende en achttiende eeuw*, Amsterdam: Bert Bakker.

Kuiper, J. (2002) *Een revolutie ontrafeld, politiek in Friesland 1795–1798*, Franeker: van Wijnen.

Leune, J.G.M. (2001) *Onderwijs in verandering: reflecties op een dynamische sector*, Groningen: Wolters Noordhoff.

Leune, J.M.G. (1995) *Het Nederlandse schoolsysteem*, Groningen: Wolters-Noordhoff.

Mayntz, R. von (2001) *Zur Selectivität der steuerungstheoretischen Perspective. MPIfG Working Paper 01/2*, May, Cologne: Max Plank Institut für Gesellschaftsforschung.

Mee, G. van der (2002) 'De HAVO is een slap aftreksel van het VWO', *Het onderwijsblad*, no. 5, 9 maart 2004, Utrecht: AOB.

Meijers, F. (1983) *Van ambachtsschool tot lts, onderwijsbeleid en kapitalisme*, Nijmegen: SUN.

Mertens, F.J.H. (2001) *Meer van hetzelfde. Over de beweging in het onderwijs*, Utrecht: Lemma.

Ministerie van OCW (2004) *Koers BVE 2*, The Hague: Ministerie van OCW.

Sas, N.C.F. van (2004) *De Metamorfose van Nederland, van oude orde naar moderniteit 1750–1900*, Amsterdam: Amsterdam University Press.

Schama, S. (1977) *Patriots and Liberators, Revolution in the Netherlands 1870–1813*, New York: Knopf.

Setten, H. van (1982) 'Opvoedend onderwijs; de vernieuwing van het volksonderwijs in het begin van de vorige eeuw', in *Comenius: wetenschappelijk tijdschrift voor demokratisering van opvoeding, onderwijs, vorming en hulpverlening*, vol. 2, pp. 5–36

Stuurman, S. (1992) *Wacht op onze daden, het liberalisme en de vernieuwing van de Nederlandse staat*, Amsterdam: Bert Bakker.

Vijlder, F.J. de (2004) 'Trajectmanagement in de transformatie van publieke organisaties', in P. van der Knaap, A. Korsten, K. Termeer and M. van Twist, *Trajectmanagement, beschouwingen over beleidsdynamiek en organisatieverandering*, Utrecht: Lemma.

Vijlder, F.J. de and Westerhuis, A.F. (2002) *Meervoudige publieke verantwoording*, Amsterdam: Max Goote Kenniscentrum.

Vos, J. and Linden, J. van der (2004) *Waarvan Akte; geschiedenis van de MO-opleidingen 1912–1987*, Assen: Koninklijke van Gorcum.

Waal, S. de (2001) *Nieuwe strategieën voor het publieke domein*, Deventer: Kluwer.

Waslander, S. (2004) *Wat scholen beweegt, over massa-maatwerk, onderwijspraktijk en examens in het voortgezet onderwijs*, Arnhem: CITO.

Wolthuis, J. (1999) *Lower technical education in the Netherlands: The Rise and Fall of a Subsystem*, OOMO reeks, Leuven/Apeldoorn: Garart.

Chapter 3

Vocational education in France

A turbulent history and peripheral role

Jean-Paul Géhin

The purpose of this chapter is not to retrace the entire history of vocational education and training (VET) in France but rather to examine certain prominent aspects using current literature on the subject (e.g. Charlot and Figeat 1985; Prost 1968; Léon 1968; Terrot 1983). This approach provides ways of interpreting the major changes and the features of VET today; it also sheds light on current aspects and debates that may appear obscure to outsiders.

In order to understand the situation and specific forms of VET in France three elements should be taken into account. The first is the significant crisis in apprenticeship that occurred at the end of the eighteenth century followed by a difficult and slow VET reconstruction process during the nineteenth and twentieth centuries. The dominance of the academic model subsequently exerted its principles and influence on the entire French education system, including the most vocational parts, and even on the organization of production. The final element was the institutionalization over at least three decades of continuing vocational training (CVT), notably in the form of major investment by business in the continuing training of their employees and the development by public authorities of educational policies focused on training the unemployed.

These historical, political and social factors form part of and contributed to the creation of French 'social cohesion', combining the education and production systems (Maurice *et al.* 1982). Stable as it may be, this coherence is not set in stone, but has occurred as a result of social and economic changes and clashes between the main organized forces in society, leading to an enduring compromise. In view of the extent and recurrence of the changes in progress, a new educational logic is suggested, described here as a French vocational education model.

The notion of a 'vocational education model' is a general concept, conditioning to a greater or lesser extent the practices of the entities involved. Such models generally work on numerous competing levels, as demonstrated by Durkheim (1938) via the concept of pedagogical inversion. The emergence of a vocational education model in France does not necessarily replace the academic model, which has demonstrated its vitality since the 1980s in raising the level of education and in extending the time given to studies. It is does, however, influence those involved and tends to orientate educational practices, whether through the development of vocational courses, reconciliation with business, the distribution of alternance-based (that is, alternating between periods of work and college) or sandwich-course training, etc.

THE CRISIS IN VOCATIONAL TRAINING AND A SLOW RECONSTRUCTION PROCESS

Under the old system education appeared divided: on the one hand general education, inspired by mediaeval scholasticism and, subsequently, humanist concepts, was reserved for the children of the aristocracy and burgeoning bourgeoisie; on the other hand VET, organized in the form of apprenticeship within corporations, constituted the sole educational option for the working classes. Naville refers to a genuine 'divide' between vocational and academic education. He notes that in the French tradition 'The purpose of apprenticeship is to learn a trade, whilst the aim of academic instruction is to acquire theoretical, abstract knowledge, independent of the practical conditions in which it will be used' (Naville 1948: 12). These concepts, which are deeply rooted in history, have for many years guided and still guide a number of public policies and the strategies of those involved in education.

Destabilization of traditional apprenticeship

Apprenticeship is a key factor in the corporate system, which was both extremely hierarchical and, in principle, governed internal mobility and access to the status of master. Apprenticeship within trade corporations was generally long term (at least 5 to 6 years) and geared to the extremely young, since the average entry age was 12 to 13. It was subject to a contract that was often – although not always – written and that specified the reciprocal obligations of the three contracting parties: the master undertook to teach all facets of the trade (including secrets) and to guarantee the apprentice, who very often also received board and lodging, a general education; the apprentice swore respect, loyalty and total obedience to his master and could not, in principle, breach the contract; the parents were often under an obligation to pay apprenticeship fees to compensate for the time devoted by the master to their child.

Apprenticeship led to the issuing of a certificate ('receipt') and concluded with a 'tour of France', generally depicted in the form of an initiation ritual, combining the technical and ethical experience of the trade, during which the future worker went from one region to another and from one employer to another. In its traditional form apprenticeship is more than just a simple technical and vocational education system; it is a general educational process offering extensive socialization and transmitting the social behaviour and values associated with a vocation.

From the second half of the eighteenth century, apprenticeship underwent a significant crisis marked by the decline of the corporate system and considerably aggravated by the deterioration in the training and working conditions of apprentices. For many years the corporate model experienced significant conflicts. First there were internal conflicts, with employers tending to deny workers access to expertise and seeking immediate profits at the expense of training apprentices (Lefranc 1975). Gradually a hierarchy based on family adherence replaced one based on vocational value (Charlot and Figeat 1985). Subsequently there were external conflicts, since alongside the so-called 'sworn' trades regulated by corporations there have always been so-called 'free' trades beyond their control. It was in the name of freedom of labour that corporations were most criticized.

In this context the French Revolution, in abolishing corporations, simply further destabilized an institution already in crisis.[1] In March 1791 the Allarde decree set out the bases of the right to work that allowed all citizens the unrestricted right to practise a vocation. In June of the same year the Lechapelier Act abolished corporations and established the principle that prohibited vocational associations. The consolidation of the right to work and expansion of contractual employment meant dispensing with the traditionally dominant systems – regulated employment and forced labour (Castel 1995).

Although not directly targeted, apprenticeship suffered the consequences and declined throughout the nineteenth century, as factories developed and the division of industrial labour and relatively unskilled jobs became more prominent. The image of apprenticeship in France was thus downgraded, offering a second-rate education geared specifically to young people (of working class or rural origin) and businesses (artisans and small businesses). This situation was a structural feature of French society, marked by a clear split between academic and vocational education. As Combes notes: 'between the liberals, in favour of on-the-job vocational training, and a mood of reform sympathetic to academic education, there is little room for apprenticeship as we know it today, i.e. there is little room for alternance' (Combes 1986: 21).

Slow reconstruction

At the end of the eighteenth century and for a considerable period afterwards VET in France, which essentially took the form of artisan apprenticeship, was therefore significantly destabilized. There was then a lengthy and slow reconstruction process, two prominent features of which are frequently highlighted by historians of education. The first concerns the overall structure of this process, which was conducted 'from above' (Léon 1968), prioritizing the education of managerial personnel with the creation of engineering and subsequently technical colleges to the detriment of the training of workers and employees, which really only took off in the 1950s. The second feature relates to the dominant form that this reconstruction adopted, which can be defined as 'academic' in so far as VET was largely taken over and implemented by academic institutions.

The establishment of vocational education in France began with the highest qualifications and thus with the training of managerial personnel. Advanced technical training was instituted, first under the old system based on a military framework and large-scale industrial sites, through the creation of the École des Ponts et Chaussées (College of Bridges and Roads) in 1747 and the École des Mines (College of Mining) in 1783, then under the French Revolution which created Polytechniques (prestigious engineering schools) and the Conservatoire National des Arts et Métiers (National School of Engineering and Technology) with the distinct aim of broadening technical culture and thus encouraging the development of a burgeoning industrial society. This structure was supplemented by the creation of the École Centrale (a prestigious college of engineering) in 1829 and of business schools at the end of the nineteenth century, commencing with the École des Hautes Etudes Commerciales (HEC) (School of Advanced Business Studies) in 1881.

France was thus the first country to provide a specific training for engineers. To a significant extent this prestigious and structured area of education further conditioned 'social coherence', both in terms of education, where it remained the prestigious route in an education system marked by republican elitism and meritocracy, and production, where managerial personnel gained numerical importance and a specific status (Maurice *et al.* 1982).

The second stage of VET reconstruction concerns technicians and 'master crafts-men', as they were called at the time. Various technical training colleges were created from the end of the nineteenth century: in 1873 the École Diderot and from 1881 several Écoles Nationales Professionnelles (National Vocational Colleges), located throughout France and based around specific sectors (mechanics, textiles, etc.). At the same time the Ministry of Industry and Commerce opened Écoles Professionnelles Commerciales et Industrielles (Commercial and Industrial Vocational Colleges).[2] A high-level technical training system was thus created and provided the foundation for what by the end of the twentieth century would become one of the specific features of advanced education in France – a major development in the initial vocational education of advanced engineers in the Institut Universitaires de Technologie (IUT) (Polytechnics) and *sections de techniciens supérieurs* (STS) (advanced engineering courses).

The final stage in the reconstruction of vocational education concerns junior employment. It was not until the beginning of the twentieth century that a benchmark national diploma for worker qualifications was created, the *certificat d'aptitude professionnelle* (CAP) (vocational training certificate), comprising numerous specialities and structured around a framework of trades. The actual implementation of worker and employee training had to wait even longer. Even though the Astier Act of 1919 provided for the organization of full-time vocational courses and evening classes for apprentices, this type of training was still fairly sparse, poorly attended and often frowned on by businesses (Agulhon 1994). It was thus not until the Second World War and the need for a skilled labour force, encouraged by the rebuilding of the country and the economy, that France would see any significant development in basic vocational education.

It took more than two centuries for a complete VET system to be re-established. This was notably marked by the intervention of public authorities and academic institutions and was created within a framework of separation from business and the production sector. It can thus be said that VET underwent a 'schooling' process that enjoyed a broad social consensus. During the 1950s and 1960s all the main organized forces involved (teachers, unions, public authorities, etc.) opted for this solution, including businesses and groups of employers who saw in it a chance to reduce their training costs (*Formation Emploi* 1989). The majority of businesses, particularly the larger ones, which had training centres or technical education establishments, thus yielded them to public education and lost interest in initial vocational training.

This organization of VET by academic institutions, relatively independent from business, still influences today's French education system.

THE PERSISTENCE OF THE 'ACADEMIC MODEL'

The prevailing education system in France can generally be classified as the academic model, which can be defined schematically by the pre-eminence of general education and discipline-based approaches, a centralized mode of management and design in addition to a relative distance from production. The persistence of this model is generally explained by historical and religious considerations.[3]

Unlike Anglo-Saxon countries (in particular Germany), France never experienced what Durkheim called 'pedagogical inversion', attributing that to the Protestant tradition (Durkheim 1938). The differing viewpoints of Catholicism and Protestantism on the human relationship with the world and matter find their logical extension in the curriculum. On the one hand, the scholastic and humanist tradition was maintained, which introduced children to the more general aspects of the heart and human mind. On the other hand, a 'realist' education was established, breaking with this tradition through the study of science and technical subjects that sought to make humans protagonists in their own destiny. With this latter viewpoint VET gained a more prestigious role, since in addition to conveying technical knowledge it sought to prepare children for the whole of the adult life for which they were 'destined' – described in German through the term *Beruf*, meaning both a profession and a vocation.

Conversely, the French academic model emphasized general education in terms of subject matter, syllabuses and selection criteria; and even more so when the humanist and universalist concepts that form the basis of the French academic model were combined with the idea of equal opportunity of access to education. The principle of equality, far from being purely incantatory, effectively shaped the structure of the education system as a whole and contributed to the gradual creation of the 'single school system', where standardization is multiple. In terms of organization it has a single, highly centralized administration to guarantee equal treatment throughout the country. Pedagogically it establishes syllabuses, examinations and national diplomas, prioritizing the most generic and theoretical knowledge and subject matter. And in social terms it reiterates the principles of equality and 'republican elitism' that tend to attach too much importance to a single model of academic excellence, the prestigious institutes of higher education, and thus implicitly to validate social selection via academic criteria.

This single school structure has disadvantages. It reinforces the internal hierarchy in the school, a feature known to and recognized by all the parties concerned and notably conveyed by the importance accorded to the diplomas obtained as exit qualifications.[4] It also helps to maintain the historic and devalued social and economic status of vocational courses, with guidelines for entry drawn up on the negative basis of lack of success in general education and with reintegration into long-term, more prestigious courses difficult and rare. Participation in vocational courses has been almost exclusively from working-class children (Charlot and Figeat 1985).

These significant features of the 'academic model', and in particular the top status accorded general education, do not imply a lack of relationship between the education and economic systems in France; quite the opposite, they guide the French production system, particularly the structure of jobs and the organizational and recruitment policies of companies. The significance and prestige of long-term education (particularly of the engineering colleges) echo the importance of management structures and jobs in French companies (Maurice *et al.* 1982). Similarly, the increased significance over several decades of advanced engineering education has undoubtedly accelerated the process of reducing the number of relatively unskilled working-class jobs, to the benefit of the middle classes.

THE INSTITUTIONALIZATION OF CONTINUING EDUCATION

In addition to these two major historical characteristics of the French education system (primacy of general education and the relative depreciation of vocational education), a third, more recent and less frequently considered, feature needs to be taken into account: the development and institutionalization in specific ways of continuing vocational training (CVT) since the 1960s.

Over a period of several decades CVT has become an extensive social and economic activity,[5] and a routine practice involving more than eight million adults each year (mainly public and private sector employees and the unemployed). This quantitative growth has led to the construction and implementation of social regulatory systems that are separate from the traditional organization of education in France.

Three prominent features of CVT in France can be highlighted (Géhin 1999; Pallazzeschi 1998).

Social compromise and the significant numbers involved

One of the major characteristics of CVT in France is its origins in negotiations between unions and employers dating from the collective agreement of July 1970. This contractual origin lies at the root of the majority of subsequent attempts to enhance or reform the CVT system (Dubar and Gadéa 1999). Based on collective agreements, adult education sets up a compromise between distinct concepts.

During the 1960s new concepts of adult education were experimented with and implemented. An Act of 1959 sought to enhance 'social development', a term that defines both the act of educating and its objective, that of offering everybody the chance to obtain new qualifications and to progress socially. Its main aim was political, to promote social mobility, enhancing the value of individual merit and effort. In this way a concept of adult education was propagated that is still very much alive and is characterized by the notion of a second chance offered to those who for one reason or another have failed at school.[6]

This ideological structure was supplemented by a liberal view of the organization of education. By classifying CVT as a national obligation and not a public service, an Act of 3 December 1966 initiated a form of regulation based on negotiation and collective agreement. The government lost its predominant role in basic training and became part of an extensive and complex system of parties including unions, employers, national authorities, business and educational bodies.

An Act of July 1971 underlines these trends, instituting both an individual right offered to all employees to pursue the training of their choice without breach of contract and a tax obligation for companies (based on the wage bill) to contribute financially to the training of their employees. It set up a compromise between two independent concepts of adult education: one relating to the development of the individual and the dissemination of culture (full-time education), and the other underlining the economic aspect of CVT.

Conceived during a period of major economic growth, the 1971 Act and the social compromise on which it was based was to be implemented in a completely different context of unemployment and internationalization. The economic dimension was to establish itself and, simultaneously, education was increasingly mobilized to combat the problems of unemployment and of socially integrating young people. A new division of tasks between government and industry took shape, with public authorities being given responsibility for educating the working population outside employment and with business responsible for employees. The areas of cultural education and social development gradually became neglected.

Co-decision and collective bargaining

CVT thereby switched its central focus to negotiation between unions and employers, co-decision and collective bargaining. Signed in a context of social crisis (post-May 1968) and a desire for political modernization ('the new society' promoted by Jean Jacques Chaban Delmas and Jacques Delors), the general multi-industry agreement of 6 July 1970 gave rise to a lengthy series of agreements between unions and employers. Negotiations concerned the creation of organizational and operational rules governing industrial training, consultation with unions and employers regarding training, the implementation of personal training leave and, subsequently, the development of skills assessment and the pursuit of co-investment in CVT between industry and employees. They also concerned access to training for job seekers and, more extensively, VET for young people, including sandwich course contracts, the modernization of apprenticeship, etc. The benefits of this long series of national inter-industry negotiations were significant: the recognition of training as an important area in vocational relations; the broadening of regulatory systems within the CVT framework towards the vocational training of young people, sandwich courses and apprenticeship; and the gradual introduction of negotiations into sectors of activity and industry, etc. (Jobert 2000).

This last aspect was boosted by the Rigout Act of 1984, which imposed an obligation to negotiate; there was thus a remarkable increase in sectoral agreements relating to VET.[7] The influence of the different sectors was underlined by the capacity of sectoral training bodies to attract a significant share of finance and establish themselves as major developers of training courses, particularly for subject matter specific to their activities. This was reinforced and stimulated by the public authorities, who awarded VET pride of place in their collective bargaining policies with unions and employers, notably through: 'forward study agreements', based on analysis of the qualifications in a sector; 'training development agreements', involving sharing the financing of continuing education between public authorities and industry; and even agreements with the aim of developing apprenticeship and sandwich courses.

Market control and the influence of business

The final prominent feature of CVT in France relates to the organization of training activities. In breaking away from the bureaucratic and centralized organization of national education, the 1971 Act did not place any restrictions on the creation of organizations. One of the Act's main pioneers, Jacques Delors, was explicit about influencing the way national education operated by experimenting with alternative forms of education:

> in view of the current limits of the education system, full-time education bears undeniable elements that contribute to a solution . . . When the change is

complete, educational institutions should be significantly modified. They will lose their imperious and invasive nature and should abandon this single model to which everyone is subjected and which is at the root of social inequality and conservatism.

(Delors 1974)

The 1970s saw the creation and development of a vast number of VET bodies. The notion of a competitive market regulating the supply of and demand for VET should, however, be put into context: cost is not a decisive variable in overall regulation; the relationship between supplier and demander is often strong and stable; the private sector has to date only evolved moderately and bodies dependent on employer organizations occupy a central and dominant position in industry-financed continuing education.

The establishment of the market model contributed to strengthening and legitimizing industrial policy; vocational education was seen as a non-material investment relating mainly to human capital and thus serving productive efficiency. A close link was thus apparently established between CVT and productivity and hence competitiveness. Statistical study failed, however, to demonstrate this link and, conversely, established clear correlations between industrial training effort, capital intensity, the level of employees' basic vocational education, etc. (Dayan *et al.* 1986).

The upshot was still a marked investment by industry in training: increased expenditure on employee training; the reinforcement by firms of their education strategies; the development of new types of organization giving more scope for apprenticeships; basic training with the development of industrial training and sandwich courses, etc. This was something new for French companies, particularly when compared with their German counterparts, which had been investing – and were undoubtedly the main force – in basic VET for many years via the dual system (Géhin and Méhaut 1993).

TOWARDS A FRENCH VET MODEL?

These historical developments represent a major turning point in the French education and training system, particularly from the 1980s onwards, influencing its scale, social composition and overall organization (Verdier 2001). They have contributed to a combination of: a sharp increase in manpower; reorientation of curricula in favour of vocational and technical dimensions; a transformation of organizational methods; the development of alternance between education and work; and above all the diversification of education policies.

The increased importance of education

The most dramatic development was undoubtedly the extension of the average duration of studies, an openly declared objective since the 1980s of successive right- and left-wing governments under the slogan '80 per cent of the young generation at baccalaureate level'. This objective is now within reach: the rate of access to baccalaureate level doubled in 20 years, standing at approximately 70 per cent in 2002. This increase has been achieved through diversification of the subjects covered: general baccalaureates (based around science, arts, economics and social affairs), predominant in the early 1980s, now only relate to about half of baccalaureate graduates. At the same time, technology-based and, above all, vocational baccalaureates, created in the mid-1980s, have experienced sustained growth and account for 21 per cent and 13 per cent of young people respectively.

Rather than democratization, which would mean reducing or even eliminating school-related social inequalities,[8] there has been a consolidation of secondary and subsequently higher education. The percentage of 20 year olds in full-time education by the mid-1990s was particularly high in France, reaching 57 per cent compared with only 35 per cent in the United States, 40 per cent in the United Kingdom and 46 per cent in Germany (OECD 1996). In France much importance has been attached to pursuing studies in higher education,[9] which currently accounts for more than two million students and experienced a boom during the 1990s, explained both by greater access to and the increased duration of advanced studies, with more and more students pursuing studies at post-graduate level.

Slight increase in vocational courses

There was another notable trend as a growing number of subjects became vocation-oriented. Over a period of three decades the development of college-based VET continued and broadened, involving the creation of national diplomas with precise qualifications and, in principle, extensive recognition within the labour market. Alongside the CAP and the brevet d'études professionnelles (BEP) (technical school certificate), which constituted a benchmark in terms of worker training, diplomas were issued that marked the successful conclusion of a two-year vocation-oriented short course in higher education after the baccalaureate, the Brevet de Technicien supérieur (BTS) (vocational training certificate) and the Diplôme Universitaire de Tecnologie (DUT). Subsequently in the 1980s vocational baccalaureates were put in place, keeping pace with the increasing technical skills required for junior employees.

These diplomas have consistently grown in importance and are now awarded to the greater proportion of young people leaving the education system. At the end of the 1990s the national education system each year awarded approximately 210,000 CAPs, 200,000 BEPs, 230,000 technology- or vocation-based baccalaureates and 120,000 advanced engineering degrees. Orienting schools towards vocations appears even more significant in so far as it extends to universities, where there has been a significant increase in vocation-based diplomas and courses: Diplômes d'Etudes Supérieures Spécialisées (one-year post-graduate diplomas in an applied subject of which about 25,000 are awarded each year), Maîtrises de Sciences et Techniques (science and engineering master's degrees), Instituts Universitaires de Formation des Maîtres (teacher training colleges), Instituts Universitaires Professionnalisés (vocation-based colleges) and, very recently, licences professionnelles (vocation-based degrees) (Verdier 2001).

Whilst two decades have seen an increasing orientation towards vocational training in education and specifically in higher education, this has not eliminated the historical influence of academic systems. Vocational qualifications are still largely gained via basic training and within the framework of the college. In 1999 more than 800,000 vocational students and nearly 360,000 students studied for an advanced engineering diploma. These all represented young people in vocational training within an academic institution against only 360,000 apprentices and approximately 100,000 young people on qualification contracts, that is part-time vocational courses managed by firms, industrial sectors, unions and employers.

The development of sandwich courses

Alternance between training and work, although far from being unified and referring to different systems and practices, affects a growing number, even the majority, of young people leaving school education (Monaco 1993). It is of three major types. The first concerns vocational courses in secondary and higher education, where syllabuses increasingly include mandatory training courses geared towards an introduction to industry and the world of work in addition to enhancing technical and vocational expertise. The second refers to young people who have left the education system without any vocational qualifications or with problems in the labour market. Numerous vocational integration/training systems have been set up within this framework, organized by public authorities or unions and management, and all based on the notion that training offers protection against unemployment (*Sociologie du travail* 1995). In the main they offer lengthy periods in firms to acquire vocational skills, as in the case of qualification contracts, which are specific labour contracts based on alternating between periods of work and training. The last and by far the oldest type of alternance is the traditionally undervalued artisan-based apprenticeship requiring an employment contract, geared to young people from underprivileged environments or of rural origin who have failed in their school career and based in small firms, in particular in the building trades, commerce, hotel management and catering, and vehicle repair. In spite of numerous attempts at modernization, which nevertheless led to enhanced organizational training and success in examinations (previously very low), apprenticeship has maintained its structural characteristics.

Not until the 1990s, under the dual influence of a public employment incentive policy for apprentices and legislation opening up apprenticeship to larger companies and higher level diplomas, was a relative improvement to be observed, including: a significant increase in workforce presence; improved levels, evident from the reduced proportion of apprentices studying for a CAP (although these still remain the majority); and the development of apprenticeship in higher education. The increased workforce relates more to an extension of the apprenticeship period, with more young people bound to several contracts, than to any increase in the numbers linked to the system. Finally, the highly regarded aspects of apprenticeship (preparation for a higher education diploma, incorporation into large companies, etc.) still remain very much a rarity.

Diversification of decision-making and management areas

We are witnessing a diversification of decision-making in education and training that may ultimately lead to significant reorientation. Whilst the Ministry of National Education has maintained a central role, new decision-makers have reinforced their functions and prerogatives, above all firms and their professional, inter-professional or sectoral organizations. From the continuing vocational training of their employees, they have gradually broadened their scope to include basic training through the development of training and sandwich courses.

At the same time, increased youth unemployment, particularly affecting those with the least training and fewest diplomas, has led to the development of specific public policies. An overall institutional structure has been gradually established, geared towards the training of the most vulnerable in the labour market and managed by the Ministry of Employment and Labour (Rose 1998).

Growing concerns about the management of employment and unemployment has led to the administrative organization of VET in France becoming increasingly complex. On the one hand, the Ministry of National Education and its decentralized administration (education authorities) have been essentially responsible for technical and vocational training with a mainly academic structure. On the other hand, the Ministry of Labour, Employment and Vocational Training and its decentralised administration tend to supervise the nascent overall system, which can be classified as 'post-academic vocational training', used by young school leavers, job seekers, people in difficulties in the labour market, etc., with a focus on employment and employability.

A third category of decision-makers in terms of VET has become apparent since the 1980s: regional councils, that is the main regional political authorities, to which responsibilities concerning CVT and apprenticeship were transferred with the regionalization process in France that began with the decentralization laws of 1983. This process was supplemented by the so-called 'five-year' Act of 1993 on labour, employment and vocational training, which sought to inspire decentralized concerted planning, consultation with financial institutions, unions and employers and the creation of numerous partners. The effect was to consolidate the forces involved, the regional councils and two decentralized public bodies – the Education Authorities and the DRTEFP – representing the education and labour administrations (Coordinating Committee 2000). Regional councils occupy a central position within this group in terms of the scope of their direct responsibilities, now covering the essential aspects of public policy on CVT and extending to the provision of facilities, information and guidance for the general public. The most significant development, however, concerns the increased importance of their coordinating role, which means that the majority of regional councils to a greater or lesser extent control the overall VET system and even, albeit indirectly, secondary and higher education. The regional councils are thus responsible for creating 'regional vocational training development plans' that seek to coordinate the various heterogeneous systems within VET.

BY WAY OF A CONCLUSION

In view of these developments, one question that arises is: are we witnessing a crisis in the academic model and its gradual replacement by a new model prioritizing vocational aspects and linking education and the economy? Although the scope of the changes in progress should not be underestimated, answering this question with a 'yes' would undoubtedly be somewhat premature, given that these changes are considerable in number, ambiguous and partly contradictory.

On the one hand, the academic model does not appear to have been significantly destabilized and remains steadfast. Thus, although quantitatively speaking their relative influence has dwindled, the most respected school courses have seen their numbers rise and, above all, their prestige remain intact, particularly science-based baccalaureates, intensive preparatory courses for the prestigious Grandes Écoles, and the Grandes Écoles (prestigious higher education institutes) themselves. The Grandes Écoles, too, maintain their position in the education hierarchy, their central role in producing elite graduates and the advantages within the executive labour market of being awarded one of their degrees. Similarly, whilst the French education system has witnessed a move towards a more vocation-based system that particularly affects its most highly valued elements such as higher education, this process does not call into question the academic institution and model because, as we have seen, this operates principally within the school.

On the other hand, the period since the 1980s has been marked by a change in the dominant features: a relative increase in the standing of vocational education or traditional courses, such as apprenticeship; the gradual recognition, via the development of employer-financed CVT and training and sandwich courses, of industry as a place for training; the challenging (through the development of training for job seekers and subsequently through the coordination and planning role awarded to regional councils) of traditional relationships between education and production, previously considered both impregnable and incompatible.

New concepts are gradually emerging and expanding concerning the legitimacy of qualifications requested by firms, the formative nature of work, and the recognition and endorsement of vocational knowledge and experience (Ropé and Tanguy 1994). The essential factor in this construction is symbolic, acknowledging French industry as a legitimate source of training or education in the same way as other institutions, such as school, the family and, to a certain extent, the professions. This question is currently unresolved and is the subject of debate between the main organized economic and social forces in society.

NOTES

1 It should be noted that the edict of Turgot of 1776 had established the principles of the right to work and the elimination of corporations but could not be applied.

2 The significant number of types and controls that govern establishments reflects the importance of the disputes and discussions around the concept of vocational education (including within the government), with the Ministry of Public Education prioritizing a 'broad, secular and republican' type of education, whilst the Ministry of Trade and Industry preferred an education in line with the needs of business.

3 The roots of the so-called academic model lie in the scholastic tradition, established in the majority of European universities from the end of the Middle Ages.

4 In France education levels control an extensive range of actions and strategies carried out by the main actors in the education system, including employers.

5 The country's total expenditure in terms of continuing education currently stands at around 1.8 per cent of gross domestic product (GDP). This constitutes an extremely significant effort that has tended to stabilize since the mid-1990s following significant growth in the 1980s and that has above all been taken up by public authorities (government and public administrations nearly 50 per cent; regional councils approximately 10 per cent) and business (nearly 40 per cent), whilst the direct contribution of households, and thus of individuals, to education would appear to be marginal.

6 The notion of social advancement suggests the possibility of going from the status of worker to that of executive; this is symbolic rather than actual, as demonstrated by the first sociological analyses on the subject (Durand and Durand 1972).

7 More than a hundred a year over the recent period, prioritizing the financing of continuing education, the creation and operation of fundraising bodies, alternance-based training contracts or joint systems, and, more rarely, prioritizing more qualitative aspects such as the objectives and priorities of education and the subject matter of vocational qualification certificates (Lindeperg 1999).

8 There has been a diversification of courses and paths to academic success. Although until the 1980s obtaining a baccalaureate and moving on to higher education constituted satisfactory indicators for understanding school-related social inequalities, it is now necessary to refine these data, particularly taking into account type of baccalaureate obtained or course of higher education selected.

9 A survey (source: MEN) of 2,119,000 students enrolled in 1998–9 revealed

1,310,000 at university (excluding IUT and IUFM), 240,000 in STS (advanced engineering courses), 115,000 at IUTs (polytechnics), 78,000 on intensive courses for the prestigious Grandes Écoles and 55,000 at engineering schools.

REFERENCES

Agulhon, C. (1994) *L'enseignement professionnel*, Paris: les éditions de l'atelier.

Castel, R. (1995) *La métamorphose de la question sociale*, Paris: Fayard.

Charlot, B. and Figeat, M. (1985) *Histoire de la formation des ouvriers: 1789–1984*, Paris: Minerve.

Combes, M.C. (1986) 'La loi de 1971 sur l'apprentissage: une institutionnalisation de la formation professionnelle', *Formation Emploi* 7, 8–16

Dayan, J.L., Géhin, J.P. and Verdier, E. (1986) 'La formation continue dans l'industrie', *Formation Emploi* 16, 7–36.

Delors, J. (1974) 'Genèse d'une loi et stratégie de changement', *Esprit* 439, 547–566.

Dubar, C. and Gadéa, C. (1999) *La promotion sociale en France*, Lille: presse universitaire du Septentrion.

Durand, C. and Durand, M. (1972) *De l'OS à l'ingénieur : carrière ou classe sociale*, Paris: éditions ouvrières.

Durkheim, E. (1938) *L'évolution pédagogique en France*, Paris: PUF.

Formation Emploi (1989) numéro spécial, 'l'enseignement technique et professionnel, repères pour l'histoire', 27–28, La Documentation française.

Géhin, J.P. (1999) 'L'explosion de la formation post scolaire en France: quelques enjeux', *Mouvements* 5, 46–55.

Géhin, J.P. and Méhaut, P. (1993) *Apprentissage ou formation continue? Les stratégies éducatives des entreprises en Allemagne et en France*, Paris: L'harmattan.

Jobert, A. (2000) *Les espaces de la négociation collective, Branches et territoires*, Toulouse: Octarès.

Lefranc, G. (1975) *Histoire du travail et des travailleurs*, Paris: Flammarion.

Léon, A. (1968) *L'histoire de l'enseignement technique*, Paris: PUF.

Lindeperg, G. (1999) 'Les acteurs de la formation professionnelle, pour une nouvelle donne', Rapport au premier ministre, Paris.

Maurice, M., Sellier, F. and Silvestre, J.J. (1982) *Politique d'éducation et organisation industrielle en France et en Allemagne*, Paris: PUF.

Monaco, A. (1993) *L'alternance Ecole production*, Paris: PUF.

Naville, P. (1948) *La formation professionnelle et l'école*, Paris: PUF.

OECD (1996) *Education at a glance: Analysis*, Paris: OECD.

Pallazzeschi, Y. (1998) *Introduction à la sociologie de la formation*, Paris: L'harmattan.

Prost, A. (1968) *Histoire de l'enseignement en France*, Paris: A. Colin.

Ropé, F. Tanguy, L. (eds) (1994) *Savoirs et compétences*, Paris: L'harmattan.

Rose, J. (1998) *Les jeunes face à l'emploi*, Paris: Desclée de Brouwer.

Sociologie du travail (1995) 'Contre le chômage, la formation?', *Variations européennes*, 37, 4, 95.

Terrot, N. (1983) *Histoire de l'éducation des adultes en France*, Paris: édilig.

Verdier, E. (2001) La France a-t-elle changé de régime d'éducation et de formation?, *Formation Emploi*, 76, 11–34.

Chapter 4

The German philosophy of vocational education

Wolf-Dietrich Greinert

(Translated by Janet Fraser)

> Most Germans are not looking for just a job, they want a *Beruf*,[1] a lifelong one, and one about which they can be passionate. And any government that does not meet that aspiration must fail, sooner or later. If you have a *Beruf* in Germany, you are someone. If you just have a job, you aren't.

So wrote Ullrich Fichtner in the weekly current affairs magazine, *Der Spiegel*, on 30 May 2005. His pithy summing-up illustrates one of the most crucial issues now facing the German labour market but also suggests that this specific understanding of the link between employment and *Beruf* reflects a long tradition in Germany. He is implying that the *Beruf*-oriented structural model of employment has become deeply embedded in the German culture of labour, illustrating that Germans understand *Beruf* to be as universal and unchanging a concept as the quintessentially German concept of *Bildung*.[2]

In this chapter, I shall attempt to show how the development and organizational structure of the 'German system' of non-academic vocational education have been shaped by the social power of these two key concepts and are still today under its influence. To recognize this is to understand many aspects of the deep-rootedness of the concept of *Beruf* in Germany. I shall also attempt to explain why Germany, with its tradition of vocational education and training, is having such difficulty in adapting smoothly to the market-oriented and technocratic principles of European vocational education and training.

GERMANY'S DUAL CORPORATIST MODEL OF TRAINING AND ITS ROOTS IN PRE-MODERN EMPLOYMENT PATTERNS

Germany's reaction to the decline of the pre-modern production model and its specific pattern of vocational education differed from that of Britain or France. Rather than developing a new, modern form of vocational education and training (VET) appropriate to a society undergoing intense industrialization, Germany largely re-established the traditional form of class-based craft education that had evolved in the High Middle Ages and that had later become the paradigm for non-academic vocational education (Stütz 1969). This was not so much a response to the driving forces of industrialization as a by-product of the policy adopted in a newly united Germany (the *Kaiserreich*) on the *Mittelstand* or petty bourgeoisie. The aim of this policy was to protect what remained of the former petty bourgeoisie – the craft sector, small shopkeepers and small-scale farmers – against further proletarianisation: capitalist competition was headed off by means of economic policy and traditional class-based privileges were re-established, strengthening the surviving *Mittelstand* as a 'bulwark against social democracy'[3] and admitting it to the ranks of 'forces supporting the state'. This piece of social engineering meant that the legislator restored to the craft sector two crucial privileges in particular: a return substantially to the organiza-tional forms it had always enjoyed; and stabilization of its centuries-old form of training, apprenticeship (Winkler 1972).

In concrete terms, this means that the majority in the *Reichstag*, the elected cham-ber of the German parliament – which between 1878 and 1897 and again in 1908 consisted of Conservatives, the (Catholic) Centre Party and the National Liberals (a breakaway faction from and less progressive than the larger Liberal grouping) – passed a number of Bills reforming both the retail and the craft sectors. These did not entirely meet the demands of the *Mittelstand* but they put on a statutory footing a clear improvement in the status of the craft sector and shopkeepers to the detriment of third parties, in particular consumers. The most important reform was what was called the *Handwerkerschutzgesetz* of 1897, legislation to recognize the common inter-ests of self-employed craftworkers by establishing trade associations as public corpor-ations (*Körperschaften des öffentlichen Rechts*). Not least because it restricted internal competition, this instituted what Rinneberg (1985) refers to as 'optional compulsory guilds' (*fakultative Zwangsinnung*). Legislation for a certificate known as the *großer Befähigungsnachweis* (literally, major certificate of competence), which made it com-pulsory for any craftsman running his own shop to have master craftsman status, was passed by the *Reichstag* in 1890 but fell when the non-elected chamber of the German parliament, the *Bundesrat*, objected. It was replaced in 1908 by the *kleiner Befähigungs-nachweis* (literally, minor certificate of competence), which was regarded as only a partial equivalent. It linked the right to offer apprenticeship training to the title of master craftsman (Coelsch 1910).

Alongside the re-establishment of the principle of self-governance in the craft sector, the 1897 reform established a completely new structure for VET. Articles 126 to 128 of the legislation laid down general principles while Articles 129 to 132 stipulated the specific principles, that is, those relating solely to apprenticeships, and this consolidated the privileged status that the craft sector had for some time enjoyed over industry in vocational education and training. A key concept here is that the legislator handed over the power to supervise and administer craft apprenticeships (including the key power to control examinations) to trade corporations or guilds, as appropriate. This 'corporatist' solution remains to this day a central plank in Germany's dual system of vocational education and training (Böttger 1898).

While the revival of the craft sector's right to organize itself and of its traditional education of the next generation of workers may be seen as a Conservative/clerical variant of policy to protect the *Mittelstand*, the attempt to institutionalize further education establishments, or *Fortbildungsschulen*, as the second locus for dual VET, may be seen as its Liberal variant. Such establishments had been in existence in Germany since the eighteenth century, both as general educational establishments for children who had completed compulsory education (what were known as 'Sunday schools') and as establishments providing more specific training, particularly craft education. As a result, these establishments were mostly privately funded, often not particularly successful, and permanently under threat (Thyssen 1954). It was not, in fact, until after 1870 that policy on *Fortbildungsschulen* quickly began to evolve in Germany as a result of rapid population growth and urbanization, especially in industrial agglomerations, as the gap in 'secondary socialisation' – that is, a lack of state influence on education between the end of compulsory schooling and military service – took on proportions that bourgeois society could no longer simply ignore. However, this first state-sponsored attempt to gain educational (for which read political and ideological) influence over young people from the petty bourgeoisie and the proletariat by means of a general *Fortbildungsschule* based on the curriculum of the elementary school was a complete failure (Greinert 1975: 21ff.).

Around 1890, this attempt at normative indoctrination and discipline came under criticism for being an overt tool of the class struggle, culminating around 1900 in a proposal from Munich's schools inspector, Georg Kerschensteiner, that these schools should be converted into establishments oriented more consistently around vocational education or students' future *Beruf*; this, he argued, would serve a *Mittelstand* policy based on vocational education but taking a more overtly educational form. Kerschensteiner's proposal (Kerschensteiner 1901) to use state-regulated VET to enlist young people from the working classes to the (still fledgeling) bourgeois nation state not only paved the way for 'vocational schools' with a public education mission but also, from an international perspective, embodied one of the most significant school reform initiatives of the twentieth century, albeit one that has in some cases been decisively rejected (see, for example, Knoll 1993).

Between 1895 and 1914, education reformers led by Woldemar Pache in Saxony and Georg Kerschensteiner himself, along with state authorities in Prussia, Bavaria, Baden, Württemberg and other states (almost all exponents of bourgeois liberalism), succeeded in substantially increasing the number of vocationally oriented *Fortbildungsschulen* and extending their coverage. They also succeeded in making them compulsory as a complement to the newly established vocational education (Harney 1980). The close ties between these establishments with their class-based concept of *Beruf*, which was expanding in the conservative social climate of the German *Kaiserreich*, and the requirement for 'civic education' that would span all classes acted, however, as a strong brake on this Liberal modernizing agenda with regard to vocational education (Geißler *et al.* 1992). The 'role model of the *Mittelstand's* identification with *Beruf* and its fundamental loyalty to the state' (Harney 1980), which the Liberals and governments had, since at least the 1890s, promoted as the binding model of education for those attending *Beruf*-oriented and compulsory *Fortbildungsschulen*, did, however, include one undoubtedly progressive element. This was the promise of occupational opportunity, a social and educational dimension that would eventually result in these establishments becoming the second pillar of the dual system (Bruchhäuser and Lipsmeier 1985).

It may be useful here to give some brief background on Georg Kerschensteiner. An education reformer, Kerschensteiner was a major contributor to the development of the modern German academic and vocational education system. His key educational concept, 'civic education' through VET provision – the core of the German philosophy of vocational education – produced a completely new establishment with a public education mission. Ultimately, this return to a pre-modern model of socialization represented a schism between two strictly class-specific forms of socialization in the new generations: the (humanist) concept of *Bildung* was to be the medium for educating the bourgeois and academic upper classes for their role in society, but for the manual working classes, *Beruf* took its place (Kerschensteiner 1901). Thus, in the early twentieth century, Kerschensteiner was the first prominent educationalist to strengthen the divide instituted a century earlier by New Humanists between a school system offering general education and a VET system governed by the concept of *Beruf* (Greinert 2003).

SUCCESSFUL INTEGRATION OF TRADITIONAL AND RATIONAL VET: APPRENTICESHIPS IN TRADITIONAL GERMAN INDUSTRY

The second phase in the development of the dual VET system in Germany was typified by an attempt to impose clearer and more modern structures on a sector that was still pre-industrial in its fundamental orientation, still largely unharmonized and offering a seemingly random combination of academic and industrial learning. Astonishingly, the various measures and initiatives survived three very different political epochs, eventually to converge in what has been a remarkable consolidation of 'dual' VET and a real system.

The last economic cycle before the First World War (approx. 1895–1913) saw the beginning of changes in industry's qualification requirements as a result of rapid growth. The pioneering companies in the mechanical engineering and electrical industries in particular were expanding rapidly and needed new methods of production, which they based on a model developed in the United States (Hanf 1987: 157ff.).

This push for rationalization, known as 'Taylorism', demanded a new type of worker in German industry, one who – in contrast to the 'artisan-craftworker' model of the past – was willing to conform to the demands and explicit constraints of new methods of production.

The new VET model that German industry was developing from around the turn of the century was, as a result, strongly influenced by F. W. Taylor's ideas of scientific management and his rational system of work organization. It had three main aspects: an *institutional* aspect, with facilities on the shopfloor and a school within factories; a *methodological* approach, including the use of psychological aptitude testing, standardized training courses and materials; and a *Beruf*-system approach, with provisions laid down in law relating to profile, VET scheme and examination requirements (Greinert 1998: 65ff.). Specialist institutions were created to develop and disseminate this modern model of VET, such as the *Deutscher Ausschuß für Technisches Schulwesen* (German Committee for Technical Education) (DATSCH), the *Arbeitsausschuß für Berufsausbildung* (Working Group on Vocational Education) (AfB) and the *Deutsches Institut für Technische Arbeitsschulung* (German Institute for Technical Employment Education) (DINTA), and their successor institutions have in some cases survived to the present day.

This represented an unprecedented systematization and refinement of the VET model compared with traditional craft education and it abolished the supremacy of the craft sector in this area when, in 1936, the sector's certification monopoly on craft education was removed. Those who emerged from this development embodied an entirely new type of qualified worker and, indeed, represented a new 'social player', one that had been moving towards a leading role in German VET since the 1930s (Ebert 1984).

A closer study reveals that industry left untouched two traditional principles of the apparently antiquated education model recreated by the *Kaiserreich*'s policy on the *Mittelstand*: first, its orientation to the concept of *Beruf* and, second, the principle that it should be largely self-governed by the trade associations that represented employers. A particular historical requirement for the 'differentiation of a self-referencing system for vocational education that was (relatively) independent of the schools system and of individual companies was the social acceptance of *Beruf* as a meaningful way of constituting and reproducing vocational education structures' in Germany (Georg 1998: 181). 'Self-referencing' here means, according to systems theory, that using the category of *Beruf* enabled a vocational qualification system also to translate social and economic problems into its own systemic logic. It is this characteristic more than any other that distinguishes the German system of VET from purely academic or, indeed, purely enterprise-based variants.

With the *Beruf* principle adopted in industry's education and employment regulations, the orientation around *Beruf* came to dominate Germany in both company recruitment and employment policy practice and in the state's and trade unions' social and labour market policy. Labour framed by *Beruf* is relevant from various but interlinked perspectives, both politically and in terms of social structures, as: a special type of social distribution of labour; a medium for the exercise and control of company power; and a special form of tackling social problems (Lempert 1981: 522ff.).

From a historical and structural perspective, *Beruf* has in many cultures – at least until they have industrialized – been a pivotal link in social structures. Its role-based nature acquires a constitutive significance in building and regulating relationships between members of a society. In this context, individuals' development of self-identity is closely linked with their adoption of specific vocational roles, although not necessarily with having a number of more or less heterogeneous jobs.

BERUF AS AN ORGANIZING PRINCIPLE IN GERMAN VOCATIONAL EDUCATION AND IN GERMAN INDUSTRIAL CAPITALISM

It was only when industry almost single-handedly integrated traditional and modern VET structures that the foundations were laid for the many positive socio-economic and educational effects of the German system. While the model had long been admired across the world, its cultural specificity was a block to its adoption anywhere else. Even more significant, however, was the fact that the embedding of the dual system in Germany's industrial culture also reflected the influence industry had in the first place had on the emergence of a VET system. There are a number of key interlinkages:

- German industrial capitalism and the German VET system reflect a strongly production-oriented economic model at whose core lies what Baethge (2000) has called a 'productionist understanding of labour' that traditionally neglected the service economy as a residual category, even when service occupations had long since come to represent a majority of jobs in the economy.
- Industrial and other skilled occupations form the basis of a specific segmentation of the labour market in Germany that is characterized by a structure of 'niche *Beruf*-based labour markets'. Transfers between these partial labour markets are governed by a system of universally accepted certified qualifications based on the tradition of professional standards (Georg and Sattel 1995: 127ff.).
- The principle of *Facharbeit* (skilled labour) is also the main factor governing the organization of labour in Germany, which is typified by relatively flat hierarchies and concomitantly reduced supervision and leadership functions. Vocational education, competence and experience, mean that the *Facharbeiter* and technician work largely independently of close supervision and management.[4] On the other hand, the ability of this type of vocational education to adapt to changed –

and changing – demands gives companies plenty of scope in deploying their workers and relieves them of the need to provide costly further training and re-training.

■ The VET system and the principle of *Facharbeit* also typify what Mückenberger (1998) has called Germany's 'labour law culture' as well as 'production relations' in Germany. The simplest manifestation of this is in individual labour law, which is explicitly framed as *Berufsrecht*, that is, based on the *Beruf*, and is, moreover, guaranteed under Article 12 of the German Constitution (its *Grundgesetz*). When it comes to collective labour law, which governs the relationship between labour and capital, the links with the *Beruf* principle are more indirect (Hesse 1984: 80ff.).

■ The German trade unions (as one specific object of collective labour law) that developed in the 19th century as interest groups for the craftsman and *Facharbeiter* have long geared themselves to principles of *Beruf* or *Facharbeit* when considering their organization and strategies. The strong position they enjoy today as 'social partners' to major employers' associations has traditionally been the fruit of their mass membership in (heavy) industry, and this is also where the unions have been most successful in implementing the specifically German concept of the *Betriebsverfassung* (Works Council Constitution), granting rights of participation, including involvement in company-level VET measures.

■ The *Beruf* principle and *Beruf*-based *Facharbeit* have also had a major influence on what is known as the standard employment relationship that has become the 'employment and social norm in industry, with employees working for one company for eight hours a day, for five or six days a week and for 40 years' (Baethge 2001: 31).

■ The traditional German system of social security is closely linked to this pattern, oriented as it is on long-term employment within a given *Beruf*. Empirical research has now demonstrated incontrovertibly that the typically German model of socialization has played an enormous role in terms of social integration (Konietzka 1999).

■ *Beruf*-based *Facharbeit* as the basis for a specific social identity of industrialism, with a quasi-standardized route for education, employment and career development, has in particular a direct impact on workers themselves, on the way their lives are shaped and on their spiritual and moral development (Beck *et al.* 1980: 199ff.). Numerous empirical studies have shown that, within German culture, workers have a strong self-identification with their *Beruf* and with its demarcation from others, which is the primary source of the identity and the self-image of workers, both as perceived by themselves and as presented to others.

As Heidegger (2004: 63) argues:

Unlike other countries, Germany still views it as positive, rather than as a sign of failure, when a student follows his or her secondary education with 'just' vocational rather than academic education. This seems in any case the only logical development in the case of modern, leading-edge roles in industry, commerce or the service sector for which, in other countries, students have to go to university. The German system also supports less demanding occupations with vocational education towards the base of the employment pyramid whose quantitative dominance ensures that vocational education is widely recognised as the central institution for young people.

The much-admired efficiency of this peculiarly German combination of an industrial model of production and a traditional *Beruf*-based and corporatist qualification system was, however, achieved at the expense of a substantial disadvantage in terms of educational structures, as indicated above in the section on Kerschensteiner. This special path was the key pre-condition for the traditional split in German education between general education and vocational education, with their different regimes and differing levels of social esteem. The existence of a comprehensive, efficient system of broad-based VET was exactly what was needed for the parallel system of highly selective elite education in academic secondary schools and universities to function smoothly. On the other hand, this system meant that industry had access to the 'best sons of the people', as sociologist Burkart Lutz epitomized them, by consistently removing the negative 'just' tag from VET. This is precisely the reason that the convinced US Democrat John Dewey so emphatically rejected the introduction of vocational schools along German lines as separate entities from general schools as a model for the USA (Knoll 1993).

THE COLLAPSE OF INDUSTRIALISM AND THE SEARCH FOR A NEW SKILLS MODEL

There is substantial evidence that the industrial labour culture model has been disintegrating for some time, and the unmistakable signs of erosion are preoccupying both public opinion and political circles. The following list includes just some of the most striking signs:

- the continued decline of the industrial sector accompanied by massive, sustained and politically damaging loss in labour capacity;
- the advance of the service economy coupled with its failure so far to compensate for job losses in manufacturing or to offer pay at the levels previously offered in industry;
- the advanced decline of the standard employment relationship in favour of more flexible forms of working;

- the threatened collapse in particular of the social security system financed, along the lines first instigated by (united Germany's first Chancellor) Bismarck, jointly by employee and employer contributions to offer pensions, unemployment benefits and sick pay, among other things;
- the structural crisis in the trade unions, the fragmentation of partial labour markets and the erosion of the qualification system, all of which point to the end of the *Facharbeiter*'s privileged position on the German labour market.

Attempts to draw out patterns from the trends now emerging in industrialized European societies can perhaps be summarized as the 'transformation of the post-war social state into a competition state' (Streeck 1998: 180). The driving force behind the process, to which the diffuse label 'globalization' is often attached, is the unprecedented technical progress of the last few decades: this has both largely freed capital from its traditional dependency on labour and made it increasingly mobile, a trend that has had a growing influence on national policies.

The viability of the German VET system is now being threatened by two main, complex trends. The first of these is what Büchter (2005) describes as the 'traditional inherent instability' of the concept of *Beruf* at times of permanent pressure to modernize. This can be defined as the acceleration of change in the content of each *Beruf* coupled with the increasingly rapid decline of old groups of qualifications and the pressure to acquire new ones (that are not always immediately relevant to the *Beruf* in question). A further factor is the limited porosity of the boundaries between one *Beruf* and another, a factor that is a particular impediment to the modern organization of work.

Germany is the only culture to have a specialist discipline called *Berufspädagogik* (literally, the methodology of teaching a *Beruf*), and for many years now, this discipline has reflected the uncertainty surrounding the *Beruf* principle with neologisms such as 'de-*Beruf*-ization' as well concerns about the 'erosion of the *Beruf*' and 'the crisis in vocational education'. Industrial sociologists also now take a more sceptical view of the *Facharbeiter* model in German industry and its basis on the *Beruf*. They argue that its rigidly specific competence boundaries are poorly suited to achieving the more flexible and efficient wealth creation and labour processes required by new principles of organization and management. Kern and Sabel (1994) refer in this context to the 'faded virtues' of the German model of industrial production and its threatened increasing dysfunctionality in the light of incontestable processes of industrial change.

German *Berufspädagogik* is, for all its beleaguered position, still focusing on a reality-oriented theory of *Beruf* (Büchter 2005), particularly since it views the concept of *Beruf* itself as irreplaceable. The *Beruf* orientation as an 'organizing principle' in the acquisition of qualifications in Germany (Deißinger 1998) is, however, coming under pressure from a second, and much more significant, trend, the European Union's VET policy. Experts – and particularly German ones – disagree on the extent to which the European Commission has a direct impact on the VET offered by Member States. The

Treaty of Rome can be interpreted as providing the Commission with a 'steering function' across the education and training field (Article 128 of the Treaty Establishing the EEC), but the European Union (Maastricht) Treaty stipulates that the principle of subsidiarity applies to VET. Specifically, Article 126(1) of the Maastricht Treaty stipulates:

> The Community shall contribute to the development of quality education by encouraging co-operation between Member States and, if necessary, by supporting and supplementing the responsibility of the Member States for the content of teaching and the organisation of education systems and their cultural and linguistic diversity.

Article 127(1) adds:

> The Community shall implement a vocational training policy which shall support and supplement the action of the Member States while fully respecting the responsibility of the Member States for the content and organisation of vocational education.

Irrespective of this clear injunction, the European Commission is attempting to create a single labour market for the whole European area and, in particular, to propagate a VET model that is based on workplace orientation and accreditation of vocational sub-competences. Back in 1992, the Council recommended in a Directive that the British accreditation system, based strictly on modularity, be adhered to in combination with the mutual recognition of vocational qualifications. This recommendation was also taken up by the Commission in its White Paper *Teaching and Learning: Towards the Learning Society* [COM(95)590 final] (European Commission 1996), firmly setting the scene for the planned creation of the 'European Qualification Frame' (EQF), the 'European Credit (Transfer) System for Vocational Education and Training' (ECVET) and the so-called 'EuroPass' as part of what is known as the 'Copenhagen process' and the implementation of a market-oriented concept of VET within the European Economic Area (Rauner and Grollmann 2004; Drexel 2005).

It is as yet unclear from the preliminary work undertaken by the Technical Working Group whether establishing an ECVET system in parallel with harmonization of university education across Europe will be a success. Indeed, some doubt seems appropriate, given that all the Commission's attempts since the 1960s to harmonize VET across the Member States have ended in dismal failure (Fulst-Blei 2003). Even if this attempt is more successful, the German system of acquiring vocational qualifications and its traditional *Beruf*-orientation will face substantial adjustment problems under the 'Copenhagen Process', given that the market model of VET that seems to be the paradigm across Europe is in many respects the exact opposite of Germany's *Beruf*-based model. In particular, the obvious solution – simply to integrate the two models, as is currently happening in Germany as the Bologna Process (the integration of European higher education) is implemented – would entail an enormous increase in bureaucratic structures.

One thing has, however, indisputably been achieved by the direction Brussels has taken on VET, especially in its orientation to current thinking as well as to general global trends and influences. From an international perspective, the last few decades have seen a violent paradigm shift in vocational qualifications and, since the 1970s in particular, the privileged, subject-oriented principles of vocational education – humanization, democratization and participation, for example – have now been pushed aside as VET has been reduced to just one element in socio-economic strategy, and preferably one that is geared around economic efficiency (Münk 1997: 92). 'Digital capitalism' is clamouring to be acknowledged in Europe, as elsewhere (Greinert 2001).

NOTES

1 Translator's note: the German term *Beruf* is one that does not have a single equivalent in English and can be rendered as 'occupation', 'profession' or 'career'. However, training and status are always involved. In this chapter, it will not be translated but left in the original German.

2 Translator's note: *Bildung* also has no single English equivalent, encompassing as it does 'training, 'education' and 'culture'. It, too, will be left in the original German.

3 The Social Democratic Party was banned in Germany between 1878 and 1889.

4 Translator's note: the *Facharbeiter* is a qualified worker with a specific role in integrated production processes, with skills and knowledge guaranteed through vocational education. For an explanation of the origins of the *Facharbeiter* and his relation to the older craftsman see Hanf in this volume (Chapter 7).

REFERENCES

Baethge, M. (2001) Abschied vom Industrialismus: Konturen einer neuen gesellschaftlichen Ordnung der Arbeit, in: M. Baethge and I. Wilkens (eds), *Die große Hoffnung für das 21. Jahrhundert?*, Opladen: Leske & Budrich, pp. 23–44.

Beck, U., M. Brater and H. Daheim (1980) *Soziologie der Arbeit und der Berufe. Grundlagen, Problemfelder, Forschungsergebnisse*, Reinbek bei Hamburg: Rowohlt.

Böttger, H. (1898) *Geschichte und Kritik des neuen Handwerkergesetzes vom 26 Juli 1897*, Leipzig: Diederichs.

Bruchhäuser, H.P. and A. Lipsmeier (eds) (1985) *Quellen und Dokumente zur schulischen Berufsbildung 1869–1918*, Köln/Wien: Böhlau.

Büchter, K. (2005) Beruf: Idee – Form – Politikum. Eine Rekonstruktion berufstheoretischer Ansätze in der Berufs- und Wirtschaftspädagogik, in: K. Büchter, R. Seubert, and G. Weise-Barkowsky (eds), *Berufspädagogische Erkundungen. Eine Festschrift für Martin Kipp*, Frankfurt am Main: Gesellschaft zur Förderung arbeitsorientierter Forschung und Bildung, pp. 255–277.

Coelsch, H. (1910) *Deutsche Lehrlingspolitik im Handwerk*, Berlin: Guttentag.

Deißinger, T. (1998) *Beruflichkeit als 'organisierendes Prinzip' der deutschen Berufsaussbildung*, Markt Schwaben: Eusl.

Drexel, I. (2005) *Das Duale System und Europa. Ein Gutachten im Auftrag von ver.di und IG Metall*, Frankfurt am Main: Hausdruck.

Ebert, R. (1984) *Zur Entstehung der Kategorie Facharbeiter als Problem der Erziehungswissenschaft*, Bielefeld: Kleine.

Fulst-Blei, S. (2003) *Im Spannungsfeld von Modularisierung und Europäisierung: Die deutsche duale Berufsausbildung im Test – Ein deutsch-englischer Leistungsvergleich*, Mering: Rainer Hampp.

Geißler, K.A., W.-D. Greinert, L. Heimerer, A. Schelten and K. Stratman (eds) (1992) *Von der staatsbürgerlichen Erziehung zur politischen Bildung (1901–1991). 90 Jahre Preisschrift Georg Kerschensteiner*, Berlin/Bonn: Bundesinstitut für Berufsbildung.

Georg, W. (1998) Die Modernität des Unmodernen. Anmerkungen zur Diskussion um die Erosion der Beruflichkeit und die Zukunft des dualen Systems, in: F. Schütte and E. Uhe (eds), *Die Modernität des Unmodernen. Das 'deutsche System' der Berufsausbildung zwischen Krise und Akzeptanz*, Berlin: Bundesinstitut für Berufsbildung, pp. 177–198.

Georg, W. and U. Sattel (1995) Arbeitsmarkt, Beschäftigungssystem und Berufsbildung, in: R. Arnold and A. Lipsmeier (eds), *Handbuch der Berufsbildung*, Opladen: Leske & Budrich, pp. 123–141.

Greinert, W.-D. (1975) *Schule als Instrument sozialer Kontrolle und Objekt privater Interessen. Der Beitrag der Berufsschule zur politischen Erziehung der Unterschichten*, Hannover: Schroedel Verlag.

Greinert, W.-D. (1998) *Das 'deutsche System' der Berufsausbildung. Tradition, Organisation, Funktion*, 3rd edn, Baden-Baden: Nomos.

Greinert, W.-D. (2001) Berufsausbildung und digitaler Kapitalismus. Eine Problemskizze, in: *Zeitschrift für Pädagogik* 47, pp. 725–737.

Greinert, W.-D. (2003) *Realistische Bildung in Deutschland. Ihre Geschichte und ihre aktuelle Bedeutung*, Baltmannsweiler: Schneider Verlag Hohengehren.

Hanf, G. (1987) Berufsausbildung in Berliner Großbetrieben (1900–1929), in: W.-D. Greinert, G. Hanf, H. Schmidt, and K. Stratmann (eds), *Berufsausbildung und Industrie*, Berlin/Bonn: Bundesinstitut für Berufsbildung, pp. 157–187.

Harney, K. (1980) *Die preußische Fortbildungsschule*, Weinheim/Basel: Beltz.

Heidegger, G. (2004) Zur Zukunft des (deutschen) Berufskonzepts – die Herausforderung durch den Bologna-Prozess, in: G. Zimmer (ed.), *Kompetenzentwicklung und Reform der Berufsausbildung. Arbeit, Qualifikation und Ausbildung in der NetzWerk-Gesellschaft*, Bielefeld: Bertelsmann, pp. 49–69.

Hesse, H.A. (1984) *Das Recht der Bundesrepublik Deutschland*, Heidelberg: C.F. Müller.

Kern, H. and C.F. Sabel (1994) Verblaßte Tugenden – die Krise des deutschen Produktionsmodells, in: N. Beckenbach and W. von Treek (eds), *Umbrüche gesellschaftlicher Arbeit*, published in *Soziale Welt, Sonderband* 9, pp. 605–624.

Kerschensteiner, G. (1901) *Staatsbürgerliche Erziehung der deutschen Jugend*, Gekrönte Preisschrift, Erfurt: Carl Villaret.

Knoll, M. (1993) Dewey versus Kerschensteiner. Der Streit um die Einführung der Fortbildungsschule in den USA, 1910–1917, in: *Pädagogische Rundschau* 47, pp. 131–145.

Konietzka, D. (1999) *Ausbildung und Beruf. Die Geburtsjahrgänge 1919–1961 auf dem Weg von der Schule in das Erwerbsleben,* Opladen/Wiesbaden: Westdeutscher Verlag.

Lempert, W. (1981) Beruf als Politikum, in: *Zeitschrift für Berufs- und Wirtschaftspädagogik* 77, pp. 519–531.

Mückenberger, U. (1998) Nationale Arbeitsrechte und soziales Europa, in: Cattero, B. (ed.) *Modell Deutschland, Modell Europa. Probleme, Perspektiven,* Opladen: Leske & Budrich, pp. 33–54.

Münk, D. (1997) Deutsche Berufsbildung im europäischen Kontext: Nationalstaatliche Steuerungskompetenzen in der Berufsbildungspolitik und die Sogwirkung des europäischen Integrationsprozesses, in: H.-H. Krüger and J.H. Olbertz (eds), *Bildung zwischen Staat und Markt,* Opladen: Leske & Budrich, pp. 91–108.

Rauner, F. and P. Grollmann (2004) Einheitliche Qualifikationsrahmen im Brügge/Kopenhagen-Prozess zwischen Schulabschluß und Kompetenz, in: *Die berufsbildende Schule* 56, pp. 159–165.

Rinneberg, K.-J. (1985) *Das betriebliche Ausbildungswesen in der Zeit der industriellen Umgestaltung Deutschlands,* Köln/Wien: Böhlau.

Streeck, W. (1998) Industrielle Beziehungen in einer internationalisierten Wirtschaft, in: U. Beck (ed.) *Politik der Globalisierung,* pp. 169–202, Berlin: edition sigma.

Stütz, G. (1969) *Das Handwerk als Leitbild der deutschen Berufserziehung,* Göttingen: Vandenhoek & Ruprecht.

Thyssen, S. (1954) *Die Berufsschule in Idee und Gestaltung,* Essen: Girardet.

Winkler, H.A. (1972) *Mittelstand, Demokratie und Nationalsozialismus,* Köln: Kiepenheuer & Witsch.

Chapter 5

The emergence and reinforcement of class and gender divisions through vocational education in England

Linda Clarke

INTRODUCTION

Vocational education is about the social development of labour, about nurturing, advancing and reproducing particular qualities of labour to improve the productive capacity of society. It is about entry into the labour market; about dividing up the potential labour force into different occupations and skills, each with a distinct quality. And it is about class and gender divisions, acting as a filter to include or exclude particular groups from particular occupations or industries and from acquiring a particular status in society.

At the same time there is a sense in which we can say that the identity of the state is formed through the social development of labour and that, as a result, vocational education is integral to the nature and development of the state; when one stagnates, so does the other. Indeed, in discussing developments in the Netherlands in this volume, Anneke Westerhuis shows how at various stages the identity of the Dutch state was formed through the education and training system and how through this system a concept of citizenship was imparted. In Britain in contrast it is a continuing puzzle to understand why the state distances itself from direct regulation of vocational education, by – as Ewart Keep shows in this volume (Chapter 12) – appearing to give unfettered control to employers, and hence fails to underpin the social development of labour.

This chapter seeks to show how, by examining the institutional structure regulating apprenticeship and vocational training in England from the sixteenth century and hence entry into the labour market – whether as apprentice or trainee – we can see how class and gender divisions of labour are structured. As Marsden (1999) explains, different institutional arrangements are associated with different skill formations. In effect, institutions and occupational hierarchies differ qualitatively with respect to the type of skill and labour market. More than this, we can also say that they differ according to class and gender relations. Chartered institutions, for example, play a key role in maintaining both what can be regarded as an almost intractable class divide between professionals and operatives and at the same time a male-dominated elite. Similarly, the town corporations of the sixteenth century were instrumental in ensuring that the crafts remained a male preserve and in restricting the employment of journeymen to maintain a hierarchy of craft masters.

The deep-rooted nature of the institutional arrangements supporting particular qualities of labour has implications for the nature and concept of skills and for skill formation. Thus the Anglo-Saxon concept of skill is of an individual physical attribute or 'property' required to fulfil particular tasks or outputs. This is as evident in the 'competences' associated with National Vocational Qualifications (NVQs) as in the writings of Adam Smith through to Braverman (e.g. Smith 1910; Braverman 1974). Such 'skill' is alien to the continental concept – whether in Germany, the Netherlands or Denmark – on which qualifications are built, of socially constructed knowledge and collective, physical and mental attributes associated with divisions and hierarchies of particular production processes. Thus in England the bricklayer's skills are associated with the physical and technical ability to lay bricks rather than seen as an integral part of a complex, dangerous and divided labour process governed by social norms and regulations and embedded in an institutional structure. How very different must be the vocational education of these two kinds of bricklayer and how very different their status once qualified!

When the quality of labour is considered in this continental sense as related to the division of labour and as institutionally cemented through schemes of education and training, then change becomes as dependent on labour and industrial organization as on specific employment and working conditions. It is not possible simply to construct a new quality or 'skill' by developing a new NVQ or to change gender and class divisions through legislation. A restructuring of the labour process and the institutional framework may be called for.

When vocational education is regarded as part and parcel of the social development of labour, it can be seen to go through qualitatively distinct stages of development. Nor can we assume that the dominant form of social relations of production at any one time is necessarily what is determinant for this development. If in the early sixteenth century the town corporation apprenticeship was the most entrenched institution for regulating entry, for skill acquisition and for reproducing the craft form of production, this did not mean that it was determinant for the further social development of labour. Indeed the craft form was superseded rather by the development of wage labour in the countryside regulated through the Statute of Artificers and involving very different processes, different means of valorization and different class and gender divisions.

The chapter therefore concerns different stages in the social development and reproduction of labour and its institutional contexts. Reference is made in particular to building which has remained a key industry throughout the centuries, one in which questions of skill formation have been especially important. In order to highlight distinct and qualitative differences, particular periods in each stage will be focused on, namely the early seventeenth and nineteenth centuries and post-World War II.

SKILL FORMATION, CLASS AND GENDER DIVISIONS UNDER FEUDALISM

Under feudalism two distinct categories of labour and hence apprenticeship are evident, one associated with artisan production regulated through the town corporations and the other with wage labour, prevalent in the countryside and regulated from 1563 through the Statute of Artificers (5 Elisabeth c4). A key difference between the two was in their respective wage forms. Payment for the former represented a price for the product or output of labour or, in other words, piecework. The wage for the latter represented a payment for the working day, that is for time, and developed both as a redemption from feudal service – whether through work on the demesne or statute labour on the roads – or as payment for occasional work.

Under the artisan system, the apprentice was controlled by a master who registered with the relevant town corporation, which in turn regulated apprenticeship, such as its length and limitations on numbers per class of master. Within the corporations exclusive liveries of large masters and merchants developed which, in contrast to the small craft masters, were less restricted in the number of apprentices they could take on. This meant that large numbers of poorly paid apprentices were to be found in some workshops whilst the craftsman who had paid an upstart fee was confined to maybe only one or two (Clarke 1999). The corporations themselves were divided according to different trades, determined by the particular product which the company had the royal privilege to sell, whether wood by the Worshipful Company of Carpenters or brick by the Worshipful Company of Tylers and Bricklayers of the City of London (Alford and Barker 1968; Bell 1938; Derry 1931). This represented the principle on which labour or 'skills' were divided and members of the corporations were not supposed to carry out the work of other trades, given their particular 'skill' privilege.

Men and women were also carefully divided as apprenticeship remained an overwhelmingly male institution. This ensured not only that property and power rested with the privileged group but that gender roles were clearly defined. Male apprentices were not, for instance, allowed to marry within the terms of their indenture. As Simonton has explained:

Apprenticeship was a period when the role of the male apprentice moved from lad to man; it was a transitional period that meant far more than 'learning a skill'. The close identification of apprenticeship with sexual development helps to identify the role of the institution as defining masculinity and conversely femininity and in excluding females from the system.

(1999: 34)

Those women who did enter the companies and practise a trade as mistresses working on their own account were invariably widows who had taken over the freedom of their husband's company. Otherwise women acted as assistants to husbands or fathers (Kenrick 1981).

In contrast to the artisan system was the wage labour system prevalent in the countryside and regulated through the Statute of Artificers of 1563 by Justices of the Peace (JPs). The statute introduced a contract of services for all hired labour, wage assessment and apprenticeship, such as a limit of three apprentices to one journeyman (Davies 1956). It was a system which extended throughout the realm aiming to integrate the landless category of labour, to bind it to a locality through the Act of Settlement, and to stem vagrancy through parish apprenticeships (Deakin 1991; Clarke 1992). No restriction with respect to the estate of parents was placed on apprenticeship.

A remarkable feature of the Statute was that it was not gender specific, referring to 'persons', 'boys and girls' and masters and mistresses' (39 Elisabeth c3; 43 Elisabeth c2). It set a framework for the parish apprenticeship system whereby males were bound to the age of 24 and girls till they were 21 or until they married. Snell (1985), in a survey of southern English counties between the seventeenth and nineteenth centuries, found that 34 per cent of parish apprentices were girls, and numbers were especially high in the eighteenth century (278). Nor were women necessarily bound to particular trades; indeed, Snell found male apprentices in 46 occupations and female in 51, including as bricklayers, carpenters, joiners and shipwrights (291).

Through the effective implementation of the statute and its extension to occupations such as brickmaking not covered by the companies, municipal trade control was weakened and the artisan craft system progressively undermined (Perry 1976). Though apprenticeship remained the rule, control by the companies could no longer be maintained. The clash between the artisan and wage labour systems came to a head around London in the seventeenth century when the Crown and the City Corporations fought against each other for control over the wage labour force congregated around the City as 'forrens', a term disparagingly applied to those not 'free' of the City (Unwin 1908). This was evident in the building trades in numerous petitions by the City companies against Crown proclamations seeking to control building activity and labour around the City (Clarke 1992). In 1636 a crisis point was reached as the Crown attempted to assert control over the suburbs by setting up a new rival Incorporation of Trades, appointed by JPs and including, for instance, the Brickmakers Company. The ensuing suits between the City and the new Corporation constituted a major grievance in the Civil War. The Rebuilding Act of 1667 after the Great Fire of London eventually resolved this particular dispute by given 'forrens' the same rights as freemen, thus symbolizing the domination of wage labour and the erosion of City powers (Reddaway 1940). This erosion is perhaps nowhere more evident than in 1673 when a girl claimed admittance to the Carpenter's Company by right of apprenticeship (Derry 1976). Nevertheless the 1688 constitutional settlement represented a compromise, establishing a system dominated by wage labour but one with strong artisanal characteristics.

From this time onwards, it became increasing common for apprentices once having served their time to just work as journeymen, taking on their own apprentices and labourers, given the difficulties of ever becoming masters. By the early eighteenth century masters were very often found employing 'forrens' or those not bound to the company or free of the city, taking on more apprentices than the ordinances allowed, and taking on apprentices in trades other than their own. The companies lost control too of individual trades or 'skills' as apprentices were bound to other companies. Throughout the eighteenth century female parish and non-parish apprentices alike were found in a wide range of overwhelmingly male-dominated trades, including as ironmongers, stonemasons, carpenters, bricklayers, butchers, blacksmiths and furniture makers (Dunlop and Denman 1912; Leeson 1979; Jupp and Pocock 1887; Pinchbeck 1930; George 1925; Snell 1985). As a consequence journeywomen were also to be found in all kinds of trades. For the building trades, for example, numerous female traders are recorded in the eighteenth century (Guillery 2000; Hewlings 2000).

By the end of the eighteenth century, however, JPs had lost control of apprentice regulation and the statutory system had become so weakened that the apprentice clauses of the Statute of Artificers were eventually repealed in 1814, despite the strong campaign mounted by the City companies in their defence (Derry 1931). Henceforth there were 'no longer statutory or legal formularies or instructions binding upon masters or journeymen in the matter of apprentices' but a 'free' agreement between the master, on the one hand, and the apprentices, his parents or representatives on the other (Howell 1877: 842). Without the protection of regulation, women too were increasingly excluded with the exception of parish apprenticeships.

THE EMERGENCE OF NEW CLASS AND GENDER DIVISIONS UNDER CAPITALISM

By the early nineteenth century many masters had never served an apprenticeship; they employed workers from trades in which they had themselves no competence, and took on apprentices as a form of cheap labour. The end of the statutory regulation of apprenticeship did not, of course, mean that apprenticeship ceased to exist, but that its institutional context was transformed. It had been opposed by the Committee of

Manufacturers as appropriate to 'feudal governance and the tyranny of the ancient barons' and as making for a rigid differentiation of trades which automatically encouraged combinations (Derry 1931). Adam Smith identified it with the 'Policy of Europe' and argued that: the government of trade by trade which it implied meant that a multitude of new occupations were not covered; the 'free circulation of labour from one employment to another even in the same place' was obstructed; it represented an exclusive privilege of corporations established to prevent reductions in price; its length and limitations of numbers restricted competition 'to a smaller number than might otherwise be disposed to enter the trade'; it gave 'no security that insufficient workmanship shall not be exposed to public sale'; and, as journeymen working by the piece, young men were likely to be more 'industrious' and to 'practice with more diligence and attention' (Smith 1910: 107–11, 122).

In the absence of legal regulation of apprenticeship, however, it was left largely to the newly emerging trade unions to enforce. Indeed George Howell in 1877 described the whole history of the trade unions as:

> One long record of persistent and sometimes not very wise efforts to maintain and enforce apprenticeship as the only means in their opinion for securing good and capable workmen.
>
> (851)

The General Union of Carpenters and Joiners set up in 1827, the Friendly Society of Bricklayers from 1829 and the Operative Stonemasons from 1831 all formed 'non-exclusive unions' of 'non-society men' and echoed the old artisan regulations in their demands for limitations in the number of apprentices taken on as a means to prevent the use of cheap labour, a seven-year term, age restrictions and no piecework. The trade unions too remained bound to traditional trades with those outside these classified as 'labourers' and not allowed into the union. Any new processes were fought over and claimed, such as the use of cement floors and breeze block partitions by both plasterers and bricklayers or gas fitting by plumbers (Hilton 1963; Postgate 1923).

Despite what might be regarded as skill protectionism, however, there was a clear transformation in the division of labour at this time, away from the old separate trade hierarchy of master, journeymen, apprentice, servant/labourer. Instead a new hierarchy emerged of capitalist employer, foreman, skilled craftsman, semi-skilled work and apprentice/labourer. This was related rather to industrial capital as the trades ceased to dominate over particular materials and the new capitalists might employ workers from a range of different trades.

The development of capitalist relations of production went together with a greatly enhanced gender division of labour. Gone were the female apprenticeships of the eighteenth century in what were regarded as 'male' trades and the proportion of female apprentices generally declined dramatically, though the number of female parish apprentices increased, especially factory apprentices and those in 'domestic' trades (Honeyman 2007). Non-parish apprenticeship became invariably confined to men and acted as a critical means of exclusion and control. This, together with the growing split between home and place of production, made for a narrowing in the possibilities for women in the labour market and increased dependence on men. The female marriage age dropped from 27 years and the proportion of women never marrying from 25 per cent in the late seventeenth century to 24 years and 6 per cent respectively by the 1820s (Snell 1985: 311).

Occupational gender segregation was very much accentuated. In 1804 the Ladies Committee for Promoting Education and Employment of Female Poor complained about the exclusion 'grievously and unjustly intruded upon by the other sex . . . confined most frequently to a few scanty and unproductive kinds of labour' (Pinchbeck 1930: 304). For parish apprentices Honeyman found that by the 1820s and 1830s a gender division of labour became generally practised and the norm was established for male apprentice wages rates to be higher than female (2007). Between 1841 and 1861 for instance virtually all 'male' trades became more male dominated – including carpenters, plumbers, glaziers and painters – whilst female trades became more heavily female, including glovers, dressmakers and ribbon makers (Snell 1985: 290). At the same time, the range of occupations open to women declined dramatically; only 5 out of 75 trades in Middlesex between 1803 and 1822 for example were mixed, the remainder being totally segregated (ibid.: 285).

An important reason for this exclusion of women from certain workplaces was the early trade union view that women should not enjoy the status of artisan and that, in effect, 'skill' was an essentially masculine quality or 'property' (Clark 1995: 119; Hobsbawm 1978: 132). Women represented 'a threat to the rates and conditions given' and 'as a class, the most dangerous enemies of the artisan's Standard of Life' (Webbs 1898: 497). The ribbon weavers even drew up an agreement with the masters that 'except in times of war, no woman or girl to be employed in making any kind of work except such work herein fixed' (George 1979: 183). And between 1806 and 1811, strikes against the employment of women took place, for instance by hatters, weavers, cotton spinners and tailors, resulting in women being restricted to subsidiary branches and processes. Women were excluded from apprenticeship and were not allowed artisan status but confined, for instance by the Spitalfields silkweavers, to subsidiary positions (Clark1995: 120). In this way, the notion of 'property in skill' was associated with a masculine quality. By the 1840s women's access to jobs had been delimited and the family wage was openly espoused as a wage paid to a married male worker adequate to raise a family, so emphasizing 'patriarchal control of the productive resources' (Kenrick 1981: 186; Pinchbeck 1930; Humphries 1987).

It is questionable whether changes in apprenticeship were really associated with the social development of labour rather than just with restricting access to the trades and maintaining wage levels. Without formal skill requirements and vocational education, the tendency was anyway to reproduce the skills of yesterday and to use apprentices as cheap labour. As the master was transformed into a capitalist employer, so apprentices were instead taught a trade by the journeyman. Indeed, it was only from the 1870s that more concerted attempts were made to develop labour, in particular following the establishment in 1871 of the City and Guilds of London Institute for the Advancement of Technical Education (Lang 1979). The trade unions tried hard to maintain standards but by 1884 the Royal Commission on Technical Instruction was complaining of a lack of skills and of apprenticeships increasingly being informal and mainly in small firms: 'at the best all that is learned in the workshop is manual dexterity and how to do things by "rule of thumb", "wrinkles and dodges" ' (Samuelson Commission 1884). Despite the clear decline in apprenticeship, an Enquiry into Apprenticeship and Training, set up in 1925, revealed that it remained in many respects entrenched, with for instance the building trades having a ratio of craftsmen to apprentices of 3.6:1 and of 7:1 in London (HMSO 1927–8: 17, 180).

Increased awareness of the need for formal vocational education for apprentices met only a patchy response, for instance through the setting up of local trade schools as local authorities gradually took over the role formerly assumed by the Mechanics Institutes (Lang 1979). Trade unions actively encouraged the technical education of apprentices and some system of practical examination (Booth 1895: 103). This was supported in the early 1900s by the Minority Report of the Poor Law Commission and the report on apprenticeship of the Education Committee of the London County Council which even called for half-time education for 15 to 18 year olds (Bray 1909: 114). There was, however, no pressure from industry before the 1930s for an extension of technical education (Cotgrove 1958: 80). By this time union proposals for reform included: joint regulation, the attachment of the apprentice to industry rather than the individual employer, the involvement of education authorities and day release as a right (Lee 1979: 39). The result of these efforts was the National Joint Apprenticeship Board set up in World War II but still on a voluntary basis, as the government continued to refuse to take responsibility for vocational education (Cotgrove 1958: 61). As reasserted in the Command of 1943 on Training for the Building Industry:

> Apart from the State's responsibility for supervising or grant-aiding technical instruction, apprenticeship unlike special adult training will not be provided and paid by the state . . . these are traditionally settled by the industry itself.
>
> (Command 6428)

THE POST-WAR DEMISE OF APPRENTICESHIP

Through this distancing of the state from vocational education the division between education and practical knowledge, between knowledge acquired outside the workplace and within, a division established in the days of the Mechanics Institutes, has been constantly reaffirmed (Cotgrove 1958: 33). It even sharpened as technical instruction rapidly expanded following the 1944 Education Act. This contained provisions for local authorities to provide further training and the setting up of National Joint Apprenticeship Boards which meant that apprentices were educated in the employer's time through day release once a week to technical college. After the war however there was increased concern about leaving training to industry, as expressed by Harold Clay, Assistant General Secretary of the Transport and General Workers Union to the British Association for Commercial and Industrial Training in 1947:

> There has got to be consideration of issues beyond the individual, beyond the firm, even beyond the industry . . . We have to get away from the idea that schemes of education and training represent something that a benevolent employer provides for his worker.
>
> (Lee 1979: 40)

This plea was heeded following the 1956 White Paper on Technical Education which outlined plans for a massive injection of funds into further education and for major reorganisation (Command 0903). And under the Industrial Training Act of 1964, representing 'the first attempt to formulate a modern industrial manpower policy', tripartite statutory Industrial Training Boards were set up, numbering 27 by 1969 (Perry 1976: xix). The remit of these was to: establish policy with respect to training, including its length, the registration of trainees and their attendance at further education college; set standards of training and syllabuses; provide advice and assistance about training; devise tests to be taken by apprentices and instructors; run training course in training centres; pay grants to reimburse firms and allowances to trainees not taken on by firms; collect levies; and borrow (Perry 1976: 101).

The levy-grant mechanism, whereby all firms except those below a certain size paid a levy and those providing training received grants, was central to the operation of the boards. Therefore when this mechanism collapsed in the early 1970s, so did the training board system, with the exception of the Construction Industry Training Board (CITB) and Engineering Construction Industry Training Board (ECITB) which still remain today. However even these remaining boards have undergone a metamorphosis in the intervening period, into employer-led bodies, catering for employers' specific demands and organized on the basis of a myriad of NVQ occupations rather than sector-wide vocational education and training schemes. Employers have reasserted managerial prerogative and the right to train and in so doing 'scotched' the traditional link between trade unions and apprenticeship (Gospel 1995: Lee 1979: 40–46). Left again to voluntarism, apprentice numbers fell dramatically, from 243,700 in 1966 to 53,000 by 1990 (Gospel 1995). In contrast to countries such as Germany, 'training' for 'skills' provides the rationale, rather than 'vocational education' for the productive enhancement of labour.

Since 1994 successive governments have sought to revive apprenticeship in the face of what has been described as the 'employers' retreat' as firms have shown increasing reluctance to make training places available (Keep 2002). The Modern Apprenticeship has been devised to cover a wider range of occupations and to be less gender and ethnically exclusive. As a result 46 per cent of Advanced Modern Apprentices are women and 4.3 per cent are from ethnic minorities. These are, however, concentrated in particular sectors: only 1.1 per cent of recruits into the construction industry and 2.8 per cent into engineering manufacturing, for instance, are women compared with 88 per cent in health and social care and 81 per cent in business administration, reflecting severe occupational gender segregation (Fuller and Unwin 2003). Modern apprentices were supposed to attain National Vocational Qualifications Level 3, though Level 2 is now the norm. Delivery is unspecified so that candidates can pursue very different routes (on- or off-the job, full or part-time) and processes to attain the same qualification. Non-completion rates are very high, with around 40 per cent of leavers from the traditional male sectors achieving an NVQ level 3 but only 15 per cent of leavers from the female sectors of hospitality and retailing (ALI 2002). In the construction sector too, where most trainees remain confined to the old traditional trades, only a minority (38 per cent) of first year trainee entrants are Modern Apprentices in firms. The majority (62 per cent) are found studying without an employer in Further Education Colleges, though here the drop-out rate is over 40 per cent and few succeed in subsequently entering employment in the construction sector as they do not have the necessary work experience (CITB 2004).

The system has remained not only distant from the national education system but also governed by quangos, public bodies which are not government departments but operate at arm's length from Ministers. Vocational Education has, since the demise of the Training and Enterprise Councils in 2002, been delegated to 47 Learning and Skills Councils, which support 15 Sector Skill Councils, in turn a merger of 72 former National Training Organizations and covering 90 per cent of the workforce (Figure 5.1) (Clarke and Herrmann 2004). These are set up as private companies under government licence as the 'UK's voice of employers', symptomatic yet again of the state's deference to private business interests. Skills recognition follows this same logic, with employer trade associations lobbying the respective Sector Skills Council to develop NVQ qualifications related to competences in their particular activity and unrelated to recognized programmes of vocational training. In this way, skills formation responds to the needs of yesterday, or rather the narrowly conceived needs of employers at the present moment, rather than forming part of a comprehensive vocational education system. At the same time, as apparent in Figure 5.1, there is no institutional link between industry and the FE colleges, between practical training and education.

Figure 5.1 *The structure of learning in the UK*

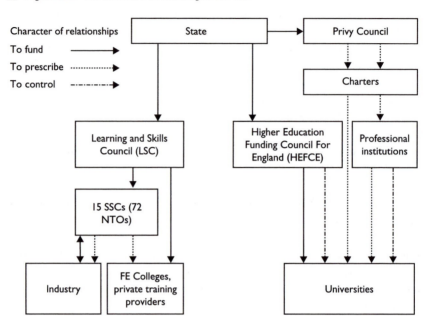

THE INSTITUTIONALIZATION OF CLASS SKILL DIVISIONS

A peculiar but critical aspect of the British system is the institutional arrangement governing the vocational education of professionals, such as engineers or architects. It is a system dating back to the early nineteenth century when professions began to emerge and set up their own institutions, such as the Institute of Civil Engineers in 1818 and the Institute of British Architects in 1834. Control over professional vocational education is exerted by these professional institutions which are accountable to the Privy Council, sitting between Cabinet government and the monarchy. The Privy Council exercises the prerogative of the Crown and is therefore outside direct ministerial and public accountability. Each institution is incorporated through a royal charter which defines its objectives and the particular 'skill' area or 'unique' profession over which it has a prerogative. This skill privilege, granted in perpetuity and only revoked if there is a breach, gives the institution the right to control entry into its respective profession via the categories of membership laid down in its by-laws and to control educational content on the condition that it serves the public interest (Privy Council 2006). The Engineering Council Charter from 1981, for instance, stipulates that:

> The objects of the corporation shall be to advance education in, and to promote the science and practice of engineering (including relevant technology) for the

public benefit and thereby to promote industry and commerce in Our Kingdom.

(Engineering Council 2006)

This arrangement has the effect of separating the training of operatives from professionals, a separation which might be regarded both as a class divide and as creating a serious barrier to permeability or to hierarchical progression from the trades into the professions. Throughout the twentieth century the use of charters in this way proliferated and there are currently over 400, more recent additions being that of the Chartered Institute of Personnel and Development in 2000 and the Institution of Occupational Safety and Health in 2002. Through their charters, the professional institutions acquire a monopoly status – not dissimilar to the traditional chartered company – in determining what members learn. Until the Second World War and even beyond this, learning was through a system of tutelage, akin to apprenticeship, whereby a surveyor, for instance, was 'articled' to a practice under contract. Such 'learning on the job' has now been replaced by academic learning undertaken by universities, with the professional institutions usually prescribing about 75 per cent of the content of the courses they accredit as core knowledge.

The serious shortcomings in this system have in recent years become increasingly apparent. In the first place, there are growing problems of overlap and fragmentation of skills as each institution claims exclusive control of a particular area of activity and knowledge. In construction, for instance, there are seven main chartered bodies plus numerous associated institutions, though in a country such as Germany there are only two professions – the architect and the engineer – covering the same areas of activity (Clarke and Herrmann 2004). An unnecessarily fragmented division of labour is thereby dictated, which is less and less appropriate to the modern production and education processes and which serves to block the dynamic development of skills. The curricula of structural engineers, for instance, overlap with those of civil engineers; architects are too focused on design; and institutions compete with each other to claim control over activities such as project management and urban design.

Other problems with the system include the restrictive roles of the universities, given the importance of professional membership to practice, with often too little room accorded to general educational and specialist content. But perhaps the most serious shortcoming is the institutional divide between professional vocational education under the monarchy and operative 'training' accountable to government. The lack of institutional links between these two systems, as shown in Figure 5.1, enforces class divisions and hinders the development of vocational education in intermediate skill areas, though in other countries these areas are precisely those which have seen significant growth (Felstead *et al.* 2002). This also means that the education of professionals is outside the remit of the state except in its role as a funding body through the Higher Education Funding Council for England.

CONCLUSIONS

Whilst the vocational education system in Britain has taken distinct forms at different periods – whether under the town corporations, the Statute of Artificers, free collective bargaining, the Industrial Training Boards or Sector Skills Councils – it has retained certain enduring features. It has remained remarkably trade-specific, built on a notion of skill tied to a particular output or work activity and the attribute of an individual, a form of property – even a privilege in the case of the modern professional – rather than an object of negotiation between employee and employer. It has also remained sharply divided, with the vocational education of the professional constitutionally separately accountable from that for the operative and the two structures operating without regard to each other. The consequent lack of permeability and underdevelopment of intermediate skill areas only reinforces and reproduces what amounts to class divisions. And, finally, with perhaps the exception of the system under the Statute of Artificers, it has remained exclusive and critical to maintaining a gender division of labour.

But perhaps the most enduring feature is the failure of the state to regulate directly vocational education and the social development of labour, even in the face of poorly developed transferable skills or underpinning knowledge (e.g. Steedman 1992). Transferable skills – as Marsden (1999) has explained – require the most institutional intervention and investment. In the absence of these and of a direct institutional link between further education and industry, the too-close adherence to practical prescriptive application, to firm-specific skills and traditional tasks, persists.

REFERENCES

Alford, B.W.E. and Barker, T.C. (1968) *A History of the Carpenters Company*, London: George Allen & Unwin.

ALI (Adult Learning Inspectorate) (2002) *Annual Report of the Chief Inspector*, Coventry: Adult Learning Inspectorate.

Bell, W.G. (1938) *A Short History of the Worshipful Company of Tylers and Bricklayers of the City of London*, London: H. G. Montgomery.

Booth C. (1895) *Life and Labour of the People in London, vol. V: population, classified by trades*, Basingstoke: Macmillan.

Braverman, H. (1974) *Labour and Monopoly Capital*, New York: Monthly Review Press.

Bray, R.A. (1909) 'The apprenticeship question', *Economic Journal*, 19, 404–15.

Clark, A. (1995) *The Struggle for the Breeches: gender and the making of the British working class*, London: Rivers Oram Press.

Clarke, L. (1992) *Building Capitalism: historical change and the nature of the labour process in the production of the built environment*, London: Routledge.

Clarke, L. (1999) 'The changing structure and significance of apprenticeship with special reference to construction', in D. Ainly and H. Rainbird (eds), *Apprenticeship: towards a new paradigm of learning*, London: Kogan Page, 25–40.

Clarke, L. and Herrmann, G. (2004) 'The institutionalisation of skill in Britain and

Germany: examples from the construction sector', in C. Warhurst *et al.* (eds), *The Skills that Matter*, London: Palgrave.

Construction Industry Training Board (CITB) (1969) *A Plan of Training for Operative Skills in the Construction Industry*, Bircham Newton.

Construction Industry Training Board (CITB) (2004) *Skills Foresight Report 2004*, Bircham Newton.

Cotgrove S.F. (1958) *Technical Education and Social Change*, London: George Allen and Unwin.

Davies, M.G. (1956) *The Enforcement of English Apprenticeship: a study in applied mercantilism 1563–1642*, Cambridge, Mass.: Harvard University Press.

Deakin, S. (1991) 'The legal origins of wage labour: industrialisation and labour market institutions in historical perspective', paper presented at the 13th Annual Conference of the International Working Party on Labour Market Segmentation, Bremen.

Derry, T.K. (1931) 'The repeal of the apprenticeship clauses of the Statute of Apprentices', *Economic History Review*, 3, 67–87.

Dunlop, O.J. and Denman, R.D. (1912) *English Apprenticeship and Child Labour: a history*, London.

Engineering Council (2006) *Royal Charter*, www.engc.org.uk

Felstead, A., Gallie, D. and Green, F. (2002) *Work Skills in Britain 1986–2001*, London: Department for Education and Skills

Fuller, A. and Unwin, L. (2003) 'Creating a "modern apprenticeship": a critique of the UK's multi-sector, social inclusion approach', *Journal of Education and Work*, 16(4), 5–15.

George, M.D. (1979, 1925) *London Life in the Eighteenth Century*, Harmondsworth: Penguin Books.

Gospel H. (1995) 'The decline of apprenticeship training in Britain', *Industrial Relations Journal*, 26(1), 32–44.

Guillery P. (2000) 'The further adventures of Mary Lacey', *Georgian Group Journal*, 10, 61–69.

Hewlings R. (2000) 'Women in the building trades,' *Georgian Group Journal*, 10, 61–69.

Hilton, W.S. (1963) *Foes to Tyranny*, London: Amalgamated Union of Building Trade Workers (AUBTW).

HMSO (1927–8) *Report of Enquiry into Apprenticeship and Training 1925–6*, vols II and III, London.

Hobsbawm, E. (1978) 'Man and woman in socialist iconography', *History Workshop Journal*, 6, autumn, 121–138.

Honeyman K. (2007) *Child Workers in England 1780–1820: parish apprenticeships and the making of the early industrial labour force*, Aldershot: Ashgate.

Howell, R. (1877) 'Trade unions, apprentices and technical education', *Contemporary Review*, 30, 833–57.

Humphries J. (1987) ' "... the most free from objection ...": the sexual division of labour and women's work in nineteenth century England', *Journal of Economic History*, 47, 929–949.

Jupp, E. and Pocock, W. (1887) *An Historical Account of the Worshipful Company of Carpenters of London*, London.

Keep, E. (2002) 'The changing meaning of skill and the shifting balance of responsibility for vocational education and training – are employers calling the shots?', paper presented at the Conference on Training, Employability and Employment, Monash University Centre, London.

Kenrick, J. (1981) 'Politics and the construction of women as second class workers', in

F. Wilkinson (ed), *The Dynamics of Labour Market Segmentation*, London: Academic Press.

Lang, J. (1979) *City and Guilds of London Institute, 1878–1978 Centenary*, London: City and Guilds of London Institute.

Lee D. (1979) 'Craft union and the force of tradition', *British Journal of Industrial Relations*, 17(1), 34–49.

Leeson, R.A. (1979) *Travelling Brothers: the six centuries' road from craft fellowship to trade unions*, London: Allen & Unwin.

Marsden, D. (1999) *A Theory of Employment Systems*, Oxford: Oxford University Press.

Perry, P.J.C. (1976) *The Evolution of British Manpower Policy: from the Statute of Artificers to the Industrial Training Act 1964*, Portsmouth: Grosvenor Press.

Pinchbeck, I. (1930) *Women Workers in the Industrial Revolution 1750–1950*, London: Routledge.

Postgate, R. (1923) *The Builders' History*, London: National Federation of Building Trade Operatives.

Privy Council Office (2006) *Chartered Bodies*, www.privycouncil.gov.uk

Reddaway, T.F. (1940) *The Rebuilding of London after the Great Fire*, London: Cape.

Samuelson Commission (1984) *Report of the Royal Commission on Technical Instruction*, no. 2096, London: HMSO.

Simonton, Deborah (1999) 'Gendered work in eighteenth century towns', in Margaret Walsh (ed.), *Working out Gender: perspectives from Labour History*, Aldershot: Ashgate.

Smith, Adam (1910) [1776] *The Wealth of Nations*, vol. I., London: Dent & Sons.

Snell, K.D.M. (1985) *Annals of the Labouring Poor: social change and agrarian England 1660–1900*, Cambridge: Cambridge University Press.

Steedman, H. (1992) *Mathematics in Vocational Youth Training for the Building Trades in Britain, France and Germany*, NIESR discussion paper no. 9, London.

Unwin, G. (1908) *The Guilds and Companies of London*, London: Methuen.

Webb, S. and Webb, B. (1898) *Industrial Democracy*, National Association of Operative Plasterers, London.

Part Two

Contrasting approaches to VET

Chapter 6

School reform in America

Can Dewey's ideas save high school vocational education?

Theodore Lewis

INTRODUCTION

High school vocational education in the United States (US) stands on shaky ground, more so now than in recent decades. Because its ethos is so different from that of the dominant academic mainstream, vocational education's standing in the curriculum has perennially been the object of contestation. It has generally been offered to minorities or more broadly to the under-classes (Ogbu 1978). Although preparation for the labour market has been its most enduring stated purpose, its sorting aspect may have been an important subterranean reason for its longevity. The subject has been an unwitting instrument of social inequality.

The dominant discourse in education in the US since the 1980s has been about how to make schools world class so that children are academically competitive with their counterparts from other developed countries (Linn *et al.* 2000). This focus has informed a standards movement, with scholars in academic subject areas completely rethinking and re-specifying their content.

Since so much of the quality of educational provision turns on the respective wealth of local communities, there have been winners and losers in the game of academic achievement, due largely to funding disparities both within and between states (Biddle 1997). To compensate for such disparities, successive recent American presidents have embarked upon policy initiatives intended to level the academic playing field (for example the elder Bush's *America 2000*, the Clinton administration's *Goals 2000* and the younger Bush's *No Child Left Behind*).

One common proposal emanating from these initiatives is the need for Opportunity to Learn (OTL) standards as concomitants of content standards. The idea is that quality benchmarks must be set not just in terms of what students must learn, but also for the resource provisions that will support their learning. This has been an area of difficulty, as state and local educators and politicians complain that the funds required are not available. While the standards movement has generally been seen in a positive light, OTL standards provoke debate, although it is argued that without them children from the under-classes will have no hope of being competitive in the learning game (Banks 1997; Darling-Hammond and Falk 1997).

The academic reform movement has implications for the conduct of vocational education, since it has become more difficult for schools to resort to this as a dumping ground for underachieving students or students outside the mainstream. The mood in recent times is that all children should have a chance to achieve academically and that greater effort must now be made by state and local communities to marshal school resources, especially federally derived resources, towards this end. As a result it has become increasingly more difficult to justify vocational education as an aspect of the high school curriculum. To survive, structural reform – more than mere curriculum change – on a whole-school scale may be required.

EARLY TENSIONS: THE DEWEY–SNEDDEN DEBATE

Vocational education in the American high school was born out of a manual training movement consisting of tool-work exercises and mechanical drawing, an idea first brought to the US as part of the Russian exhibit at the Philadelphia exposition of 1876. Its foremost early advocate was Calvin Woodward, who built a model school for adolescent boys in St Louis and was responsible for the subject's widespread adaptation in the elementary and high school (Woodward 1882). By the turn of the twentieth century an Industrial Education movement promoting a federally supported separate school system for vocational education took form. Its advocates believed that manual training was not sufficiently responsive to the needs of a growing industrialism. Among those advocating a separate school system, with a curriculum derived from and geared to industry, was David Snedden, state Commissioner for schools in Massachusetts. Snedden is recognized as the most influential figure in American vocationalism in the twentieth century.

Arguably the most prominent American philosopher of the twentieth century, John Dewey, held a different point of view. He saw the subject chiefly in liberal terms, helping children to understand the forces of progress around them but not in the service of employers. Commenting on the formation by the US Congress of a Commission on National Aid to Vocational Education, Dewey opined that the impetus for this industrialized curriculum focus seemed to be German economic competition but that, although Germany had systematized its approach to education, trade and commerce, such systemization was in the service of the state not of citizens (Dewey 1915). In *Democracy and Education* he wrote that it is not the business of education to inculcate skill at the expense of meaning. That:

> there is the danger that vocational education will be interpreted in theory and practice as trade education; as a means of securing technical efficiency in specialized future pursuits . . . Education would then become an instrument of

perpetuating unchanged the existing industrial order of society, instead of operating as a means of its transformation.

(Dewey 1916)

As Wirth points out in a classic work, Dewey and Snedden held diametrically opposed views on the question of whether schools should be doing the bidding of industry (Wirth 1980). Reflecting on his efforts in Massachusetts to vocationalize the curriculum, Snedden set forth 11 principles that had now been established, including: 'That vocational education is futile and harmful whenever it is mixed up in a kind of blend or hash with general education . . .' (Snedden 1916: 3)

Snedden had expanded upon this latter point in a piece entitled 'Fundamental distinctions between liberal and vocational education' writing that:

vocational education differs from general, or liberal, education fundamentally as regards its essential aims and that, therefore, it will differ also, fundamentally, as regards the means and methods of instruction, as well as the administrative agencies which are intimately related to means and methods of instruction.

(Snedden 1914: 152)

Earlier he had articulated a logic for selecting children for vocational education, based upon three criteria, namely 'native capacity', 'economic conditions of the family' and 'probable educational destination' (Snedden 1908: 2). These selection criteria were to be cornerstones of American vocationalism for most of the twentieth century and one recent study has shown them still to be factors influencing vocational participation (Agodini et al. 2004).

Two polar views of vocationalism were therefore in contention early in the last century, Snedden's social efficiency approach, where the state was the unit of focus, and Dewey's social reconstruction approach, where individuals were. In 1917 the US Congress passed the Smith–Hughes Act that gave aid for secondary and post-secondary vocational education – a triumph for the Snedden camp. The Act legitimized job-specific vocational education in the high school, which Dewey found abhorrent but which remained the dominant concept for the greater part of the twentieth century.

Kliebard contends that the triumph of vocationalism for most of the twentieth century stems not from economic outcomes, but rather from the fact that as a concept it is etched in the American psyche, deriving 'in large measure from the symbolic meaning that Americans have attached to work as central to their identities' (Kliebard 1999: 229). He argues that much of what passes as advocacy for vocational education redounds little to the benefit of children and more to the status interests of advocates themselves, who signal to vocational clients that 'at least nominally' their concerns have been officially addressed. The vocational education lobby in the United States is formidable and is especially vigilant on federal funding. Traditionally that lobby has avoided critical assessment of the subject, especially with respect to its sociological aspects. This traditional apathy has to change now.

VOCATIONAL EDUCATION AND CURRICULUM TRACKING

For much of the twentieth century, job-specific vocationalism prevailed in the American high school, the primary criterion for its efficacy being whether such a curriculum led to jobs. Some studies have confirmed that when high school vocational graduates found jobs related to their training they earned higher wages than their non-vocational peers and that participation in vocational education tended to reduce the dropout rate (e.g. Bishop 1989).

But participation in vocational education was also based on socio-economic and racial factors. The weight of evidence is that curricular tracking in schools remained one of the last bastions of racial segregation, with black children being more likely than white to be selected for vocational education (Ogbu 1978; Oakes 1985). Curriculum differentiation in schools perpetuates opportunity differentiation in communities. Apple writes that schools serve a reproductive function by helping to select and certify a workforce (Apple 1985).

The use of vocational education as a tracking mechanism continued to be well documented into the last decade of the twentieth century (Oakes and Guiton 1995; Wells and Serna 1996). Oakes showed that tracking led to racial and socio-economic segregation in schools and that African–American and Latino students are placed in the lowest status classes even where they have superior test scores or grades (Oakes 1985). Oakes and Guiton found that, as communities became more racially and ethnically diverse, the view was that the vocationalist component of the curriculum had to be expanded accordingly.

Wells and Serna (1996) provide empirical evidence of resistance of local elite parents to attempts to de-track the curriculum. They found that the primary variable at issue was power – the struggle to hold on to a privileged status. Thus, advanced placement courses were for the privileged, while vocational courses were for the disadvantaged. Welner and Oakes contend that there is now enough compelling research demonstrative of the fact that tracking is 'pedagogically ineffectual', discriminatory and disproportionately harmful to non-white students (Welner and Oakes 1996).

REFORM AND A NEW VOCATIONALISM

Since Dewey's very early objections, arguably the next serious challenge to the vocational education status quo in the twentieth century came indirectly with the publication of *A Nation at Risk* (National Commission on Excellence in Education

1983), whose context was American deindustrialization (Bluestone and Harrison 1982) characterized by declining competitiveness in sectors such as steel and electronics. The authors argued that new workplace realities and global economic competitiveness demanded greater focus on academic rigour in the high school curriculum.

A Nation at Risk had a ripple effect in American education, engendering important reform not just of schools but of teacher education. In 1989 the elder President Bush, along with governors of states, convened a summit to discuss education and the economy out of which came National Education Goals, two of which referred to all children. Academic goals were set for the end of grades 4, 8 and 12 (National Education Goals Panel 1999: 5).

First wave reforms

As schools strove to bolster academic subjects, so enrolment in vocational education declined (National Assessment of Vocational Education Independent Panel 1994). Faced with the prospect of a diminished role, vocational advocates countered that the subject area bore significant complementarities with the academic curriculum. Thus a first wave of vocational education reform was triggered, based on broad, intrinsic purposes (Lewis 1991). With their backs to the wall, American vocationalists had come to embrace a new vocationalism with features more consistent with Dewey's version of the subject. Arguably the new vocationalism began with the publication of *The Unfinished Agenda*, a reprise of *A Nation at Risk*, commissioned by the National Center for Research in Vocational Education and contending that vocational education in the high school yielded liberally inspired ends (National Commission on Secondary Vocational Education 1984: 3).

Second wave reforms

Shortly after publication of *A Nation at Risk* a second evaluation of the kind of education that was required to make the US competitive began to crystallize. The focus now was on the non-college bound. In *Head to Head*, Thurow (1992) cautioned that the US was not investing sufficiently in students not going on to university, and competitors such as Japan and Germany were much more successful in producing mid-level workers agile enough to operate new flexible systems in the workplace.

This argument meshed well with a growing chorus in the mid-1980s that American high school graduates not going on to four-year college did not have bridging structures in place to help them make a smooth transition into the world of work (Parnell 1985; William T. Grant Foundation Commission on Work, Family and Citizenship 1988). Parnell proposed a model for connecting high schools to two-year technical and community colleges by having students pursue articulated course work. This model, called 'Tech-prep' (short for technical preparation), has been a critical aspect of successive iterations of the vocational education legislation since the mid–1980s.

One ironic feature of the second wave of school reform, with its focus on the non-college bound, was that the practical relevance of traditional knowledge came under scrutiny. Some pointed to a disconnection between school knowledge (said to be too abstract) and real world knowledge (said to be contextualized) (Resnick 1987). Conceptions of the skills needed in workplaces tended to de-emphasize discipline-based knowledge, favouring instead generic competences such as communication and problem solving (see especially Carnevale *et al.* 1988; Secretary's Commission on Achieving Necessary Skills (SCANS) 1991).

The new reasoning that reform should focus greater attention on the non college-bound led to consideration of models that help youth transition from school into the workplace, especially German-style youth apprenticeship (Hamilton 1993). Transition from school to work became entrenched in policy with the passage of the School To Work Opportunities Act of 1994 providing funding incentives to encourage communities to fashion programmes that would structure the transition from school into jobs (United States Congress 1994). Recent findings show that transition into the world of work after high school is the more successful the more education one receives and that the stability of the experience varies by gender and ethnicity (Yates 2005).

New models

The period since the publication of *A Nation at Risk* has been one of innovation. We have seen creative attempts to provide programmes that are informed not just by employer needs, but also by the well-being of students. Invariably the new models seek to connect vocational and academic learning. One new model is the 'Career academy' in which the curriculum is thematic, revolving around a cluster of related careers in a particular discipline (Stern *et al.* 2000). Another is 'High Schools That Work', offering vocational students challenging academic course sequences (Bottoms 2002). A third is 'Tech-prep', discussed above, and a fourth is the 'dual enrolment' approach, where students take course work in post-secondary two- and four-year colleges while still in high school.

Collectively, studies show that new vocationalism programmes are making some difference, including persistence in school, increased academic course-taking and improved chances of graduating (Bragg *et al.* 2002). Because they seek to break down walls between academic and vocational knowledge, they are felt to constitute a belated concession to Dewey's vocationalist ideals (Grubb 1996). But Dewey's critique went beyond epistemological considerations. At its core his concern was sociological. Thus, it was not so much how to make the vocational curriculum more liberal, but beyond that how to make it less an instrument of inequality. Such a disposition would mean that reform of vocational education begins with critical examination of the mechanisms and assumptions that dictate who shall be its primary participants.

RECENT RESEARCH FINDINGS

Where new vocationalism approaches exist, changes have been largely within vocational education rather than across curriculum tracks. Vocational education, after two decades of reform, is still recognizable by the type of student who opts or is selected for it. The most recent National Assessment of Vocational Education (NAVE) reported that enrolment decline had been stemmed and that vocational courses are attracting more academically talented students than in the past (Silverberg *et al.* 2004). However, schools with high concentrations of racial minority students in high poverty areas were less likely to offer new vocationalism initiatives such as Tech-prep; and African–American students earned more vocational education credits on average than students of other racial and ethnic groups. This racial disparity cannot be attributed to overt school practice, since vocational courses in the high school are offered electively. However, schools signal to minorities through counselling and other mechanisms what their abilities purportedly are and what curricula best suit them. Yonezawa and colleagues contend that curriculum tracks are 'political spaces' created by the identities of the students within them, formed on the basis of past untoward educational experience (Yonezawa *et al.* 2002). Many prefer low track classes because these are socially safer than high status classes in which they would be racially isolated.

There is evidence that the practice of organizing schools into mutually exclusive curriculum tracks is declining but that *de facto* tracking persists, since academic courses continue to be offered in stratified ways with high and low versions of the same subject being offered as equal options (Lucas 1999). Lucas and Berends (2002) found, however, that when prior achievement was controlled for in public schools, socio-economic determinants of tracking persisted. Agodini and colleagues found that participation in vocational education was determined by low academic achievement, low educational aspirations and low socio-economic status (Agodini *et al.* 2004).

Notwithstanding the findings of Lucas (1999), tracking still substantially exists as a way of organizing schools. A study by this author examined what factors predict which of the three typical tracks (academic, vocational and general) is dominant in the high school (Lewis and Cheng 2006). The finding was that what predicted the dominant track was the socio-economic composition of the student population. The more affluent the children, the more likely was the academic track to be dominant compared with the vocational track.

Socio-economic status appears to have overtaken race as the primary basis of track assignment. Poverty is a prime determinant of socio-economic status in the US and members of racial minority groups, especially blacks, are more likely to be numbered

85

among the working poor than whites (Mosisa 2003). Race continues to lurk as a factor to be reckoned with.

NO CHILD LEFT BEHIND: PROSPECTS

Both the elder President Bush and President Clinton had set the year 2000 as the target date by which measurable academic improvements had to be shown nationally. However, the National Center for Education Statistics (NCES) report card for mathematics achievement in 2000 showed that, while scores for both black and Hispanic students were higher in 2000 than in 1990, they were lower than average scores for white and Asian–Pacific Islander students (Braswell *et al.* 2001). Lee shows that the black–white and Hispanic–white socio-economic gap closed in the 1980s but then widened into the 1990s, as mirrored in the academic achievement of children from these groups (Lee 2002). Gamaron predicts inequality as a condition of American education deep into the twenty-first century (Gamaron 2001). Kaestle and colleagues have found that significantly higher levels of black and Hispanic adults performed at the two lowest proficiency levels of prose, document and quantitative literacy (Kaestle *et al.* 2001). These data helped to explain the poor showing of the American labour force in international adult literacy comparisons (OECD 1995).

The No Child Left Behind (NCLB) Act of the younger Bush's administration acknowledges the existence of an academic achievement gap in the society and seeks to attack the problem by changing the culture of schooling (United States Congress 2001). Its basic logic is: that schools must offer challenging, standards-based curricula to all students; and that those ill-prepared to compete academically be provided with the extra help they might need and given the opportunity to learn. Paraphrased, Title I Sec.1001 of the Act sets as a goal that 'all children have a fair, equal, and significant opportunity to obtain a high-quality education'.

These principles are in keeping with Dewey's democratic ideal. The Act has been controversial, mainly on the count that it constitutes an unfunded mandate. But that aside, the societal conditions to which it responds are real. If educational provision continues to be dictated by the wealth of communities, then the outcome of such education will be to the detriment of the poor. Education is too critical a variable in the shaping of the post-high school work experiences of students to be left to factors outside their control (Yates 2005).

The principles embedded in NCLB mean that once again vocational education must be reformed to avoid extinction. What now are the possibilities for the subject? A White Paper entitled *Rigor and Relevance: A New Vision for Career and Technical Education* (CTE) recommended that high school vocational students would take core academic courses along with electives within a broad career area (Brand 2003: 7). Basically the vision here is for continuation of vocational education in the high school on terms that bring the academic and CTE curricula closer together.

Several contributions to an Office of Vocational and Adult Education (OVAE-Sponsored) High School Symposium resonated strongly with the notion that challenging academic course work must be the first priority of schools and that this priority is consistent with goals of vocational education (Bottoms 2002; Jacobs and Grubb 2002; Bailey *et al.* 2002). Bailey and colleagues offered support for dual enrolment programmes, where students spend part of their high school time taking courses in two-year colleges, as a plausible way in which low-achieving students can be exposed to high-level challenging courses that lead to college (Bailey *et al.* 2002). Jacobs and Grubb pointed to shifts in emphasis in the kinds of skills needed in the job market today and the inappropriateness of the high school as the site of such preparation. Taken together, these papers offered practical scenarios to the OVAE, illustrative of the mutuality of vocational education and challenging academic curricula. Their effect is quite noticeable in notes on the Secondary and Technical Education Excellence Act of 2003, in which glimpses of what the Bush administrations intended as the future of vocational education in the high school could be seen. Here, the (now former) Assistant Secretary of Education proposed that:

> A completely new approach is necessary – one that improves high school academic preparation for all students, AND that draws upon the strengths of community colleges collaborating with high schools to create high quality technical options.
>
> (D'Amico 2003: 2)

TOWARDS DEWEY'S IDEAL

John Dewey's ideas for vocational education as set forth in his *Democracy and Education* are often cited as the philosophical foundation of the new American vocationalism. He proposed an alternative conception to remind advocates of what education was for. Vocation was not merely an economic construct. Thus the vocational curriculum had to provide the competence that citizens in a democracy needed to be able to integrate their work, family and community lives. The new American vocationalism has approached Dewey's ideal. But because the subject is still dispensed asymmetrically in the curriculum, that ideal remains yet to be attained.

When schools are pressured to improve the academic performance of all students, that dispensation works especially to the good of those traditionally left behind in vocational education classes. Academic-driven reform gives schools no place to hide. The ideal they should strive for is the prospect of a de-tracked curriculum in which vocational education takes its place mainly as education about rather than for work (Lewis 1997 and 1998). The curriculum would be offered to all students, and could provide context for the teaching and learning of other school subjects while being of epistemic integrity in its own right (Bell 1980).

What should students know and experience about the world of work that can prepare them for responsible and critical citizenship? The answer could yield models that are configurations of cross-cutting experiences. The aim of a curriculum so derived would be vocational literacy, a synthesis of the knowledges, experiences and dispositions of the students gained from participation in activities pertaining to the world of work. It could include: short modules on topics that provide glimpses of workplace commonplaces, such as 'What makes an automobile work?', or 'Sexual harassment in the workplace'. The activities could range beyond the economic to include service-learning. Students could participate in short internships in actual workplaces, in job-shadowing or mentor-ships. The wider school curriculum could benefit from collaborations across disciplines, featuring vocational knowledge.

Ultimately, if vocational education is to survive in the high school amid persistent calls for increased academic content and for leaving no child behind, it has to demonstrate that it poses intellectual and creative challenges for children across the spectrum of abilities and interests. This approach is quite different from reflexively responding to the skills that employers want. The subject in the American curriculum that comes closest to embodying these principles is technology and design education (Layton 1994; Lewis 1995). Students enrolled in this manipulate tools and machines and solve practical design problems in realms such as manufacturing, construction, and power and energy.

Vocational education in the American high school ought not to respond necessarily to the needs of employers. It should not be instrumentally focused. Rather, it should be liberally conceived and taught in authentic contexts in ways that educate students about the world of work and careers. The main challenge here is political, premised on complete abandonment of curriculum tracking in all its forms. There is no second tier set of watered-down academic courses to be set aside for students deemed to be vocational concentrators. All students receive a challenging curriculum within which they are exposed to the world of work. But to attain the ideal, communities need to fight off the strong force of tradition regarding what constitutes normative practice in dispensing school knowledge.

REFERENCES

Agodini, R., Uhl, S. and Novak, T. (2004) *Factors That Influence Participation in Secondary Vocational Education*, Princeton, NJ: Mathematica Policy Research, Inc.

Apple, M.W. (1985) *Education and Power*, Boston: Ark Paperbacks.

Bailey, T.R., Hughes, K.L. and Karp, M.M. (2002) 'What role can dual enrollment programs play in easing the transition between high school and postsecondary education?', paper presented at the Office of Vocational and Adult Education Conference convened, 'Preparing America's Future: The High School Symposium', Washington, DC, 4 April.

Banks, C.A.M. (1997) 'The challenges of national standards in a multicultural society', *Educational Horizons*, 75(3), 126–32.

Bell, G.H. (1980) 'Industrial culture and the school: some conceptual and practical issues in the schools-industry debate', *Journal of Philosophy of Education*, 14(1), 175–89.

Biddle, B.J. (1997) 'Foolishness, dangerous nonsense, and real correlates of state differences in achievement', *Phi Delta Kappan*, 79(1), 8–13.

Bishop, J. (1989) 'Occupational training in high school: when does it pay off?', *Economics of Education Review*, 8(1), 1–15.

Bluestone, B. and Harrison, B. (1982) *The Deindustrialization of America: plant closings, community abandonment, and the dismantling of basic industry*, New York: Basic Books.

Bottoms, G. (2002) 'Raising the achievement of low-performing students: what high schools can do?', paper presented at the Office of Vocational and Adult Education Conference convened, 'Preparing America's Future: The High School Symposium', Washington, DC, 4 April.

Bragg, D.D., Reger, W., Brown, C.H., Orr, M.T. and Dare, D. (2002) 'New lessons about tech prep implementation: changes in eight selected consortia since reauthorization of the federal tech prep legislation in 1998', St Paul, MN: University of Minnesota, National Research Center for Career and Technical Education.

Brand, B. (2003) *Rigor and Relevance: a new vision for career and technical education*, Washington, DC: American Policy Forum.

Braswell, J.S., Lutkus, A.D., Grigg, W.S., Santapau, S.L., Tay-Lim, B. and Johnson, M. (2001) *The Nation's Report Card: Mathematics 2000*, Washington, DC: National Center for Educational Statistics.

Carnevale, A.P., Gainer, L.J. and Meltzer, A.S. (1988) *Workplace Basics: the skills employers want*, Washington, DC: US Department of Labor/American Society for Training and Development.

D'Amico, C.A. (2003) *Secondary and Technical Education Act Fact Sheet*, Office of Vocational and Adult Education, US Department of Education, Washington, DC.

Darling-Hammond, L. and Falk, B. (1997) 'Using standards and assessments to support student learning', *Phi Delta Kappan*, 7(3), 190–99.

Dewey, J. [1915] (1977) 'On industrial education', *Curriculum Inquiry*, 7(1), 53–60.

—— (1916) *Democracy and Education*, New York: Macmillan.

Gamaron, A. (2001) 'American schooling and educational inequality: a forecast for the 21st century', *Sociology of Education* (extra issue), 135–53.

Grubb, W.N. (1996) 'The new vocationalism: what it is what it could be?', *Phi Delta Kappan*, 77(8), 533–46.

Hamilton, S.F. (1993) 'Prospects for an American style youth apprenticeship system', *Educational Researcher*, 22(3), 11–16.

Jacobs, J. and Grubb, W.N. (2002) 'Implementing the "education consensus": the federal role in supporting vocational-technical education', paper presented at the Office of Vocational and Adult Education Conference convened, 'Preparing America's Future: The High School Symposium', Washington, DC, 4 April.

Kaestle, C.E., Campbell, A., Finn, J.D., Johnson, S.T. and Mikulecky, L.J. (2001) *Adult Literacy and Education in America*, Washington, DC: US Department of Education.

Kliebard, H.M. (1999) *Schooled to Work: vocationalism and the American curriculum, 1876–1946*, New York: Teachers College Press.

Layton, D. (1994) 'A school subject in the making? The search for fundamentals', in D. Layton (ed.), *Innovations in Science and Technology Education*, vol. V, Paris: UNESCO.

Lee, J. (2002) 'Racial and ethnic achievement gap trends: reversing the progress toward equity?', *Educational Researcher*, 31(1), 3–12.

89

Lewis, T. (1991) 'Difficulties attending the new vocationalism in the United States', *Journal of Philosophy of Education*, 25(1), 95–108.

—— (1995) 'From manual training to technology education: the continuing struggle to establish a school subject', *Journal of Curriculum Studies*, 27(6), 621–45.

—— (1997) 'Towards a liberal vocational education', *Journal of Philosophy of Education*, 31(3), 477–89.

—— (1998) 'Vocational education as general education', *Curriculum Inquiry*, 28(3), 283–9.

Lewis, T. and Cheng, S. (2006) 'Tracking, expectations, and the transformation of vocational education', *American Journal of Education*, 113, 66–99.

Linn, M.C., Lewis, C., Tsuchida, I. and Butler-Songer, N. (2000) 'Beyond fourth-grade science: why do U.S. and Japanese students diverge?', *Educational Researcher*, 29(3), 4–14.

Lucas, S.R. (1999) *Tracking inequality: stratification and mobility in the American high school*, New York: Teachers' College Press.

Lucas, S.R. and Berends, M. (2002) 'Sociodemographic diversity, correlated achievement, and de facto tracking', *Sociology of Education*, 75, 328–48.

Mosisa, A.T. (2003) 'The working poor in 2001', *Monthly Labor Review*, 126(11–12), 13–19.

National Assessment of Vocational Education Independent Panel (1994) *Interim Report to Congress (1994)*, Washington, DC: US Department of Education.

National Commission on Excellence in Education (1983) *A Nation at Risk: the imperative for reform*, Washington, DC: US Government Printing Office.

National Commission on Secondary Vocational Education (1984) *The Unfinished Agenda: the role of vocational education in the high school*, Columbus, OH: National Center for Research in Vocational Education, Ohio State University.

National Education Goals Panel (1999) *Data Volume for the National Education Goals Report*, Washington, DC: US Government Printing Office.

Oakes, J. (1985) *Keeping track: how schools structure inequality*, New Haven: Yale University Press.

Oakes, J. and Guiton, G. (1995) 'Matchmaking: the dynamics of high school tracking decisions', *American Educational Research Journal*, 32(1), 3–33.

Ogbu, J.U. (1978) *Minority Education and Caste. the American system in cross-cultural perspective*, New York: Academic Press.

Organization for Economic Cooperation and Development (OECD) (1995) *Literacy, Economy and Society: results of the first International Adult Literacy Study*, Paris: OECD; Ottawa: Statistics Canada.

Parnell, D. (1985) *The Neglected Majority*, Washington, DC: Community College Press.

Resnick, L.B. (1987) 'Learning in school and out', *Educational Researcher*, 16(9), 13–19.

Secretary's Commission on Achieving Necessary Skills (SCANS) (1991) *What Work Requires of Schools: a SCANS report for America 2000*, Washington, DC: US Department of Labor.

Silverberg, M., Warner, E., Fong, M. and Goodwin, D. (2004) *National Assessment of Vocational Education*, Washington, DC: US Department of Education.

Snedden, D.S. (1908) 'Differences among varying groups of children should be recognized; and the period at which this recognition takes place may constitute the beginnings of secondary education', *Manual Training Magazine*, 10(1), 1–8.

—— (1914). 'Fundamental distinctions between liberal and vocational education', *Proceedings and Addresses of the Fifty-second Annual Meeting of the National Education Association*, session of 1914, held at St Paul, Minnesota, 150–61

—— (1916) 'Vocational education in Massachusetts: some achievements and some prospects', *Manual Training Magazine*, 18(1), 1–4.

Stern, D., Dayton, C. and Raby, M. (2000) *Career Academies: building blocks for reconstructing American high schools*, Berkeley, CA: University of California at Berkeley.

Thurow, L. (1992) *Head to Head: the coming economic battle among Japan, Europe, and America*, New York: William Morrow and Company, Inc.

United States Congress (1994) *School to Work Opportunities Act of 1994*, Washington, DC: United States Congress.

—— (2001) *The No Child Left Behind Act of 2001*, Washington, DC: United States Congress.

Wells, A.S. and Serna, I. (1996) 'The politics of culture: understanding local political resistance to detracking in racially mixed schools', *Harvard Educational Review*, 66(1), 93–118.

Welner, K.G. and Oakes, J. (1996) '(Li) ability grouping: the new susceptibility of school tracking systems to legal challenges', *Harvard Educational Review*, 66(3), 451–469.

William T. Grant Foundation Commission on Work, Family and Citizenship (1988) *The Forgotten Half: non college bound youth in America*, Washington, DC: William T. Grant Foundation.

Wirth, A. (1980) *Education in the Technological Society: the vocational-liberal studies controversy in the early twentieth century*, Washington, DC: United Press of America.

Woodward, C.M. (1882) 'The function of an American training school', *Proceedings of the National Educational Association*, Session of the year 1882 at Saratoga, Boston: Alfred Mudge Printers, 140–57.

Yates, J.A. (2005) 'The transition from school to work', *Monthly Labor Review*, 128(2), 21–32.

Yonezawa, S., Wells, A.S. and Serna, I. (2002) 'Choosing tracks: "freedom of choice" in detracking schools', *American Educational Research Journal*, 39(1), 37–67.

Chapter 7

Under American influence?

The making of modern German training in large Berlin enterprises at the beginning of the twentieth century

Georg Hanf

This chapter is concerned with the conditions under which modern German vocational training in industry came into being in Berlin, with reconstructing the situation in which what was new and innovative evolved. Its focus is three leading enterprises in Berlin's crucial electrical and mechanical engineering industries, each of which played a pioneering role in one area: plant vocational schools, training workshops and systematic courses. I will concentrate on the period between 1900 and 1920, because by that time the essential elements of industrial training, which were to become more widespread from the 1920s onwards, were already fully developed in the capital. Formal institutions and codified rules with associated organizational structures are socially devised and a closer look at the main actors, individuals and organizations around 1900 in Berlin shows how modern German skill formation was created.

The following, to a certain extent, illustrates what has been dealt with more analytically by Kathleen Thelen (2004). She draws attention to the question of how institutions develop and evolve over time and finds that institutional survival is often strongly laced with elements of institutional adaptation and even sometimes transformation of the sort that brings inherited institutions into line with changing social, political and economic conditions. Institutions follow a certain path, but there are dynamic processes that sustain them. Looking at history, moments of openness and critical junctures are to be found.

In the case of German training, the core 'innovation' around which the German system came to be built was the *Handwerkerschutzgesetz* of 1897, a piece of legislation designed to shore up a reactionary artisan class that could serve as a bulwark against the surging working-class movement. Shortly after, there was legislation on compulsory schooling up to the age of 18 for young workers. Berlin at that time was a centre of 'diversified quality production', dependent on highly skilled workers. Industry was breaking away from the craft model of training, but then single companies and organizations adapted craft practices to form their own training based on this model – surprisingly inspired by American examples of company training.

THE HISTORY PRIOR TO 1900: PUTTING AN END TO 'ARTISTIC DAWDLING'!

Before industry started shaping human capital for its purposes, with the aid of training, it had no choice but to work with the labour power of the traditional craftsman from which it planned to become independent. Siemens provides a particularly good example of a company that underwent this evolutionary process (Kocka 1969; Behr 1981).

When the mechanics workshop of Siemens & Halske began making telegraphs and ringing devices on 1 October 1847, there were ten employees working there, most of them locksmiths and mechanics by training. The work was done to order and some of the apparatus was made by a single craftsman from start to finish; there was as yet no stringent separation between design and manufacture. Halske, who was a mechanic by profession, had initiated the craft orientation of the company for the first twenty years of its existence, in terms of both production and sales strategy. During this period the 'artist's dawdling' of the mechanics in the company was a continuous cause for complaint for Werner von Siemens. This complaint was justified. These mechanics were well and truly artists, a sparsely populated, sought-after occupational group, trained in draughtsmanship in the Academy of Arts in Berlin (Preußische Akademie der Künste 1850; Hanf 1985). Werner von Siemens' brother Carl had advised his brothers to take the radical step of replacing handicraft work with mass production processes. Werner finally took heed of this advice when the 'founder years' (after the unification of the German Reich in 1871) led to the placing of large-scale orders and the business took on dimensions that the craftsman Halske could no longer comprehend. He left the firm in 1867. It was now time to become independent of the artist mechanics and to replace them by 'house servants', as Carl von Siemens maliciously put it. But how?

The answer was found just around the corner in 'Ludwig Loewe & Co. AG Limited Shares Partnership for the Manufacture of Sewing Machines', a company established in 1870, which had introduced totally new methods into production processes (Ludwig Loewe & Co. AG 1930). Ludwig Loewe & Co. AG, the leader in weapons manufacture soon after its foundation and later in machine tool manufacturing, was one of the first companies not only in Berlin but in all of Germany to apply 'American methods' to the production process. Not long after it was founded, the owner set off with his factory engineer on a study trip to North America. From this trip they brought back a wealth of experience that was immediately put to use in production. In the first business report for the year 1870, the principles that characterize the enterprise are already set forth (Wegeleben 1924).

Machines were no longer to be built German-empirically, but scientific-systematically, with strictly monitored mathematical precision. This meant 'that all parts were to be made with the help of tools, strictly excluding all manual work' (Wegeleben 1924: 163). The manufacturing installations were to be designed in such a way that they 'actually represented total automatons producing totally uniform and reliable parts, without the influence of the worker operating them being necessary or even permissible'. Werner von Siemens had a personal relationship with Ludwig Loewe who had come to Berlin in 1862 to trade in machine tools and had immediately joined the Progressive Party (today we would call it 'liberal'), for which he had himself elected to the city council and finally to the Reichstag. Loewe was thus politically allied with Werner von Siemens, who had been one of the founders of the Progressive Party. For Siemens, which was suffering from a shortage of labour during the 'founder boom', Loewe arranged the procurement of American milling machines, drills and planers, which were set up in 1871/1872 in the so-called 'American Hall'. A Siemens worker was instructed in the operation of the machines in the Loewe firm. After that, Werner von Siemens was convinced 'that our future salvation lies in the use of the American methods' (Kocka 1969: 126) He saw the standardized sewing machine, Loewe's first product, as an excellent example of the potential of mass production.

In the 1880s, qualification was no longer of interest to Werner von Siemens. His negative comments on training culminated in the remarks he made at the meeting of the *Verein zur Beförderung des Gewerbefleißes in Preussen* (Prussian Association for the Promotion of Industrial Diligence) on 1 June 1885. Here as Privy Councillor he found words of praise for the initiatives of the Ministry of Commerce and Trade to regulate apprenticeship training in the State Railways, but took a strong stand against transferring that experience to industry: 'I do not consider it advisable for large factories to concern themselves with the actual training of apprentices as a matter of principle. I consider that to be wrong and I have therefore prohibited it in my factory' (Kocka 1969: 126).

AT THE TURN OF THE CENTURY: 'DO YOUR OWN TRAINING!' LOEWE, SIEMENS AND AEG TAKE THE INITIATIVE

From the mid-1890s the Berlin economy and the German economy as a whole had been passing through a phase of tumultuous growth. This was celebrated in Berlin by the great industrial exhibition of 1896 at which the electrical industry in particular showed how strong it had become. Production sites were re-located to spacious grounds on the outskirts of the city. The expansion and acceleration of production were accompanied by the introduction of completely new production methods and new forms of labour organization and company management. These measures, summed up under the term 'rationalization', also called for a different way of handling labour power. The ultimate target of rationalization was the elimination of the independent will of the worker and of the subjective assessment of the work by the master craftsman. These were replaced by central rules, targets and controls.

Nevertheless, under the conditions of rapid growth, skilled craftsmen remained necessary for the continuity of production. They were not however available in unlimited supply. The fact is that the dynamic of the business boom released a dynamic of aspirations in addition to the long-term structural loosening of social ties. The wish 'to change, to improve oneself' became the most frequently cited motive for the job-hopping registered in the 'Studies on selection and adaptation of the workforce in closed large industry' in 1908 and the years that followed (Verein für Socialpolitik 1919–1912). The individual desire to become 'something' was satisfied by way of further education. The collective will of workers to improve their position was expressed in the trade unions and the *Sozialdemokratische Partei* (Social Democratic Party). One way of bringing aspirations for change back to company level and to tailor the horizon of expectations to the horizon of the enterprise was to provide systematic training in the large firms, which they themselves organised.

The Ludwig Loewe & Co. AG: rationalization and welfare agencies

Ludwig Loewe & Co. AG was the precursor and model in Berlin, and for the whole of northern Germany, for systematic apprenticeship training organized in the company itself. The Royal Prussian Government and Industrial Councillors praised its establishment in 1902 and acknowledged its exemplary character. Why Loewe? What predestined this company for such a leadership role? In what historical context did the first Berlin plant vocational school come into being?

By the 1890s the former backyard sewing machine factory had turned into a mechanical engineering firm with a world-wide reputation. Planning and implementation were in the hands of the new director, Pajeken, who had worked in America for a long time and studied advances in machine and factory construction there in the 1890s. He completed the modern production complex with the help of American engineers. Exemplary social and welfare facilities were integrated from the start, including the plant school and its library.

The principles of rationalization were put to effect from the outset. The range of products was halved (specialization); the plant was given its own standards office, generating Loewe standards that were adopted by many other firms; total production cost calculation and control by the costing office were consistently applied to the whole production process. The first product-testing department in German machine tool manufacturing began its work at Loewe in 1902 (Hausen 1981: 208).

This reorganization had a dramatic sociological impact on production, depriving workshop foremen of their power. In the old factory it was they who prescribed the work schedules and piecework quotas and hired workers. These functions shifted to the hands of office engineers. Even the foremen's once exclusive domain, the training of recruits, became the task of the plant engineer, Georg Schlesinger, known as a 'master of rationalization', who became the organizer and first plant vocational school teacher at Loewe. Later he held the machine tool manufacturing chair (from 1904 onwards) at the Charlottenburg Technical University, the first such university in

Germany. The Loewe school was up and running in January 1900 (Reichelt 1906; Waldschmidt 1913; Schlesinger 1930). At first it was an enabling facility for a small number of apprentices aged 16 and over, the yardstick being that these constituted 4 per cent of all employees (engine makers, lathe operators, toolmakers, planers, milling workers, smiths, pattern makers and moulders). In 1905, further education up to the age of 18 became obligatory in Berlin and the school was recognized from the start as an alternative school (Magistrat der Stadt Berlin 1906). In 1906 an additional fourth year was added to the three existing years for the 'really ambitious' students.

The year 1908 saw a fundamental new setting of the scene for industrial training in Germany: in this year the *Deutsche Ausschuß für das Technische Schulwesen* (*DATSch*, German Committee for Technical Education) was co-founded by the *Vereinigung Deutscher Maschinenbauanstalten* (*VDMA*, Association of German Machine-Building Firms) and the *Verein Deutscher Ingenieure* (*VDI*, Association of German Engineers). For thirty years this organization was the driving force for structuring the system of VET in Germany (Herkner 2003).

The DATSch also obviously triggered the major reorganization of the training at Loewe in 1909. The apprenticeship quota was raised to 10 per cent, the school and the newly established training workshop received a full-time director, and the range of subjects offered was diversified. The engine-makers school was bolstered by an additional training school for unskilled and semi-skilled young people and special classes for commercial and technical trainees. A year later there were also further training and masters' courses. Beginning in 1913, particularly ambitious engine makers could train as fitters and installers in the fourth year of training. So even before World War I a diversified range of in-company educational opportunities was to be found at Loewe.

A whole series of social pedagogic facilities were dedicated to resolving the difficult problem of integrating the apprentices into a company universe. The aim of the company was 'to strengthen the *esprit de corps* of young people' (Waldschmidt 1913: 842). The facilities included an apprentices' library, evenings of entertainment with artistic performances, a savings bank, Sunday outings, an extended annual excursion, and finally the Loewe Sports Club set up in 1910. Early efforts were made at Loewe to reconstruct a spirit of sociability and community alongside the rationalized work process. However, it was left to the international Siemens group to revive the old European concept of the 'whole house' ('*Das ganze Haus*') in a large enterprise.

Siemens: migration to the outskirts, compulsory schooling and labour struggles. How do you recruit a loyal core workforce?

After 1897 Siemens–Halske acquired spacious, undeveloped property in Spandau on the outskirts of Berlin. In his memorandum on the choice of location the Director, the building surveyor Carl Dihlmann, mused about the disadvantages of locating plants far removed from the city (Siemens-Archiv-Akten 1897):

- greater travelling distances meant that higher wages had to be paid to attract skilled workers;
- the farther the plant was from the city the weaker the position of management in potential labour struggles.

First (in 1899) the cable plant was moved to Spandau and in 1905 and 1906 the entire production was relocated. A Berlin–Hamburg railway station was opened nearby on the application of Siemens in 1905, shortly after production began. In addition, Siemens soon began promoting housing construction near the plant. But distance from the city still brought with it labour recruitment problems. The mass of workers commuted. It was a long distance from their home neighbourhoods and from the city-based further training and crafts schools. Almost simultaneously with the site relocation in 1905, compulsory attendance at the further training school in the Spandau district was decreed. In view of the long distance from the plant to the nearest further training school and of the fact that lessons took place during the day, a major deduction in working time was called for. And so the coincidence of migration to the outskirts and of compulsory schooling was the stimulus for Siemens–Halske to establish a plant school of its own (1906) and to begin systematic training.

Another reason for organizing the training of recruits itself was the labour struggles that flared up in the years 1904, 1905 and 1906 as the old company patriarchy broke up (Kocka 1969: 354). Conflicts over wages, overtime and holidays escalated to such an extent in 1906 that the company management felt compelled to fire about 4000 'red workers', 'namely agitators', as Wilhelm von Siemens called them (Kocka 1969: 359). What was to be done?

Provide their own training! In the year 1908, when this phrase appeared in the minutes, the practical training of apprentice mechanics began in a central training workshop at Siemens–Halske. As in the case of the introduction of the first American machines, intended to replace the 'artists', Ludwig Loewe AG was Siemens' model for establishing the 'workshop school'.

The curriculum of the school started with German, arithmetic/mathematics, and drawing, but shifted from year to year towards more ambitious subjects until the last year when only special occupation-related subjects (physics, technology, electrical engineering) were taught. Instruction was given solely by those officials of the plant with technical or commercial training who possessed 'pedagogic skill' and 'teaching talent' (Siemens & Halske AG 1913). Practical training in the training workshop began with filing metal cubes; after 5–6 weeks apprentices were expected to be able to make the most essential tools for their own use by themselves. After one year they were transferred to workshops on a six-monthly basis and in the last six months especially capable apprentices were trained in toolmaking or in the 'experimental workshop' (testing innovations).

Siemens–Halske pursued a special policy, deviating from that in large industry elsewhere, with regard to the examining of skilled workers. Whereas enterprises like

Loewe considered it beneath their dignity to have their apprentices appear before a body nominated by the locksmiths' guild in accordance with the 1908 Law on the Master Crafts Certificate of Competence (*Befähigungsnachweis*), Siemens apprentices were able from the beginning to take their test at the Chamber of Handicrafts so as 'not to place restrictions on them for the future' (Voss 1911: 294). An 'examination committee of precision mechanics and electrical engineering' was formed of representatives of handicrafts and industry in 1912 through which the firm exerted its influence on the organisation and management of the examinations (Siemens & Halske AG 1913: 26).

If statistics on where the apprentices ended up are to be believed, the goal of 'creating a core of high-performing skilled workers' (ibid., 27) was attained: in 1930, more than two-thirds of those trained since 1908 were still employed in the plant (Siemens-Archiv-Akten 14/Lr 492 1930).

AEG: from standardization of production components to the production of standardized training documents

The development of apprentice training at AEG is a good example of how a late developer can suddenly be up front. The rise of AEG has often been referred to as 'fantastic'. Emil Rathenau, one of the partners who was briefly a draughtsman at Borsig, the renowned locomotive manufacturer, after attending the Polytechnic, purchased a small machine factory in the north of Berlin which did not survive the 'founder crisis'. Armed with a small fortune, he travelled in the 1870s to the USA, going from one international exhibition to the next until he finally found in the Edison patents the starting-point for viable and promising mass production. He became the First Director of the German Edison Society, founded in 1883 and known as AEG (*Allgemeine Electricitaets-Gesellschaft*) from 1887. Up until World War I the production range included not only almost all branches of the electrical industry (with the emphasis on heavy current engineering) but also locomotives, cars, ships, aeroplanes and so on.

AEG too changed its location, but it retained its main headquarters near the old machine-building quarter in Wedding, north of the city centre. The Ackerstrasse appliance factory (1888), the second site, became the nucleus of a factory area in the workers' quarter. The first large machine factory of 1896 was already considered to be a model of transparent, functional labour organization with a delicately ordered bureaucratic superstructure. After a phase of tumultuous growth the company entered a 'period of systematic refinement and inner smoothing-out' (Allgemeine Elektricitaets-Gesellschaft 1956: 176) in the years between 1908 and 1913. In a lecture on 'modern mass production' in January 1912 Dolivo-Dobrowolsky, the director of the appliance factory claimed that the success of modern mass production depended on a fast flow of materials, low material consumption, and constant precision. This meant, however, 'making sure that the product was as little as possible at the mercy of the worker' (Dolivo-Dobrowolski 1912: 2). From the standpoint of modern industry, this is a definite settling of accounts with individual manual work, seen as the converse of mass production. It may have its place in art, but in the production of consumer goods it only got in the way. The machine yielded more 'precision and quality' in any desired amounts than any 'individual manual work could ever provide'. As a 'stopgap measure', 'human hands . . . would still have to help' until they could gradually be replaced by 'sufficiently perfect copying machines'. The human being as a makeshift substitute for suitably built machines would, however, 'have to function as such, even if it is not a very precise machine' (ibid.).

Dolivo-Dobrowolsky was boldly thinking ahead. The aim was to eliminate the worker from production: 'The less work, or more precisely man hours, is expended on a given manufactured item, the less schooled personnel is required, the more perfectly the human being and his mind will be excluded from where it does not belong and diverted to its real purpose, namely to proposing and disposing' (ibid.) – which means, we might add, to offices. The offices applied the bulk of their mental energy to the 'standardization of components'. To ensure their uniformly precise production, however, good tools were needed, and Dolivo-Dobrowolsky realized that that meant a third group between the proposers and disposers, on the one hand, and human machine substitutes on the other: quality workers. In their hands were to be placed drawings, specification tables and ancillary devices and hence responsibility, removed from the actual manufacturing process.

In his lecture Dobrowolsky underscored the increased importance of quality workers. Their recruitment, he said, should no longer be left to the plant environment: thus, in the year following the lecture (1913), AEG installed its first training workshop in the Ackerstrasse appliance factory (Bünger 1919).

By this time (1911) the DATSch had finally adopted its governing principles for vocational training. It was possibly also the geriatric illness of Emil Rathenau – a staunch opponent of company training workshops all his life – that facilitated the start. In 1913 the training workshop was opened for 100 apprentices (mechanics, toolmakers, lathe operators) who during their four years of training were obliged to attend the compulsory further training school and the 'trade hall' – a technical school for metal workers. Under the pressures of the skilled labour shortage that set in when the war began and the production losses caused by improper operation of expensive machines by semi-skilled workers, the other AEG manufacturing sites also began systematic training. The 'Apprentice School' in Brunnenstrasse, established in 1915, a combination of training workshop and vocational plant school with Adolf Heilandt as full-time director, became the centre of training (Heilandt 1918). This was an elitist affair with an apprenticeship rate of less than 2 per cent of the workforce. But the school was characterized from the beginning by a high level of rationality (AEG 1917).

It was not only the production components that were energetically standardized before World War I. AEG was a major force behind the founding of the German

Institute for Industrial Standards, and this meant that the stipulations, the standard sheets themselves, were given a standardized layout in 1913. Modelled on these standard sheets, the 200 standardized instructions, the model drawings for the tasks for the first year of training in the Brunnenstrasse AEG vocational plant school, were prepared. These constituted the main part of the curriculum for the training of industrial apprentices at AEG. In 1918 its director, Adolf Heilandt, assumed the chairmanship of the DATSch commission for apprentice training and after slight modifications the AEG course became the first DATSch course for machine builders in 1919. In the following years, on the AEG model and mostly on the basis of documents from Berlin companies (Loewe, Siemens, Borsig, Fritz Werner, whose training directors sat on the DATSch subcommittees as responsible expert advisors), courses for other occupations were developed. Thus the rationalisation principle of standardization found its way into training in the form of these courses.

AN AMERICAN INVENTION? APPRENTICESHIP TRAINING IN THE USA BEFORE WORLD WAR I

Were these beginnings of systematic training genuine achievements of the Berlin enterprises or were there other models? There were the dedicated pioneers, MAN (Maschinenfabrik Augsburg-Nürnberg) and Schuckert, certainly. The Berlin enterprises, however, turned their eyes to the USA just as did the VDI and the DATSch. The USA?

Even when he visited the Chicago World Fair in 1893, the Berlin City School Chief Inspector Bertram was still talking about 'one of the dark sides of American life' during a meeting of the Association for the Promotion of Industrial Diligence in Prussia; 'In general', he reported, 'there are no apprentices' (Bertram 1894). Twenty years later, in June 1913, the Director of the General Electric Corporation in West Lynn, Massachusetts, M.W. Alexander, read a paper to the German Committee for Technical Education in Berlin on 'The Practical Training of Skilled Workers and Technical Officers in the Mechanical Industry of the United States of America' (Alexander 1914). He referred to the 'solid design' of German wares at the Chicago Fair as what actually prompted consideration of industrial apprenticeship training in the USA. The process was accelerated, Alexander said, by a change in the immigrant population around 1900, when the regions of origin shifted eastwards and the less developed agrarian countries provided hardly any workers with craft and technical skills. Taking up the tradition of craft training in England and Germany, they had in 1902 begun a private initiative to develop a recruiting system of their own. Loewe AG was for a time closely associated with General Electric through its Union Electricitäts-Gesellschaft and introduced many GE practices into its own training, as did AEG later.

The volume of 'Research Work in the Field of Engineering' with the paper by Alexander also contained a travel report by Conrad Matschoß, the Managing Director of the DATSch, 'On the Intellectual Means of Technical Progress in America' (Matschoß 1914). In it and in a series of descriptions written at the same time by VDI emissaries on 'Worker and Apprentice Training in the United States' or 'The Practical Training of Technicians and Factory Apprentices in North America' (Mühlmann 1912; Schuchardt 1913), efforts were made to ascertain how training could be combined with 'American methods' following the adoption of the DATSch governing principles. By 1913 the DATSch was compelled to acknowledge that precisely in the field in which Germany thought it was invincible, namely the qualification ('quality') of its workers, the USA was about to take the lead with new forms of industrial training.

INDUSTRIAL PSYCHOTECHNOLOGY: THE COMMENCEMENT OF SCIENTIFIED INDUSTRIAL VOCATIONAL EDUCATION AND TRAINING

In the period before World War I, after a phase of international competition in which a relative tie was reached in the permanent race in the field of production methods, questions of how to increase the 'efficiency of the workforce as a whole' moved to the forefront. In 1913 the 'Principles of Scientific Management', F.W. Taylor's main work, was translated into German and the VDI made these principles the subject of its 54th general assembly. The main speaker, together with Dodge, an American, was Georg Schlesinger, the first plant school teacher in Berlin. He began his lecture on 'Business Management and Scientific Management' (Schlesinger 1913) by referring to 'selection' as an important but neglected principle of management. Here, in the selection of the right person for the specific industrial purpose, he felt that science had failed. Workers were still not being hired very objectively, on the basis of certificates and superficial impressions. The problem of getting at those internal processes that play a decisive role in the performance of the 'manual worker', such as attentiveness, memory, imagination, etc., seemed to be impossible to resolve. For Schlesinger, finding methods by which suitability for the specific occupation could be tested prior to hiring still seemed to be an unattainable goal.

A name already existed for the science that was to make this possible: 'industrial psycho-technology', and its programme had already been outlined during the 1910/1911 winter term at Berlin University by the German-American Hugo Münsterberg (1912). But this discipline was not generally adopted until World War I. Under the tremendous pressure of time, the right man or woman could only be quickly put in the right place with the help of formalized methods (and characteristically it was above all the 'speed jobs' – transport/communications – in which aptitude tests were first carried out). Schlesinger gained his first experience with vocational aptitude tests in the context of his work on limb replacements for war invalids: here the gap between the individual human body and the machine had to be bridged. Schlesinger did not just find a technical solution to this problem. He also began making comparative studies concerning occupational suitability and performance of people with different disabilities. He personally carried out motion studies and developed specification catalogues for a whole series of occupations as a basis for decision-making on the reinsertion of invalids into the world of work. He thus succeeded in taking the first step towards a science of 'industrial psycho-technology' (Schlesinger 1920).

Schlesinger subsequently strove energetically to anchor this science into the teaching field and associated testing areas. He founded the 'Research Society for Scientific Management Procedures' (Forschungsgesellschaft für betriebswissenschaftliche Arbeitsverfahren 1918) in May 1918 for this purpose – with himself and Loewe director Waldschmidt on the board of directors – and somewhat later the *Arbeitsausschuß für industrielle Psychotechnik* (Study Group for Industrial Psychotechnology) in the Berlin regional VDI. In October 1918, with the participation of the main ministries and the relevant influential associations, the first University Institute for Industrial Psychotechnology (IIP), the nucleus and model for most of the testing stations established later in the Reich, was set up at the Charlottenburg Technical University. Schlesinger had reached his goal: in his first post-war publications he referred to industrial psychotechnology as the crowning keystone of the scientific management edifice, the basis for the industrial plant engineer's task of 'sorting out the workers' (Schlesinger 1919/20: 4), a problem solved 'shoulder to shoulder' with the practical psychologist.

In several respects industrial psychotechnology (IPT) is of significance for the development of industry-typical apprenticeship:

- IPT provided 'objective' methods of regulating access to training.
- The test was preceded by thorough job analyses, the basis for later 'job descriptions'. Schlesinger himself had already worked out a tableau for the metal sector in 1919 (Schlesinger 1920: 100); the first analysis of the occupation of locksmith was carried out in the Berlin IIP by Adolf Friedrich (1921/22).
- Schemata of reality were drafted for the test itself and served as practice training material.
- The work on validation of the testing procedure yielded methods to monitor learning progress during training.

And those tested? How did they digest this thrust towards rationalization? Through the objective procedure they could be sure that they had found their due place in the system of occupations. War and its aftermath had done away with the political barriers to selection that had existed for a time as part of Taylor's rat race system. Berlin's first Social Democratic town councillor (from 1915), Sassenbach, had included the aptitude test in the principles for reform of the apprenticeship system at the Nuremberg Trade Union Congress in 1919. Selection was now good and democratic: 'clear the way for the competent' and 'to each according to his abilities'. Where the works councils had a voice in the prostrate economy, they too had an interest in the most comprehensive economy of human resources possible.

REFERENCES

Alexander, M. W. (1914): *Die praktische Ausbildung von gelernten Arbeitern und technischen Beamten in der mechanischen Industrie der Vereinigten Staaten von Nordamerika*. In: Forschungsarbeiten auf dem Gebiete des Ingenieurwesens. Berlin: Verein Deutscher Ingenieure.

Allgemeine Electricitaets-Gesellschaft (1917): *Ausbildung gewerblicher Lehrlinge. Lehrplan. Werkschule der Fabriken Brunnenstraße*. Berlin.

Allgemeine Electricitaets-Gesellschaft (1956): *50 Jahre AEG*. Berlin.

Behr, M. von (1981): *Die Entstehung der industriellen Lehrwerkstatt. Materialien und Analysen zur beruflichen Bildung im 19. Jahrhundert*. Frankfurt/Main: Campus.

Bertram, H. (1894): *Amerikanisches Schulwesen*. In: Sitzungsberichte des Vereins zur Beförderung des Gewerbefleißes 1894. Berlin.

Bünger, W. (1919): *Die Lehrlingsausbildung in der AEG-Apparatefabrik*. In: AEG-Mitteilungen 15 (1919), no. 2.

Dolivo-Dobrawolsky, M. (1912): *Die moderne Massenfabrikation in der Apparatefabrik der AEG*. In: AEG-Zeitung 14 (1912), no. 8.

Forschungsgesellschaft für betriebswissenschaftliche Arbeitsverfahren (1918): *Bericht über die Sitzung der Forschungsgesellschaft für betriebswissenschaftliche Arbeitsverfahren am Sonnabend, dem 4. Mai 1918*. Berlin: Archives of Technical University.

Friedrich, A. (1921/22): *Die Analyse des Schlosserberufs*. In: Praktische Psychologie 3, pp. 287–299.

Hanf, G. (1985): *Handwerkerausbildung in Berlin während der industriellen Revolution (1787–1873). Eine Untersuchung zur Frühgeschichte des beruflichen Schulwesens*. Dissertation Technische Universität Berlin.

Hausen, K. (1981): *Ludwig Loewe – Pionierunternehmen des Werzeugmaschinenbaus*. In: Karl Schwarz (Hg.), Berlin. Von der Residenzstadt zur Industriemetropole Ein Beitrag der Technischen Universität zum Preußenjahr 1981, vol. 1. Berlin: Technische Universität.

Heilandt, A. (1918): *Die Werkschule der AEG-Fabriken Brunnenstraße*. In: AEG-Mitteilungen 14, no. 12.

Herkner, V. (2003): Deutscher Ausschuß für Technisches Schulwesen. Untersuchungen unter besonderer Berücksichtigung metalltechnischer Berufe. Hamburg: Dr. Kovac.

Kocka, J. (1969): *Unternehmensverwaltung und Angestelltengesellschaft am Beispiel Siemens 1847–1914. Zum Verhältnis von Kapitalismus und Bürokratie in der deutschen Industrialisierung*. Stuttgart: Klett.

Ludw. Loewe & Co. Aktiengesellschaft (1930): *Ludw. Loewe & Co. Actiengesellschaft. Berlin 1869–1929. Herausgegeben zum sechzigjährigen Jubliäum der Firma von der Gesellschaft für elektrische Unternehmungen*. Berlin.

Magistrat der Stadt Berlin (1906): *Verwaltungsbericht des Magistrats der Stadt Berlin für das Etatjahr 1905. Spezialetat Nr. 9, Bericht über das Städtische Fach- und Fortbildungsschulwesen*. Berlin (p. 4).

Matschoss, C. (1914): *Die geistigen Mittel des technischen Fortschritts in den Vereinigten Staaten von Amerika*. In: *Forschungsarbeiten auf dem Gebiete des Ingenieurwesens*. Berlin: Verein Deutscher Ingenieure.

Mühlmann, G. (1912): *Die praktische Ausbildung der Techniker und der Fabriklehrlinge in Nordamerika*. In: Technik und Wirtschaft 5, pp. 629–638.

Münsterberg, H. (1912): *Psychologie und Wirtschaftsleben. Ein Beitrag zur angewandten Experimental-Psychologie*. Leipzig: S. Hirzel.

Preußische Akademie der Künste (1850): *Akten der Preußischen Akademie der Künste* Reg. 2 Abt. 29 no. 50.

Reichelt, H. (1906): *Die Arbeitsverhältnisse in einem Berliner Großbetrieb der Maschinenindustrie* (= Vol. 4 der Untersuchungen über die Entlöhnungsmethoden in der deutschen Eisen- und Maschinenindustrie). Hgg. im Namen des Centralvereins für das Wohl der arbeitenden Klassen von dessen Kommission. Berlin: Duncker & Humblot.

Schelsinger, G. (1913): Betriebsführung und Betriebswissenschaft. In: Technik und Wirtschaft 6, pp. 525–568.

Schlesinger, G. (1919/20): *Betriebswissenschaft und Psychotechnik*. In: Praktische Psychologie 1, p. 4.

Schlesinger, G. (1920): *Psychotechnik und Betriebswissenschaft*. Leipzig: S. Hirzel.

Schlesinger, G. (1930): *60 Jahre Edelarbeit*. In: Ludwig Loewe & Co. Actiengesellschaft. Berlin.

Schuchardt, Th. (1913): *Arbeiter- und Lehrlingserziehung in den Vereinigten Staaten*. In: Werkstattstechnik 7, pp. 323–402.

Siemens & Halske AG (1913): *Die Lehrlingsausbildung bei der Firma Siemens & Halske A.-G., Wernerwerk*. Berlin.

Siemens-Archiv-Akten 4LK45 (1897): *Dihlmann 11.3.1897*. Munich: Siemens Archives.

Siemens-Archiv-Akten 14/Lr492 (1930): *Bericht aus der Lehrwerkstatt*. Munich: Siemens Archives.

Thelen, K. (2004): *How Institutions Evolve: The Political Economy of Skills in Germany, Britain, the United States and Japan*. Cambridge: Cambridge University Press.

Verein für Socialpolitik (ed.) (1910–1912): *Untersuchungen über Auslese und Anpassung (Berufswahl und Berufsschicksal) der Arbeiter in verschiedenen Zweigen der. Großindustrie* (= Schriften des Vereins für Socialpolitik Bde. 133–135). Berlin: Ducker & Humblot.

Voss, R. von (1911): *Zur Frage der Ausbildung von Lehrlingen für die Großindustrie*. In: Werkstattstechnik 5, p. 287.

Waldschmidt, S. (1913): *Erfahrungen aus der Werkschule der Firma Ludw. Loewe & Co. AG*. In: Technik und Wirtschaft 6, pp. 836–846.

Wegeleben, F. (1924): *Die Rationalisierung im Deutschen Werkzeugmaschinenbau, dargestellt an der Entwicklung der Ludwig Loewe & Co. AG*. Berlin: Loewe.

Chapter 8

Towards a new paradigm of vocational learning

Paul Hager

This chapter begins by showing that for most of its history vocational learning was an on-the-job activity. With the rise of compulsory formal education systems late in the nineteenth century, vocational learning was gradually absorbed into formal arrangements that were in the process of being reconceptualized around influential assumptions that have shaped formal education systems and wider public understandings of learning. It is argued that the result has been that recent growing interest in on-the-job learning has been warped by unconscious adherence to inappropriate formal education assumptions. The deficiencies of recent competence initiatives are traced to these kinds of assumptions. Hence, the conclusion that we need a new understanding of vocational learning.

THE GENEALOGY OF VOCATIONAL LEARNING: ON-THE-JOB LEARNING

Of necessity, vocational learning was originally an on-the-job phenomenon – as early humans struggled for survival as hunters and gatherers, the younger family and clan members were doubtless inducted into what were literally 'life skills' by their elders. It is likely that some were more adept at the mentoring of novices than others, so it was natural for them to assume roles as mentors/tutors. If so, this was an early example of work segmentation and specialization. With the rise of agricultural practices, people could live successfully in one place, hence the growth of villages and towns. Thus, viable farming practices accelerated the segmentation of the labour force into diverse occupations and the institution of apprenticeship was born. The coming of the industrial revolution further enhanced these trends, as towns grew into cities and villages into towns. Throughout all these developments, vocational learning remained an on-the-job phenomenon. Certainly, with the rise of apprenticeship, such learning was made more formal in various ways, but it was still essentially something that occurred on-the-job. It was well into the nineteenth century before the first moves occurred to shift vocational learning decisively towards off-the-job delivery. This was ultimately to lead to the rise of formal vocational education and training (VET). A main theme in this rise of VET was the centrality of morally uplifting knowledge in off-the-job vocational learning. In this there was no conception that workers were learning skills that would directly enable them to do their job better; rather, the aim was for workers to become better persons by acquiring the scientific, disciplinary knowledge connected with their occupation.

These developments will be illustrated by considering the case of Australia, which before the twentieth century began was a series of British colonies. Not surprisingly, the developments in Australia closely followed a similar sequence in Britain. This account of the rise of formal vocational learning in Australia draws on Murray-Smith (1965, 1966), the acknowledged doyen of historians of Australian technical education up until the 1970s.[1]

According to Murray-Smith, until 1965 Australian technical education went through five distinct periods. These mirrored similar developments in Britain. The first period, from the founding of the colony of New South Wales in 1788 to about 1850, is marked by 'intellectual, middle class ideas on the social usefulness of instructing the intelligent artisan in the scientific principles underlying his trade' (Murray-Smith 1965: 171).

The first half of the nineteenth century saw the establishment of mechanics' institutes in many parts of Australia. This movement was accompanied by prominent slogans imported from Britain, such as 'self-improvement for the labouring classes'. Crucially, this movement, which marked the beginnings of formal VET provision, did not see itself as providing workers with the knowledge necessary for them to carry out their occupation: 'Education was a moral and often a charitable question, but hardly one of practical utility' (Murray-Smith 1966: 5).

This first period of VET in Australia: 'sprung less from a direct and uncomplicated response to a real lack of skills in the community than from a complex of strongly-held philosophical, moral and social ideas' (Murray-Smith 1966: 6).

Organizations of many kinds sprang up dedicated to the diffusion of useful knowledge to the working class. Although the mechanics' institutes and related organizations flourished to a greater degree in Australia than in Britain, 'their educational ambitions never succeeded' (Murray-Smith 1966: 8). This was because they presented lecture series offered by volunteers teaching what interested them personally, rather than a programme based on what the students might want or need. The result was that classes seldom lasted for longer than a few weeks at a time. In most cases, it seems, the pedagogy was woeful.

In Murray-Smith's second period, 1850–90, haphazard developments 'coalesce into a well-defined stream' (Murray-Smith 1965: 171). One by one Australian colonial state governments set up 'semi-autonomous government instrumentalities' to direct the mechanics' institutes, schools of mines, etc. Importantly, over this period of initial government involvement 'the moral content of the "diffusion of knowledge" movement leached away but its social and physical implications remained' (Murray-Smith 1966: 9).

The focus was gradually shifting to a conception that skilled workers at least, as citizens, were entitled to receive some form of systematic education. This was the era when compulsory primary education was being instituted. So the mechanics' institutes, etc., became a sort of 'poor persons' university at a time when there was minimal state provision of secondary education.

In this second period, the 'old slogan of "self-improvement" is not so much being dropped, but is metamorphosing'. Morality is still a consideration, but 'the framework in which it applies is now much harder-headed. Advancement, mobility, a sense of national purpose are becoming much more a part of the ethos of the community' (Murray-Smith 1966: 13).

In 1862, John Wooley, foundation professor of the University of Sydney, stated: 'The cry of our fathers was for "the general diffusion of knowledge"; ours is its "utilisation" ' (quoted by Murray-Smith 1966: 10). Education for economic advancement was an idea beginning to take hold.

But the point I really want to emphasize here is that in all of these developments the focus is single-mindedly on knowledge that represents a background to work, rather than on learning how to perform work itself. For that, on-the-job learning is viewed as essential:

> It was the theory underlying trades and crafts in which the institutes hoped the working man [sic] would be interested, not the practical applications. It was held that skills themselves were a matter for the workshop . . .
>
> (Marcus Clarke 1871, quoted in Murray-Smith 1966: 8)

By the end of Murray-Smith's second period, this idea of the social benefits of education for trades and crafts people had what the Melbourne *Age* called a 'firm hold . . . on the public mind' (quoted by Murray-Smith 1965: 171). It had become a major election issue.

However, poor organization persisted. Aims were ill-defined and lack of resources meant that often courses were adapted to popular non-vocational requirements, thus drawing criticism that the institutes were failing to meet their main purposes. For instance, the *Age* in 1887 complained vociferously that 'the parliamentary vote to schools of mines, designed to produce practical miners, was being "expended", in a large measure, in teaching young ladies the accomplishment of landscape and animal drawing' (Murray-Smith 1965: 179).

In these circumstances, the states inevitably intervened to provide more direction. This marks Murray-Smith's third period, 1890–1914, during which governments sought to impose more order and purpose on VET and to position it in relation to primary education, secondary education and universities. However, at the same time, a series of external developments saw the public interest in VET start to wane, as did the urgency for governments to place it on a better footing. These developments included:

- the severe depression of the 1890s which greatly cut funding;
- the rapid decline of mining in Australia;
- the retreat of Australian industry behind tariff barriers and a reduction in inter-state economic rivalries, both brought about by federation.

So the result was that any VET progress in this period was very slow, while teachers remained 'untrained, overworked and ill-paid' (Murray-Smith 1965: 183). VET schools were also badly located to meet pressing needs, and course offerings were poorly planned and conceptualized. Overall it is a plausible view that 'the assumption of control of technical education by the state departments about the year 1890 was a serious setback to its development' (Murray-Smith 1965: 182).

Nevertheless, 'by 1914, technical education had clarified its function' and assumed its shape for the next half century (Murray-Smith 1966: 22). In the process though 'the academic bias of the high schools, and the influence of the state examination systems, tended to impart to technical education a "second-class" prejudice that we still linger under today' (Murray-Smith 1965: 186).

The result of arriving finally within the educational mainstream, but with 'second-class' status, was that VET from now on was frequently dubbed the Cinderella of the educational system. It seems that things were little different in Britain. As Connell observed:

Technical education in England was the Cinderella of education. It was unplanned, inadequately financed and looked on without enthusiasm by employers, employees, and educators. A government report of 1918 estimated that in 1914 only seven per cent of the male population was receiving any kind of technical instruction.

(Connell 1980: 50)

The main point for now is that henceforward the assumption that had characterized vocational learning throughout its previous history, that it is essentially an on-the-job activity, starts to be revised. Rather than providing background understanding of principles that underpin work, thereby offering further education, the role of VET gradually shifts to one of preparing people for work. Moreover, this role is increasingly perceived in terms of assumptions about learning that characterize the formal education system as a whole.

The incorporation of vocational learning into the formal education system leads to Murray-Smith's fourth period, which spans the interwar years. This period is 'one in which achievements are modest and the pace of development slow' (Murray-Smith 1965: 171). In fact, this period is the culmination of what Murray-Smith dubs 'a long sleep of half-a-century' for VET (Murray-Smith 1966: 1). His final period is one in which interest in vocational learning is reawakened – leading eventually to the major reforms of the 1990s.

VOCATIONAL LEARNING INCORPORATED INTO THE FORMAL EDUCATION SYSTEM

As vocational education and learning became incorporated more and more into the formal education system, albeit as the poor cousin, so they came to adopt typical formal education assumptions and a supply-side focus. These formal education assumptions become so strong that their unsuitability for vocational learning is now but dimly recognized. These assumptions centre on a story about learning – the 'common sense' account – that goes something like this. The best learning resides in individual minds not bodies; it centres on propositions (true, false; more certain, less certain); such learning is transparent to the mind that has acquired it; so the acquisition of the best learning alters minds not bodies. Subsidiary threads of the story include: the best learning can be expressed verbally and written down in books, etc.; the process and product of learning can be sharply distinguished; and, although residing in minds and books, the best learning can be applied, via bodies, to alter the external world.

There are a number of basic presuppositions about learning that underpin this story. The main one is:

■ There is one best kind of learning, the furnishing of minds with true propositions.

Although it is recognized that learning comes in distinct kinds, according to this assumption the relative worth of all types of learning is to be judged against the best, viz acquisition of propositions by minds. This major presupposition centrally underpins the above story. Closely related to it are two other presuppositions, as follows:

■ *Learning centres on the stable and enduring*: Since true propositions are in some sense unchanging and enduring, the best kind of learning remains relatively stable over time.
■ *Learning is replicable*: If the best kind of learning is something that is stable and enduring, then the learning of different learners can be literally the same or identical (Hager 2005).

Taken together these three presuppositions represent a focus on 'adding more substance' to the mind. Viewing learning as the accumulation of mental products is what

109

Bereiter (2002) dubs the 'folk theory' of learning. One effect of this emphasis on the products of learning is that performance of human activities that have a substantial theoretical base is thought of as involving two distinct components. First, the mind is thought to acquire the requisite quota of theoretical items. Second, performance is thought to involve the application of these theoretical items. It is assumed that lack of these theoretical items will entail unsatisfactory practice. But, particularly as the twentieth century unfolded, the requisite theoretical base of most of the occupations catered for by VET was perceived to have expanded greatly. Hence the theoretical content of typical VET courses grew apace.

This account of what is needed to acquire occupational proficiency, shaped by the learning-as-product assumption, has come to dominate VET systems in the following ways.

- *Selection of students*: Admission criteria that are based overwhelmingly on individual performance on written tests of propositional knowledge and that, in effect, test the individual's mental capacity.
- *Curriculum*: Course content that is overwhelmingly propositional knowledge logically ordered via disciplines and subjects. Any non-propositional learning, such as workshop practice or laboratory skills, is driven by the propositional, that is, it involves application of theory covered previously in the classroom. If not, this is regarded as a flaw in curriculum structure.
- *Teaching methods*: The major focus is on presentation of verbal and written propositions for individual student acquisition and understanding, hence the dominant use of lectures, tutorials and textbooks.
- *Assessment/progression methods*: Learning is demonstrated by individuals reproducing verbal or written propositions in appropriate combinations in response to set questions in examinations, preferably unseen, and written assignments. There is a focus on universal, context-free knowledge, with numbers and grading to quantify the amount of learning demonstrated.

Taken together, these academic processes support the 'front-end model' of occupational preparation. The term 'front-end model' refers to

> any instance of vocational preparation that is based on a period of formal education and/or training that needs to be completed by entrants to the occupation before they can be regarded as qualified workers. The formal education and/or training usually take place in classrooms remote from the workplace.
>
> (Beckett and Hager 2002: 99; see also Hager 2004a)

The reason for using the term 'front-end' is that it implies that all of the *formal* learning that is needed for a lifetime of practice has been completed.[2] The front-end model has become dominant in vocational preparation of all kinds. This is most obvious in professional and sub-professional occupations where a period of some years study in a formal educational institution such as a university is typically a prerequisite for entry into the occupation. However, the front-end model has been influential also in the area of the trades and other skilled occupations where there has been more recognition of the importance of on-the-job learning for novices. In these and other occupations a mandatory period of formal education or training has become increasingly common.[3]

So VET systems have been shaped markedly by the assumptions of the learning-as-product view that has been highly influential in shaping formal education systems.

THE RECENT REVIVAL OF ON-THE-JOB LEARNING: THE PENDULUM SWINGS BACK

There are various reasons for the recent revival of interest in on-the-job learning. The two major ones will be considered here. First, the learning-as-a-product view is under increasing critical pressure for a variety of reasons, both theoretical and practical. Current problems/issues in educational theory and practice questioning this view are discussed briefly below.

Failures of theory/practice accounts of performance

If, as the common sense story of learning suggests, the most valuable learning resides in minds that are essentially passive spectators, then this will be the basis for understanding human performances that are significantly cognitive. Hence the view that such performances are practices that involve the application of previously acquired theory. Long ago Ryle (1949) pointed out the futility of this view, which effectively seeks to reduce practice to theory. Though still the common sense view of performance, the theory/practice account is increasingly seen to be implausible, thanks to research on expertise and the rise of the knowledge society, both of which emphasize the creation of valuable knowledge during the performance of work. Better concepts that involve more relevant assumptions might yet produce a viable conceptual understanding of practice (Beckett and Hager 2002: 130–2).

Failures of the front-end model of vocational preparation

These include:

- the increasing realization that front-end courses in themselves are insufficient to prepare novices for a lifetime of practice;
- the growing rejection of the technical-rationality assumption that underpins many front-end vocational preparation courses;

111

■ growing doubts about the capacity of the front-end model to prepare practitioners for accelerating change (Beckett and Hager 2002: 101–5).

Research in higher education learning

Resting on concepts such as surface vs. deep learning, a range of research has found that much learning in higher education is far from optimal (for example, Bowden and Marton 1998; Prosser and Trigwell 1999). It is often found that 'despite students' having successfully negotiated the assessment system, little understanding of fundamental concepts has been gained' (Bowden and Marton 1998: 61). Perhaps the conclusion from this is that even learning a traditional discipline is a gradual *process* of growing understanding, rather than bit-by-bit mastery of discrete *products*. I suggest that gaining high level proficiency in a discipline more resembles the gradual clearing of a fog in a landscape than atom-by-atom acquisition of content.

New directions in psychology

There is a clear move away from learning as a mind being stored with contents (for example, Bereiter 2002; Bruner 1996):

> everyday cognition makes more sense if we abandon the idea of a mind operating on stored mental content and replace it with the idea of a mind continually and automatically responding to the world and making sense of whatever befalls it. I call this the 'connectionist view of mind'.
>
> (Bereiter 2002: 196–7)

Learning transfer research

Learning transfer research has led to recent proposals to reconceptualize transfer and, by implication, learning (e.g. Bransford and Schwartz 1999; Schoenfeld 1999). Researchers see the institution of formal education being underpinned by the basic assumption that transfer is a ubiquitous phenomenon. However, despite the increasing power of experimental techniques, transfer 'seems to vanish when experimenters try to pin it down' (Schoenfeld 1999: 7). As Bransford and Schwartz (1999) conclude, from reviewing nearly one hundred years of increasingly sophisticated research, transfer is indeed rare if it is restricted to *replicative* transfer, which involves both the stability and replicability assumptions that were noted above. However, they propose that we broaden the notion of transfer by including an emphasis on *preparation for future learning*, the ability to learn in new environments. So the point of transfer is not replication of a product, but new learning.

Each of these problems/issues involves rejection in one way or another of the learning-as-a-product view and directs attention to on-the-job learning as an interesting phenomenon in its own right.

This brings us to the second main reason for the recent revival of interest in on-the-job learning, the concern to better align learning in formal courses with the knowledge and skills required in workplaces. This has been accompanied by interest in such matters as the transition from novice to skilled practitioner, a process that seems to require some form of on-the-job learning. One main manifestation of the attempt to bridge on- and off-the job learning has been the so-called competence agenda. In many countries, occupational competences have been developed as part of policies that sought to revitalize vocational education and training, usually with the stated overriding aim of becoming more competitive in the globalized economy. These developments have drawn strong criticism from many educators, and in some cases have resulted in dubious education and training offerings. Much of the confusion about competence can be traced to both its proponents and opponents variously sharing certain questionable assumptions about learning that revolve around viewing it as a product. The result is ambiguity and equivocation as both camps run together items that are logically and conceptually distinct. In particular, to advance these matters I maintain that we need to make consistently a tripartite distinction between:

- performance and its outcomes;
- the underpinning constituents of competence (capabilities, abilities, skills);
- the education, training or development of people to be competent performers (Hager 2004b).

Performance and its outcomes

Precision is possible and attainable for descriptions of performance and its outcomes. (The term 'performance' relates to human activity of some kind.) Humans have worked successfully with many kinds of performance descriptors long before the advent of the competence agenda. Road rules, driver certification criteria, the rules of golf and cricket averages are familiar examples. An important feature of performance descriptors is that they can be made as precise as necessary to meet their purpose. There is a trade-off however. The more precise they become, the more they abstract from the overall experience of the activity that they describe. For instance the rules of golf determine very exactly the number of strokes in a round, what to do when the ball is hit into the river, etc. However, they are an abstraction from the overall experience of the game of golf in that they provide little idea of what it is like to play golf. Nor are they much help for someone seeking to improve their game. This point applies generally to performance descriptors (Hager 2004b).

The underpinning constituents of competence (capabilities, abilities, skills)

Unlike performance descriptors, no such precision is attainable for the constituents of competence (capabilities, abilities, skills). These capabilities, abilities, and skills are attributes or properties of people. As such, much about them, e.g. knacks, feels and bodily know-how, remains tacit. As Polanyi famously observed, 'we can know more than we can tell' (quoted by Lum 1999: 410). Likewise the work of Hubert Dreyfus (e.g. Dreyfus and Dreyfus 1986) provides strong arguments for the view that skilled performance can neither be reduced to a set of rules nor be fully explicated theoretically. Of course, we do try to explicate the capabilities, abilities and skills involved in performance but this remains territory where contestation is inevitable. In trying to explicate capabilities, abilities and skills we use common language that incorporates dubious assumptions about them, such as the idea that skills are physical but not mental. A view more consistent with the available evidence is that skills are embodied and seamlessly integrate cognitive and psychomotor dimensions.

The education of competent performers

The education, training or development of people to be competent performers is a completely different dimension from the other two, since the development of competence is a curriculum *process*. At best, performance descriptors refer to outcomes of this process, but not to the process itself. The capabilities, abilities, and skills all need to be fostered and developed during the curriculum process. But because they are, at least partially, tacit, opinions on how best to do this are inevitably divided.

This chapter has argued that basic principles of on-the-job learning clash with formal education assumptions. Competences illustrate this clearly. Various errors abound. First, formal education systems are used to construing learning as a product. The knowledge that students need to acquire can be tightly specified. The same assumption carries over to formal VET provision. So this means that competence needs to be specified in detail. This can be done, as long as it is realized that what can be unambiguously specified is *performance and its outcomes* (tasks, processes, functions). Many competence statements are of this kind. However, the more minutely and precisely they specify, the more they abstract from the phenomenological wholeness of the activities that they describe. One common error is to overlook this inescapable abstraction and pretend that competence statements describe the whole. This is why so many sets of competence statements make practice in their field appear to be thin, repetitious and routine.

But there is a worse error, which equates performance and outcomes with skills and capabilities. This error mistakenly imputes the precision and accuracy of performance descriptors to descriptions of abilities, capacities and skills. As Lum puts it, this is the error of thinking that 'human capabilities can be unequivocally described and accurately communicated by means of language' (Lum 1999: 410). For the reasons given above, this is an unfounded hope. Yet many competence initiatives run together or confuse these two distinct categories. This leads to supposedly 'objective' lists of abilities and skills that students are expected to acquire as discrete units. Competence in the particular vocation then becomes a sum of these discrete abilities and skills.

Once again, viewing learning as a product is the problem. It discounts as inferior learning that is non-transparent. Hence the natural slide into thinking that the worker's competence (capabilities, abilities or skills) can be directly specified. It is precisely because skills, etc., involve tacit components, that they need to taught in supervised training or work situations (e.g. apprenticeship), rather than in formal classrooms. Overall, although competence approaches were supposed to bring vocational education more into line with on-the-job learning, they have widely foundered on these errors that are rooted in the common formal education assumptions that learning is transparent, is a product, etc.

THE NEED FOR A NEW ACCOUNT OF VOCATIONAL LEARNING

The competence agenda as an attempt to bridge on- and off-the job learning has failed because of assumptions taken over uncritically from formal learning situations. So we need a new understanding of vocational learning. I suggest three key ideas are necessary for this.

First, learning needs to be viewed as an ongoing process. This requires more understanding than hitherto that learning from the practice of an occupation is at least as important, if not more important, as the formal learning that precedes full entry into the occupation. Learning being an ongoing process is quite consistent with performance descriptors being devised for various stages or levels of the ongoing learning process and learners being assessed against those performance descriptors for various purposes.

Dewey was a pioneer of the concept of learning as a process (or, more accurately, as a dialectical interplay of process and product (Dewey 1916) – but for simplicity I shall refer to 'learning as process'). The sharp distinction between process and product of learning is plausible whenever learning is separated from action. However, when learning is closely linked with action, the two are not sharply distinguished at all. The process facilitates the product, which at the same time enhances further processes and so on. Dewey's ideas were widely noted and discussed. However, they cannot be said to have transformed educational thought, let alone practice, as shown by the ongoing persistence of the learning-as-product view. But recent developments in educational thought have brought the notion of learning as a process into new prominence. Some were discussed earlier (e.g. Bereiter's connectionism, the Bransford and Schwartz concept of preparation for future learning). Also, influential contemporary approaches to understanding learning view it as a process, (Lave and Wenger 1991; Engestrom 2001).

115

Second, a new understanding of vocational learning needs to recognize that, in an important sense, learning is wider than the individual learner. Learning reshapes the learner and the environment, that is, it sets up a network of relations that extends beyond the individual learner. So, while some learning can be seen as residing in individuals, other important learning occurs at the level of teams and organizations. This is why 'transfer' is actually most often new learning as the learner/environment combination is seldom the same or very similar. The significance of the social nature of learning also needs consideration.

Third, a new understanding of vocational learning needs to think much more widely than mere skill or propositional learning. What we have is an integration of cognitive, conative and affective capacities, as well as other abilities and learned capacities such as bodily know-how, skills of all kinds and so on. Not all of these components are expressed verbally or written down, but all are conceivably involved in making and acting upon judgements that reflect a capacity for successful acting in and on the world (Beckett and Hager 2002: 150).

A system of vocational learning that centred on these three features would differ significantly from current arrangements.

CONCLUSION

This chapter began by showing that for most of its history vocational learning was an on-the-job activity. Public understandings of the nature of learning, shaped by compulsory participation in formal education systems, are less than helpful for understanding on-the-job learning. So, we urgently need a new account of vocational learning, one that recognizes the value of on-the-job learning. Some likely features of such an account have been briefly outlined.

NOTES

1　The term 'technical education' was used in Australia until the 1970s when it was replaced by Technical and Further Education (TAFE). By the 1990s the wider term 'VET' had gained currency.

2　A kind of front-end model can also be seen as being virtually the only one shaping primary and secondary schooling. In this case the vocation is 'adult member of society' and some minimal period of schooling is deemed both essential and sufficient for preparation of all youth for this role.

3　In Australia, for example, a system of one-year traineeships that include a formal education component has been instituted since the 1990s for a wide range of occupations not covered by apprenticeships. These occupations previously lacked a formal training component.

REFERENCES

Beckett, D. and Hager, P. (2002) *Life, Work and Learning: Practice in Postmodernity,* Routledge International Studies in the Philosophy of Education 14, London and New York: Routledge.

Bereiter, C. (2002) *Education and Mind in the Knowledge Age,* Mahwah, NJ/London: Lawrence Erlbaum Associates.

Bowden, J. and Marton, F. (1998) *The University of Learning,* London: Kogan Page.

Bransford, J.D. and Schwartz, D.L. (1999) 'Rethinking Transfer: A Simple Proposal With Multiple Implications', *Review of Research in Education,* 24: 61–100.

Bruner J. (1996) *The Culture of Education,* Cambridge, MA/London: Harvard University Press.

Connell, W.F. (1980) *A History of Education in the Twentieth Century World,* Culture and Curriculum Series, Canberra: Curriculum Development Centre.

Dewey, J. (1916) *Democracy and Education,* New York: Macmillan.

Dreyfus, H.L and Dreyfus, S.E. (1986) *Mind Over Machine: The Power of Human Intuition and Expertise in the Era of the Computer,* New York: Free Press.

Engestrom, Y. (2001) 'Expansive Learning at Work: Towards an Activity-Theoretical Reconceptualisation', *Journal of Education and Work,* 14(1): 133–56.

Hager, P. (2004a) 'Front-Loading, Workplace Learning and Skill Development', *Educational Philosophy and Theory,* 36(5): 523–34.

Hager, P. (2004b) 'The Competence Affair, or Why Vocational Education and Training Urgently Needs a New Understanding of Learning', *Journal of Vocational Education & Training,* 56(3): 409–33.

Hager, P. (2005) 'Philosophical Accounts of Learning', *Educational Philosophy and Theory,* 37(5): 649–66.

Lave, J. and Wenger, E. (1991) *Situated Learning,* Cambridge: Cambridge University Press.

Lum, G. (1999) 'Where's the Competence in Competence-based Education and Training?', *Journal of Philosophy of Education,* 33(3): 403–18.

Murray-Smith, S. (1965) 'Technical Education in Australia: A Historical Sketch', in E.L. Wheelwright (ed.), *Higher Education in Australia,* Melbourne: F.W. Cheshire.

Murray-Smith, S. (1966) 'Technical Education: The Lines of Development', in C. Sanders (ed.), *Technical Education for Development,* Nedlands, Western Australia: University of Western Australia Press.

Prosser, M. and Trigwell, K. (1999) *Understanding Learning and Teaching: The Experience in Higher Education,* Buckingham/Philadelphia: Society for Research into Higher Education and Open University Press.

Ryle, G. [1949] (1963) *The Concept of Mind,* Harmondsworth: Penguin.

Schoenfeld, A.H. (1999) 'Looking Toward the 21st Century: Challenges of Educational Theory and Practice', *Educational Researcher,* 28(7): 4–14.

Chapter 9

14–19 and lifelong learning

Distinguishing between academic and vocational learning

Richard Pring

THE CONTEXT

Only in the 1970s was a comprehensive system of education introduced into England and Wales. Even then it was never completed. Parts of England retained their grammar schools – 164 in all, maintaining a division between those who were thought capable of an 'academic curriculum' and those who were not. But the 'common school' became the ideal and, in many cases, the reality for young people. The organizational 'bridging' of the erstwhile divide between academic and non-academic later developed into a common national curriculum up to the age of 16, consisting of ten subjects. Again, there was no division between the academically able and the rest. Vocational preparation (in the sense of providing skills relevant to specific occupations) would be postponed to age 16, when, general education having been completed, the young person could go to colleges of further education, or take a job with work-based training. Schools were for education; colleges and apprenticeships for vocational training.

Something, however, was lost in this admirable attempt to find a common curriculum for all in a non-selective system – and, indeed, in that distinction between, and that consequent separation of, the academic and the vocational. The comprehensive school had respected the value of practical learning, not just as a form of learning for those who were less academic, but as an important way of understanding, and of working intelligently within, the physical and social worlds students were to inhabit. Future engineers need more than an 'academic education'. Practical 'doing' can be as demanding intellectually. It can incorporate or embody theoretical understanding, and lead on to yet further reflection and theorizing. Indeed, as Bruner (1960) so cogently argued, the route to the 'symbolic mode' of representing reality best proceeds through, first, the 'enactive', and, second, the 'iconic'. Above all, one should not isolate the academic approach to learning from the practical, experiential and imaginary modes of representing the world.

GOVERNMENT POLICY

There have been various ways in which this greater integration of the practical and the academic modes of learning, as a preparation for more vocationally oriented studies later, has been attempted in recent years. In the 1970s, the Further Education Unit (FEU) situated in the Department of Education and Science (DES), provided guidelines for vocationally oriented courses which were not occupationally specific and which embodied general education within the context of vocational interests. Again, the 1980s saw the development of Technical and Vocational Education Initiative (TVEI) courses, under the aegis of the Manpower Services Commission, which emphasized the importance of more practical and experiential modes of learning at the centre of education across the ability range.

However, old habits and fixed modes of thinking die hard. A clear distinction between the 'academic' and the 'vocational' (confused so often with the 'practical') constantly reasserts itself, and this is reflected in many government initiatives and papers. In the 1980s, a three-track system emerged post-16, reflected in a system of awards: the academic route for those capable of pursuing 'A' (Advanced) Levels, mainly on their way to universities; an occupationally specific or 'strongly vocational' route for those who were to acquire the skills relevant to the workplace (reflected, at different levels, in the National Vocational Qualifications or NVQs); and an 'in-between' or 'weakly vocational' route in which young people would pursue a general education, albeit embodied within a vocational area to give a sense of relevance and to contextualize the kowledge (General National Vocational Qualification or GNVQ). And these distinctions soon began to start earlier as Foundation levels to the GNVQ could be pursued prior to 16 and as the more occupationally related, competency-based vocational studies were encouraged in the workplace for those 'disengaged' from the more academic pre-16 courses. These developments are a re-assertion of the three-track mentality which has shaped educational provision following the introduction of secondary education for all with the 1944 Education Act (Tomlinson 1997).

The rationale for these 'categories of courses' and for the distinctions between them varies, as is reflected in a proliferation of government papers and initiatives. These vary from an emphasis upon the centrality of nurturing and training in employment-related skills for the good of the economy, to what is perceived to be different types of learning and motivation suitable for different types of young people – through, for example, the importance attached to the widening of choice.

For example, the government's White Paper, *Schools: Achieving Success* (DfES, 2002a), had a chapter devoted to 'meeting individual talents and aspirations at 14–19'. The message was that the educational and training system does not meet the needs of so many young people. Those needs would be met when it

- opens up real choice for young people, and thus creates more opportunities;

119

- provides that choice and those opportunities by creating more vocational routes;
- ensures greater status to vocational studies and awards;
- gives priority to basic literacy and numeracy where there is under performance.

It was envisaged that such vocational routes, starting for some at the age of 14, would include work-related learning.

This White Paper reflected a focus of government policy developed within a series of policy documents (DfEE 1996a; DfEE 1997; DfEE 1999; DfES 2002b). It was clear, however, that this focus upon 14–19 was by no means 'enclosed' or without reference to lifelong learning. There was a link to the adult literacy and numeracy strategy, identified in the 2001 White Paper, *Skills for Life*, which would target 16 year olds with poor basic skills (DfES 2001). And the vocational courses would lead also into further and higher education.

Those White Papers had been preceded by others which assumed two things: first, that there was a distinctive phase of education and training for 14–19 year olds (e.g. DfEE 1996a); second, that such a phase would include from age 14 onwards a greater emphasis upon work-related relevance and vocational learning – thereby improving the economic efficiency of the individual and of society. But after the 2001 White Papers, there has been a rush of documents from the DfES and other Departments, developing the same message. The 2002 Green Paper, *14–19: Extending Opportunities, Raising Standards* (DfES 2002b), proposed a new 'matriculation diploma' or overarching award at three levels with a common core, greater flexibility with the national curriculum post-14 to permit vocational qualifications, and choice through individual learning plans. The 2003 White Paper, *14–19: Opportunity and Excellence* (DfES 2003a), endorsed these proposals, announcing the development of Vocational GCSEs (General Certificates of Secondary Education) and Advanced Vocational CSEs (Certificates of Secondary Education), looking to the long-term development of a unified framework of qualifications, and setting up a working party, under Mike Tomlinson, to implement this. Subsequently, another 2003 White Paper, *The Future of Higher Education* (DfES 2003b), tackled the implications of these developments – the enlarged and more diverse cohort thought able to progress into higher education and the greater vocational background of that expanded cohort – with the creation of Foundation Degrees and more flexible pathways. And a further White Paper (DfES 2003c), *Realising our Potential: 21st Century Skills*, emphasized stronger links between education and employers (and their representatives through the Sector Skills Councils).

Subsequently the Tomlinson Group reported in 2004, advocating a unified and flexible framework of academic and vocational qualifications, enabling progress through different levels and thereby leading on, with relevant qualifications, to further training, higher education or employment (Tomlinson 2004). Shortly afterwards, the

2005 White Paper, *14–19 Education and Training* (DfES 2005), in effect rejected Tomlinson and proposed academic and vocational routes with their respective qualifications – the academic being much as now under the system of GCSEs and A Levels, and the vocational one requiring 14 separate vocational diplomas, the first five of which should be ready for teaching in 2008.

Therefore, a 14–19 phase, with more integrated development across the 'divide' at 16, within but not across both vocational and academic areas, would now seem to be firmly entrenched in the English system. The Welsh Assembly Government has established its own 'Learning Pathways 14–19', leading to the Welsh Baccalaureate.

However, in all these government consultation papers, government White Papers, and working papers from interested groups, there seem to be four fundamental difficulties:

■ *The seduction by rather impoverished language* (or, at least, by an unreflective use of language) into too simplistic an analysis of the problems. It is a case of 'language idling' (to misuse Wittgenstein) and it is one job of philosophy to look more carefully at that language and the meanings embodied in it.

■ *The lack of historical perspective* reflected in a use of language which fails to recognize the historical and social context in which key words are used.

■ *The lack of educational vision* or aims to support the unified system of qualifications which the government wants.

■ *The failure to see the appropriate institutional framework* within which a coherent 14–19 framework of education and training can be developed.

ACADEMIC, VOCATIONAL, CHOICE AND LIFELONG LEARNING: A CASE OF LANGUAGE 'IDLING'

The word 'academic' is variously described. *Roget's Thesaurus* links it to 'irrelevant' and 'scholarly'. The *Oxford English Dictionary* equates it with 'scholarly', (and by implication, abstract, unpractical, cold, merely logical). 'Vocational', on the other hand, has the double meaning of 'answering a call' (the priesthood or nursing as a vocation) or being related to a specific job or career. Hence, in both cases, the words have a range of meanings, some not quite so pleasing as is supposed in much educational discourse. What school would be proud of its academic reputation where that means it produces lots of pupils who are unpractical, cold and merely logical?

The confusion is reflected in the unreflective attribution of certain activities or subjects to either 'academic' or 'vocational'. Thus, academic 'subjects' include English, science, law, mathematics. On the other hand, it is not clear why they should not be regarded as vocational – that is, related to, and often pursued with a view to, certain jobs or careers. An English degree at Oxford is seen as a good preparation for journalism – being able to write fluently on any subject under the sun whether or not one knows anything about it. Law is regarded as an academic subject and yet it is quite clearly geared to the preparation of lawyers. Theology is one of the oldest established academic subjects, but it always was the necessary prerequisite for the priestly vocation.

Perhaps, then, we should fall back on the importance of 'abstract' – the importation of theory, of conceptual frameworks, of ideas (such as those which would have been examined in Plato's academy). But that itself has its difficulties. Is the *doing* of art or the *playing* of music (where one is not intending to be an artist or a musician) academic in this sense? And the person going through the drudgery of learning off by heart a multitude of laws might well bemoan the lack of ideas and scholarly study. (Many law degrees find no room for jurisprudence.) Furthermore, a lot of 'academic learning' is simply contrasted with practical learning – the learning from books, from libraries – the product as well as the source of learning being the written word (not the spoken word, not the words in action). Indeed, in that respect (preparing for written examinations whilst remaining practically useless) gives a pejorative meaning to 'academic'.

If one approaches it from the other end (namely, the activities and the subjects which are normally regarded as 'vocational') the problem does not evaporate. 'Carpentry' or 'cookery' would (under current proposals) be regarded as vocational, although they are given academic respectability by being called 'Design and Technology' or 'Domestic Science'. But why are they vocational? Of course, carpentry is a useful background to becoming a carpenter, but, first, there is or could be a great deal of background knowledge and ideas about the qualities of different sorts of wood, or about the aesthetic potential of different products, and, second, it is an activity which could be pursued because of the intrinsic joy and satisfaction which it gives.

Perhaps 'intention' is the key to the distinction. 'Academic' is that which is pursued or is valued for its own sake, with no career or job in mind. But that is hard to sustain. Many, if not most, pupils pursue the 'academic subjects' not for their intrinsic pleasure but for the certificates they thereby obtain – as a necessary step to further qualifications and better careers. And, in any case, where 'intention' is the defining characteristic, then it would be difficult to divide subjects between the academic and the vocational. The same subjects would be vocational for some, merely (and regrettably) academic for others.

The point of the foregoing analysis is twofold. The first (the less important) is that so much of the analysis of educational failure, and so many of the proposals to remedy that apparent failure, are based upon a rather impoverished way of talking about and thus of conceptualizing education and training. The second is that these words take on a meaning within certain traditions, within certain ways of understanding the aims and values of learning, and within the wider social and economic context of learning.

What is worrying about present proposals is the lack of such philosophical thinking – the taking for granted of certain distinctions which do not stand up to scrutiny. It is for that reason that some of the most significant developments in schools and colleges – developments very often arising from the insights of teachers as they think deeply about what it *means* to educate *these* children in *their* social context – have achieved so little foothold within the educational system. But first it is necessary to look at the traditions which underpin the false dichotomy between the 'academic' and the 'vocational'.

England, particularly, has inherited a divided educational system – one in which a certain kind of learning, and a certain kind of subject matter to be learnt, are seen to be the province of an intelligent few and in which the rest must either struggle along the same path if they are to be deemed educated or do something very different, something more practical, something more relevant to the jobs they will eventually perform.

There are, in other words, two quite different traditions: the one which is often called 'academic' and the other which is called 'vocational'. The academic tradition is seen as the hallmark of a liberal education. It is distinguished by the pursuit of intellectual excellence, as that is reflected in the mastery of different disciplines of enquiry, or in the relatively unchanging subjects that we are familiar with through the grammar school curriculum. There is an emphasis upon the acquisition of an agreed content of knowledge, including the often abstract grasp of the concepts and prin-ciples that make up that content. There is an emphasis, too, upon the facility with which that content might be expressed in a *written* form.

Such a tradition should not be derided. At its best, it represents the most econom-ical way of introducing the scientific and humane ways in which experience has been organized, understood and applied – in which a new generation might be introduced to the arguments and debates, to the discoveries and imaginative insights of previous generations as they too have tried to make sense of the physical, social and moral world. There is an inheritance of thinking, feeling, enquiry, criticism which we must pass on to the next generation.

But too often that distillation of the 'best that has been thought and said' in science and the humanities is so abstracted from the *processes* through which the world is understood scientifically, or through which experience is illuminated within the arts and humanities, that its significance is lost on the young learner. 'Academic' does take on the pejorative meaning of 'abstract', 'dry', 'irrelevant'. It fails to educate. Furthermore, there are often whole areas of human understanding which are omitted – the practical and technical grasp, the moral appraisal, the economic and social awareness of the world in which they live. It is as though the abstractions of the academic tradition have, for so many young people, lost touch with their concrete and practical world. But, furthermore, this academic tradition not only is sadly out of the grasp of the less able; it too often provides an impoverished experience for the academically able, because, although intellectually involved, they fail to see the rele-vance to their own developing lives. Above all, however, in its abstraction, such a tradition is relaying the message to so many young people that education is irrelevant to their interests and needs. There is a failure to make *personal* that which arrives in textbook or artefact in *impersonal* packaging.

By contrast, there is a vocational tradition which derives the objectives and content of learning from very different premises – from what is necessary for getting a job done rather than from an analysis of intellectual discipline, from a listing of specific skills and competences rather than from the judgement, understanding, imagination, creativity called upon in mathematical or scientific or historical thinking. Intellectual excellence gives way to practical utility, personal development to personal effectiveness.

There are, then, different languages about education – the language of intellectual excellence for some and the language of vocational competence for the others. Occasional attempts are made to overcome this divide by making everyone academic (a grammar school education for all in Harold Wilson's terms), or by vocationalizing the liberal ideal, or by simply declaring the two to be equal or to have 'parity of esteem'. Differences are smudged by calling GNVQs 'Vocational A Levels' (Advanced Vocational Certificates of Education) or by rewriting A Levels in the language of competences or by persuading universities to see GNVQ as an alternative route into higher education. But deep down, few are deceived by all this. The philosophical assumptions of NVQs – using the inadequate language of outputs and competences, of assessment-led learning and performance indicators – will never be accepted by those who protect a tradition of liberal education which is concerned with judgement, imagination, understanding and critical enquiry, and which sees merit in uncertainty and open-endedness.

For John Dewey this distinction between the 'academic' and the 'vocational' was one of the many distinctions he railed against – a dichotomy beneath which were assumptions about the aims of education, about the nature of knowledge and about its acquisition, which he thought were highly questionable. Let us take, for example, his defence of 'vocational education' in Chapter 23 of *Democracy and Education*. John Dewey defended 'vocational education' as follows:

> A vocation means nothing but a direction of life activities as renders them perceptibly significant to a person because of the consequences they accomplish, and also useful to his associates. The opposite of a career is neither leisure nor culture, but aimlessness, capriciousness, the absence of cumulative achievement in experience, on the personal side, and idle play, a parasitic dependence on the other on the social side. Occupation is a concrete term for continuity.
>
> (Dewey 1916: 307)

The choice and pursuit of a career was in effect the pursuit and choice of a particular form of life, the adoption of particular values. Education was principally about that gradual development of the ideas, through which one organizes experience, shares the future, comes to value certain things and courses of action – and that development takes place through the reflection on experience, the interaction with others (including the 'others' as they appear in the books they have written or the art they have performed). 'Vocation' (and vocational preparation) was part of that more general development of the person through which one hopefully finds fulfilment in the way of life one chooses (in which one's occupation plays an essential part). It is difficult to separate me – the person I am, the views I hold, the values I espouse – from the vocational route I have taken or from the occupation (with its attendant values) to which I have committed myself.

If one looks more broadly at the education of young people – enabling them intelligently and responsibly and effectively to take their place in society, to play an active and shaping role within that society and to find personal fulfilment within it (including fulfilling personal relationships) – then that which is to be learnt and the mode of learning take on a different significance. The humanities – the study of literature and of drama, of history and of the social studies – take on a new significance, one which is relevant to their making sense of their humanity and of the social context in which that humanity can be respected. Literature and drama, history and the social studies, the arts become the resources upon which young people draw in addressing questions of deep personal significance – relationships between the sexes, the tolerance of poverty, the phenomenon of racism, the need for but the limitations of civic authority, the prevalence of injustice, the promotion of war and so on.

Furthermore, within such a more broadly conceived educational aim, reflection upon, and preparation for, the kind of occupation one would like to pursue would play a key part. And that would, more often than not, lead to the recognition of the need to acquire particular skills and knowledge.

HISTORICAL PERSPECTIVE

The work of the Further Education Unit (FEU) in the late 1970s, addressing the problems of young people who were seeking an extension of their education, but who neither wanted the subject-based A Levels nor had specific vocational routes in mind, tackled the problem of education and training from a very different angle – neither from an analysis of the intellectual disciplines nor from an analysis of the competences needed for specific jobs. Rather it asked the two questions: What personal qualities do young people need to acquire in order to cope, imaginatively and intelligently, with a future which is unpredictable and often hostile? What qualities do they need in order to contribute to the wider social and economic well-being? (FEU 1979)

Clearly the answers to both questions are related. Personal well-being is not disconnected from the capacity to earn a living; social and economic well-being is not disconnected from a sense of dignity and personal fulfilment, arising out of worthwhile learning. But they provide two dimensions to the basis upon which thinking about the style and the content of learning should be built.

125

In answering those questions, the FEU argued for a range of curriculum principles – that the learning should address questions of moral value, helping young people to develop defensible moral judgements on matters of profound personal and social concern; that it should enable them to be economically and politically aware; that it should sensitize them to matters of justice and fairness – to equal opportunities – in our institutional arrangements; that it should extend the capacity to communicate in different ways to different audiences; that it should encourage co-operative and open-ended learning; that it should equip them in attitudes and skills to be weaned off an over-dependence on teachers for the continuation of learning; that it should open them up to the satisfaction to be found in music and art and dance.

Of course, the content of traditional subjects is relevant – it provides the cultural resources upon which the students are enabled to draw as they strive to make sense of the physical and social world and as they seek a personal fulfilment in their reading and in the arts. But the perspective is different. The perspective is essentially that of making the impersonal personal, of seeing the significance in personal terms of that which is so often presented and assessed in an impersonal manner.

The FEU reflected and articulated a tradition in teaching which is too often neglected by those who, in positions of power and in positions to impose their theory of the curriculum, feel able to ignore the wisdom of practice. In a National Curriculum dominated by precise attainment targets or in vocational qualifications dominated by lists of competences, there is little room for those transactions between teacher and learner, the outcomes of which are so unpredictable. And yet in the 1970s and 1980s, through the City and Guilds 365 Course, the Business and Technology Education Council (BTEC), the Certificate of Prevocational Education, the many Technical and Vocational Education initiatives, one saw how teachers strove to reassert the central importance of the 'personal significance' in what too often remained an impersonal curriculum relevant only to the few.

BRIDGING THE ACADEMIC/VOCATIONAL DIVIDE: CURRICULUM PRINCIPLES

Those courses, within a 'prevocational' tradition, and one which, I am sure, would have received the blessing of John Dewey, might be characterized by the following principles.

First, the curriculum (no doubt different in significant respects from school to school) had to show *relevance to vocational need*. Vocational need could be interpreted generously – not limited to focus on a specific job, nor the acquisition of highly specific competences. Rather, did it refer to that gradual development of what was felt to be worth pursuing in life – the kind of life worth living – of which a particular kind of education, training and occupation would be part.

Second, was the requirement that, against this need for relevance, there should be a much more central place for *guidance and counselling*, no doubt with the help of work experience, from the age of 14. Life choices cannot suddenly be made wisely; they arise from both an awareness of opportunities and an awareness of one's own talents, interests and limitations.

Third, the dominance of content, of knowledge and of the relentless coverage of content, should give way much more to the *process of learning*, to the joy and pleasure to be found in learning, to the identification and solving of problems, to the styles of learning which would hold one in good stead for further learning. In particular, it needed to recognize the importance for many, if not all, of *practical learning* – learning from doing. Intelligent politicians learn more from engaging intelligently in political activity (no doubt helped by a mentor) than they do from reading books on political theory. There was an emphasis on practical modes of learning – what Bruner referred to as the enactive and then iconic – as a prelude to the symbolic.

Fourth, the prevocational principles emphasized the benefits of *information technology* as a source of learning – well before the modern advances in interactive internet and web boards. But it foresaw the way in which learning – and the possibilities of continued learning – could be transformed, though with it the role and the authority of the teacher as that was traditionally conceived.

Fifth, there should be a *technological component*, both specific as a way of acting upon the world but general as a way of understanding how society advances in terms of material improvement. Such a technological interest had too frequently been ignored in an academic education rooted in its classical past.

Sixth, there was an emphasis upon *personal effectiveness* – the personal confidence in oneself to achieve (so often deflated by a sense of failure), the skills and confidence to *communicate* to different audiences and through different means, the *social and interpersonal skills* that arise from purposeful interaction with other people, often working together in teams. Co-operative learning and team work rather than competition and individualization.

Seventh, the curriculum should be more *community conscious*, related to the wider society – to what are now referred to as the various stakeholders within that society. Hence, the school or college should draw much more upon the experience of those within the community who might provide the stimulus and the resources which schools are seldom able to provide.

Eighth, emphasis was placed upon *equal opportunities*, countering the imbalance, and the gender and racial stereotypes, encouraging ambitions which previously had seemed impossible to realize.

Finally, such principles of curriculum thinking – such a bridging of the traditional divide between the so-called academic and the vocational – would be reflected in a *system of assessment* which would record what had been achieved in all its breadth and depth. Such a system of assessment would involve the students themselves. Much work was undertaken in the development of profiles, and indeed (still surviving from that era) there remain the awards of ASDAN[1] which are taken by nearly half the

127

schools in the country. This is a way of recording the key skills achieved by pupils (Crombie White 1997).

To summarize these criteria, and to see a distinctive set of ideas beneath the wide range of prevocational practice, is not easy. But perhaps it is best summed up by the concept of 'relevance'. Distinctive of a particular and contrasting liberal tradition was the view that education was primarily concerned with the 'perfection of the intellect', with the development of intelligence in its various disciplined forms (mathematical, scientific, historical, etc.); such a 'perfection of the intellect' could ignore the practical relevance of what is learnt or, indeed, reference to the world of work; the well-trained mind would, so it was held, later be turned to whatever life had in store. But it was precisely that separation of the theoretical from the practical, of the intrinsically worthwhile from the useful, of understanding from skills and personal qualities, of 'knowing that' from 'knowing how', of the intellectual virtues from the practical dispositions required in the non-academic world, which was challenged by the prevocational principles and practice. And that challenge was reflected in the renewed importance attached to 'relevance' – the relevance of what is learnt (and how it is learnt), first, to the felt needs of the learner, and, second, to the needs of society for which the learners were being prepared. Hence, central, though often not clearly articulated, was a distinctive view about what needed to be learnt, and how learning should be pursued, in preparing young people appropriately for the later twentieth century.

All that experience, and all the thinking which helped to form it, have gone unnoticed by those who once again seek to address the 14–19 curriculum and the institutional framework within which it is to be 'delivered'. It is as though, dominated by a limited concept of 'academic' and 'vocational', the government and its agencies are embarked upon an attempt to reconcile the two which is bound to fail. It will 'bridge the gap' either by a system of learning experiences and qualifications which are stuck together in a so-called unified system of qualifications – a fragmented smorgasbord of bits and pieces – or by a distortion of the more practical modes of learning by subjecting them to the rigours of assessment taken from the academic (as was the case with GNVQs).

What is missing is a reflection of the innovative and creative attempts to provide a much more person-centred educational experience which was deeply rooted in personal and social needs in the different learning styles through which young people performed well, in the development of personal qualities and values which would sustain them in future, and in a connectedness to the community, social and economic, in which they were eventually to earn their living and take on responsible roles.

AIMS, VISION, CHOICE AND LIFELONG LEARNING

A key word in the government document is that of 'choice'. The modular learning frame and the different routes through it not only will provide greater choice (which is regarded as a good thing in itself) but also will open up opportunities for making choices about career and occupation, lifestyle and relationships. The idea of personal choice has not been extensively covered. Of course, one is able to choose one course of action rather than another – unless one is an out-and-out determinist where choice is really a matter of self-deception.

But choice (of subjects to be studied, of courses to be taken, of friends to link up with, of career to be followed) is necessarily limited, not simply by what is available, but by the ideas and values and preferences which one brings to the choosing. There are severe limits on how far anyone can claim to be autonomous. One inherits from family and friends ways of seeing and thinking about oneself – and oneself in relation to further possibilities. Hence, the careers guidance, which simply reveals the 'choices' to you, may not really be creating or extending choice at all.

To that extent, the whole of the curriculum should be in the visions it opens up through the arts and humanities, in the personal confidence it nurtures, in the critical engagement with dominant ideas – a preparation for making responsible choices in life, including the determination to pursue interests beyond the classroom and into further education and training. And this might so easily be negated by the so-called range of choices limited to selection between self-contained modules of 'academic' and 'vocational' learning.

Again, lifelong learning is constantly seen as a readiness to take up new courses, to acquire new skills in order to keep up with the changing market in jobs. It is recognized that, for many, there is a constant need for re-skilling – and hence a need to upgrade, as it were, the qualifications that one has.

But this is a very limited idea of lifelong learning. In one sense, it is a nonsensical notion. Continued prosperity, indeed existence, requires that one should constantly be learning – acquiring new habits, appreciating new friends, coping with new experiences, adjusting to new environments. And these in turn require either acquiring new concepts or applying old concepts to new situations. Learning, in that central sense, is and must be life long. What is missing – and what can arise on the whole from a much more person-centred education – is that sort of lifelong learning which comes from an openness to critical debate, a curiosity about world affairs, an urge to solve the technological problems that beset one, an engagement with the world of ideas through which one's humanity and one's place in the universe are defined and shaped.

It could be the case that, in failing to address the impoverished notions of 'academic' and 'vocational' or in failing to bridge the gap between the different traditions which they represent, in failing to see the 'personal' at the centre of education, the present proposals might indeed prepare young people for lifelong learning in the limited sense of a readiness to go on courses in order to get jobs. But they are in danger of atrophying lifelong learning in any life enhancing and worthwhile sense.

Indeed, this lack of vision, this lack of any exploration of the aims and values which should shape the learning experiences provided, is reflected powerfully by its absence in the 2005 White Paper, *14–19 Education and Training* (DfES 2005). That paper spells out two main aims, although a third, economic efficiency, is implicit throughout. The first is that the education and training system should enable young people to realize their potential; the second is that they should be 'stretched' (in various grammatical forms) 63 times. But what potential should be realized? Not surely the potential to commit robbery? Such empty phrases are a substitute for thinking, and yet there is a need for a continuing debate about the kind of person and the kind of society which the educational system should be nurturing. What, in this day and age, is an educated 19-year-old, irrespective of the specific talents which he or she has received? What understandings and knowledge, virtues and qualities, skills and competences, ideals and interests should be nurtured in schools, colleges and workplace?

INSTITUTIONAL FRAMEWORK

There are some oddities in the institutional arrangements for all this. The establishment of the Learning and Skills Council in 2001 brought responsibility for all post-16 learning (academic and vocational) under one authority for the first time with its own distinctive funding arrangements. This clearly has its drawbacks where one is then trying to develop a coherently progressive policy and set of practices from 14 to 19. Nonetheless, it did ensure links – both in policy and in practice – first, between what happens post-16 and the lifelong learning which the LSC is responsible for promoting, and, second, between schools, colleges and employers. Partnerships and collaboration were seen in so many of the government papers referred to above as the thing of the future, for no one school or college had the resources and the expertise to provide the range of courses or the flexibility of routes which were seen to characterize the 14–19 phase.

However, partnership in theory is not so easy to put into practice. Different partners (schools and colleges) are in England, but not now in Wales, funded on a different and unequal basis for the same work. Timetabling is different in different institutions, making collaborative teaching often impossible. Co-ordination and transporting across providers are costly, although, properly organized, they produce considerable savings. Local politics often supports autonomous institutions and militates against co-operation (as in campaigns 'to save our sixth form'). The institutional reporting of examination results leading to positions in league tables, supports competition rather than co-operation. And the recent policy to create 200 Academies, differently funded and with different admissions arrangements outside the Local

130

Education Authority (LEA) framework, undermines both symbolically and in reality local partnership.

CONCLUSION

Recent years have seen a vigorous attempt to develop a 14–19 phase of education. But such an attempt is bereft of any deeper consideration of the kind of learning which is to be valued, the kind of qualifications which will reflect that learning, the kind of institutional framework which will support it and thus the ways in which progress can be ensured into higher education, further training and lifelong learning. Policy and planning are trapped in an impoverished dichotomy between academic and vocational. There is little sense of a more generous tradition of education, reflected in developments in the 1970s and 1980s, where the focus of concern lay in the education and development of persons. Such a tradition would see the academic and the vocational in proper perspective and create the possibility of an integrated system of education and training, reflected in an appropriate and uniform framework of qualifications.

NOTE

1 Award Scheme Development and Accreditation Network, a not-for-profit organization, representing the consortia of participating schools, colleges, etc.

REFERENCES

Bruner, J. (1960) *The Process of Education*, Boston: Harvard University Press.

Crombie White, R. (1997) 'The ASDAN Award Scheme: A Celebration of Professional Practice', in Tomlinson, S. (ed), *Education 14–19: Critical Perspectives*, London: Athlone Press.

Dewey, J. (1916) *Democracy and Education*, New York: Macmillan.

DfEE (1996a) *Learning to Compete: Education and Training 14–19 Year Olds*, White Paper, London: DfEE.

DfEE (1996b) *Equipping Young People for Working Life*, London: DfEE.

DfEE (1997) *Qualifying for Success: A Consultation Paper on the Future of Post-16 Qualifications*, London: DfEE.

DfEE (1999) *Preparing Young people for Adult Life: A Report by the National Advisory Group on Personal, Social and Health education*, London: DfEE.

DfEE (2000) *Opportunity for All*, London: DfEE.

DfES (2001) *Skills for Life: The National Strategy for Improving Adult Literacy and Numeracy Skills*, London: DfES.

DfES (2002a) *Schools: Achieving Success*, White Paper, London: DfES.

DfES (2002b) *14–19: Extending Opportunities, Raising Standards*, Green Paper, London: DfES.

DfES (2003a) *14–19: Opportunity and Excellence*, White Paper, London: DfES.

DfES (2003b) *The Future of Higher Education*, White Paper, London: DfES.

DfES (2003c) *Realising our Potential: 21st Century Skills*, White Paper, London: DfES.

DfES (2005) *14–19 Education and Training*, London: DfES.

FEU (1978) *A Basis for Choice*, London: DES.

Tomlinson Report (2004) *Curriculum and Qualifications Reform*, Final Report of the Working Group in 14–19 Reform, London: DfES.

Tomlinson, S. (1997) 'Education 14–19: Divided and Divisive', in Tomlinson, S. (ed.), *Education 14–19: Critical Perspectives*, London: Athlone Press.

Part Three

Valuing VET

Chapter 10

Vocational education, work and the aims of economic activity

Christopher Winch

A powerful objection to liberal vocational education might go as follows: 'The proper aim of vocational education is to provide individuals with the skill to earn their living, thus supplying one of the conditions for economic prosperity. No one wants to work unless they have to. Vocational education prepares people to earn a living through work. It does not prepare them to enjoy life or develop their personality through working because work does not generally offer opportunities for self-fulfillment.'

If this claim is valid then liberal vocational education is misguided. Economies are run to maximize consumption by circulating goods and services. Prosperity comes from creating the conditions for this and there are a limited number of actions that governments can take to create employment, including the removal of artificial barriers to the take-up of vocational education. However, anything else, such as creating aims for vocational education that could interfere with this take-up, will threaten the aim of economic activity. Individuals will invest in their vocational education up to the point where (discounted) future benefits, increased individual purchasing power, no longer exceed expenditure (Ashton and Green 1996). If work is a disutility, the only point in investing in education is to augment one's income (Marshall 1890: 117).

Liberal vocational education is thus dreamed up by those who wish to extend liberal education into inappropriate fields. In this chapter I seek to defend a version of the liberal ideal in relation to the way we consider the purpose of economic activity.

In Keynes's words, echoing Adam Smith: 'Consumption, to repeat the obvious – is the end and object of all economic activity' (Keynes 1973: 137; Smith 1981: 660). In one sense this is obvious and uncontroversial. Consumption is certainly instrumentally valuable. Without food, clothing and shelter we are unable to survive, let alone enjoy life. Very often consumption is not just an instrumental but an intrinsic good. We do not just eat to stay alive, for example, but because eating good food in the company of others is one of the activities that make life worth while. Thus consumption is the overriding aim of economic activity, not only because it ensures survival but also because it is partially constitutive of a worthwhile life. What we are really after is not

135

consumption as such but a life worth living. Some may consider that consumption is what makes life worth living. Fine. But we should not assume that this is what everyone wants. Arguably consumption for most people, while it may compose a very significant part of what makes life worthwhile, is by no means the whole.

The worthwhileness of life also consists of the opportunity to exercise our active powers in such activities as raising a family, friendship, pursuing and acquiring skills and knowledge, engaging in co-operative projects, etc. It is through activity that we gain much of our well-being, which consists not only in the absence of material deprivation but in living in a worthwhile way. This is not just a subjective matter. It is true that, in order to live a life worth living someone must feel, at least for much of the time, that life is worth living. But it is not enough to feel this to make one's life worth while. People making a good living out of drug dealing may feel that their life is worth living. Most of their fellow-citizens would disagree. But even if they spent their lives consuming drugs without directly harming anyone else, most of us would say that they were not leading a worthwhile life, for they would not only be harming but morally degrading themselves. We want to see them developing and using their talents to benefit their fellow creatures. Well-being is, then, partly constituted by developing one's active powers and co-operating with other people in something worth while that contributes to a worthwhile life; that not only includes enjoyment but also some contribution to the common good (however that is conceived). This extended sense of worthwhileness includes how we think it is proper to live, and our views about this may vary over time and place. In some societies leisured contemplation might be seen as the highest form of human existence, in others it may be religious observance and in others again it may be the creation of works of art. In our civilization we attach some importance to being active as a means of social and self-validation and of exercising distinctively human powers of planning and creation (Marx 1970: 178).

Not all activities constitute work, so we cannot yet say that work is necessary to well-being, let alone paid work. There is not much point in trying to distinguish work from non-work activities in any general sense (White 1997; Marshall 1890: 54). It is claimed, for example, that work activities have an object outside themselves, whereas not all activities do. But there are leisure activities that have objects beyond themselves, for example a couple decorating their child's bedroom in their spare time. Likewise a performer in the town square is not producing anything but an enjoyable spectacle but is getting paid for it. It would be tempting to say that the object of the performance, that is what makes it work, is the payment that it gains, but she could, in appropriate circumstances, do so for the intrinsic enjoyment or to entertain her friends. Even when pay is the motive, there may be other significant reasons why she has chosen to perform rather than follow some other occupation. She may enjoy performing, working outdoors or entertaining people and these motives may be decisive. It would not be an option as paid work if she could not earn a living this way; she would rather do this than something else to earn a living. Her work does not just have instrumental value but also has intrinsic value. Of course, her endorsement of it as worth while is not sufficient or even necessary to make it so. If, however, others regard this as a worthwhile occupation for those with the temperament and talent and if it is regarded as contributing to the worthwhileness of other people's lives, then it is a worthwhile activity.

WORK IS NOT SOMETHING THAT PEOPLE, IN ORDINARY CIRCUMSTANCES, WISH TO DO

What is the relevance of all this to political economy? The example above goes against the thinking that work in itself has only disutility. Paid work is something undertaken for our livelihood, to provide otherwise unattainable necessities. While work is a disutility as opposed to, say, staying in bed, staying in bed and starving as a result would be a far greater disutility. If it is worth our while to avoid starvation by working, then according to this line of thought we will work – but not for any other reason. It follows that vocational education and training are undertaken for instrumental reasons, not as a preparation for anything intrinsically valuable. Employment policy should ensure that as many people work as possible, irrespective of whether they enjoy working. There are plausible grounds for thinking like this. First, much work is physically unpleasant and dangerous. Second, those dependent on a wage very often have to do work they do not wish to do. Third, the conditions of work often leave them little room for the exercise of judgment (Smith 1981: 785–6). Finally, economic conditions may mean they have to work too long and hard for their working lives to be enjoyable. Some or all of these conditions are true for most people at least for some of their working lives and help to account for the view that work is a disutility. They are not, however, essential to work itself, either paid or unpaid. If people seek to avoid work because of the conditions just mentioned, then it is reasonable to assume that they would be less likely to avoid it, and perhaps even to seek it out, if it lacked these features.

SMITH'S CONCEPTION OF ECONOMIC ACTIVITY AND ITS RELATION TO VET: WORK HAS INSTRUMENTAL VALUE AND IS A DISUTILITY

Adam Smith appears to have thought that work is only of instrumental value. It is tempting to think that Smith argued that people find work undesirable in the conditions of the extreme fragmentation of the labour process that he describes in *Wealth of Nations*. He did indeed consider work in these circumstances to be not only tedious but mentally degrading by dulling one's intellectual faculties (Smith 1981: 785–6). However, there is evidence that he took what Verdon has called an Aristotelian view of human activity, that the natural state of a human being, like that of a physical body in

137

Aristotelian cosmology, is to be at rest (Verdon 1996). This is an unfortunate piece of terminology, since Aristotle believed that the natural state of humans was to exercise their natural capacities (Aristotle 1924). Smith's attack on apprenticeship and the attitude of apprentices (Book I) and his dim view of the state-paid schoolmaster, 'who would soon learn to neglect his business' (Book V), bear this out (Smith 1981: 139, 785). A self-interested person would, other things being equal, rather stay in bed. Work is to be avoided except where necessary. Vocational education, then, should ensure that work is sufficiently remunerative to justify expenditure on it. For individuals, discounted rewards should outweigh costs and for employers it should increase profits beyond what could be gained by employing untrained workers. No other factors are relevant. The fragmentation of the labour process merely increases the unattractiveness of working rather than makes what is intrinsically attractive unattractive.

If the 'inertial' view of work were right, unskilled labour would be more attractive than skilled. Exercising a skill requires alertness and effort. If skilled work were more enjoyable than unskilled, some forms of effort would be preferable to others. This in turn suggests that people like to exercise their active powers and that paid employment is unattractive when it is unpleasant, boring, dangerous and poorly remunerated. It does not suggest that work per se is intrinsically unattractive. Indeed, if people find some activities intrinsically attractive then arguably work, in certain circumstances, is intrinsically attractive.

It is difficult to maintain that all activities only have instrumental value. If some activities are valuable beyond what they are instruments for, then they must, in some sense, be valuable in themselves. This is part of what we mean by saying that something has intrinsic value. People value all kinds of things for themselves: works of art, buildings, company, food and drink, pets, etc. Maybe these only have value in so far as they contribute to human pleasure. This is debatable but even were we to accept it we would simply have located another possible source of non-instrumental value: pleasure.

The concern of economics with utility reflects this. Some utilities are instrumental, in that they are a means to a further end, but some are valued for themselves.[1] However, many philosophers have doubted that pleasure is the sole source of intrinsic value. Even Mill distinguished between higher and lower pleasures, roughly corresponding with sensual pleasure in the latter case and aesthetic, moral and intellectual pleasure in the former. He speculates that workers at a certain level of education and prosperity will gain satisfaction from the management of their own enterprises that would involve them in the exercise of their intellectual and social powers (Mill 1994). Rawls terms this the Aristotelian Principle whereby well-being is partly constituted through the employment of our active powers (Rawls 1971: 426). However, not all activities that have intrinsic value are significantly worth while. The slaking of my thirst is pleasurable beyond its instrumental value of providing me with much-needed liquid, but few would say that drinking for pleasure is wholly constitutive of a worthwhile human life. Even in moderate quantities most people would say that pleasures of this kind have a relatively minor role in contributing to the worthwhileness of life. Those activities of intrinsic value that are also partially constitutive of what it is to lead a worthwhile life are what Raz calls of 'ultimate value' (Raz 1988: 177–8). One plausible claim is that a range of possible activities is partially constitutive of a worthwhile life. Some will be paid, others unpaid. Some will involve large degrees of skill and knowledge, others not. The key point is that a large range of activities requiring mental or physical effort may be partially constitutive of worthwhile human lives. Those activities that exercise a range of our abilities in relatively congenial circumstances are more likely, other things being equal, to be worth while than those that do not.

Both Keynes and Smith draw attention to the importance of consumption as the supreme end of economic activity. Does this not contradict what I have been arguing for? Not necessarily, for it is instrumentally necessary that we consume to achieve states and carry out activities that are valuable in themselves. In addition, both wished to draw attention to the fact that exchange by itself could not be the ultimate aim of economic activity, since exchange is usually only instrumentally worth while in furthering consumption. Nevertheless something more does need to be said, particularly when consumption at a comfortable level has been secured (Rawls 1971: 426).

Consumption is necessary but not sufficient for a worthwhile life. Being active in various ways is one of the most important means by which life is made worth while. If, for one reason or another, paid employment continues to be central to the maintenance of a healthy and competitive economy, then it is likely to be one of the ways in which life is made worth while. In prosperous societies then, in which more or less demanding activities are thought to be partially constitutive of a worthwhile life, providing worthwhile work ought to be one of the central aims of economic life, providing something of ultimate value over and above consumption. Work is thus one component of worthwhile life. If well-being is one of the aims of economic activity, we might call societies that recognize and promote it as a desirable aim of economic activity, work-eudaemonist.

IMPLICATIONS OF WORK-EUDAEMONISM FOR ECONOMIC POLICY AND EDUCATION

Work-eudaemonism differs from Aristotelian self-sufficiency. Aristotle's view was that contemplation, not in conditions of extravagance but of self-sufficiency, constituted the supremely worthwhile life. Such self-sufficiency, whatever its intrinsic merits, is simply not a practical possibility within an integrated global system of capitalist economies. Work-eudaemonism in our societies is predicated on the assumption of international economic competition and growth, together with the maintenance of competitive advantage through a 'high skill equilibrium' or HSE (Brown *et al.* 2001).

In terms of trade in goods and services, the only point of maintaining an HSE is in order to ensure competitive advantage. If employees are satisfied as well, then that is a welcome by-product; intrinsic value comes from the consumption of goods and services alone, even when one takes into account the Listian concept of productive powers to include potential for production as well as production itself (List 1991: 143–4). On this view, all the elements that constitute productive powers have instrumental value: churches, musicians and hospitals are, in economic terms, to be valued on the basis of their capacity to contribute to production for consumption.

However, this is one-sided. The aim of many economic activities is the production of something of intrinsic value, even if it is nothing more than a good meal. It is something to be valued, at least partially, for its contribution to well-being rather than merely for its utility in promoting a further good.

VOCATIONAL EDUCATION AND A WORK-EUDAEMONIST CONCEPTION OF ECONOMIC ACTIVITY

The promotion of an HSE thus not only has the instrumentally valuable role of making an economy productive and competitive but also of promoting a form of work-based well-being.[2] Can such diverse objectives be pursued jointly in a commercial context where profitability continues to be the crucial determinant of economic success? If vocational education has instrumental value, how can it maintain this in the face of a demand that it prepare people for work that has intrinsic or even ultimate value? The answer is that economic and eudaemonistic considerations are not really independent of each other.

Movement from a low-skill equilibrium (LSE) to an HSE is a co-ordination problem in the game-theoretic sense, and the 'training problem' is one aspect of that, as apparently accepted by the British government (HM Treasury 2002: 15). Societies have achieved an HSE in ways that reflect different cultural and social priorities and traditions. Although the solution of such problems appears to require a co-ordinating authority, such as a state that passes legislation for a training levy or licence to practise, this is not necessary if civil society combines to solve the problem with only limited help as is largely the case in, for example, Germany. On the other hand, a society that relies strongly on the state will tend to look to it for the solution, as is the case with France. Societies look to solutions that suit their own cultures, traditions and values. They may for these reasons, despite the apparent economic advantages, forgo the chance to move to an HSE or may move to one for nationalistic as well as strictly economic reasons. They may also seek competitive advantage in certain sectors through a mix of skills that includes a high-skill elite and a low-skill base.

140

Economic policy balances calculation of advantage, taking into account the values and traditions of the society.

A decision to move to an HSE often has cultural, ethical and educational as well as economic motivations. This can be seen in the tendency of some economies run largely as HSEs to maintain strong occupational categories within established industrial structures (Brown *et al.* 2001: 79; Streeck 1996: 145). Vocational education takes place through introduction to occupations within the industrial context in which the occupation is situated. A bricklayer is thus not only a member of an occupational category, but works within the construction industry in which the occupation of bricklayer and others, such as that of carpenter, work together. To have an occupational identity is to occupy a social and moral as well as an economic position. Thus a mechatronics fitter in contemporary Germany has not only technical skill but also attitudes, values and skills related to citizenship, including leadership abilities and sensitivity to the environment (Brown *et al.* 2001: 170). Occupations have their own values and traditions which involve not only technical virtues, such as pride in one's work, attention to detail, curiosity and the pursuit of perfection, but also occupational virtues, such as honesty, sociability, co-operativeness and concern for one's colleagues and the public (Kerschensteiner 1964).

Many HSE societies value occupational categories rather than jobs and tasks that exist outside occupational boundaries because occupational identity is a very effective way of maintaining the skills and virtues that belong to certain jobs, of maintaining their standing with the public and clients, and of forming new workers. These occupations, in turn, derive their identity and manage their relationships with each other within an industrial context. However, there are models that do not require strong occupational categories. One can envisage, for example, an economy dependent on graduates with a broad education whose managerial and supervisory functions did not require industry-specific training. In such an economy, a skilled elite, financial or scientific in training, is critical. There may also be, in sectors not specializing in products and services requiring very high-skill inputs, a large stratum of graduate managers equipped with generic managerial skills that supervises relatively unskilled labour. However, this model only provides a partially high-skilled workforce, relatively few workers with intermediate level qualifications and a large number of low-skilled employees. As a general point, one cannot assume that the availability of a certain category of labour (for example graduates) will guarantee that there is graduate-level work available. A given skill equilibrium only exists when the supply of skilled labour matches demand. An alternative, arguably found in Japan, is to invest the enterprise itself with some of the attributes of an occupation.

On the other hand, in an HSE based on craft and technical work it is likely that occupational status will be important. First, there will inevitably be a degree of historical continuity between older and contemporary occupations, even in conditions of technological innovation.[3] Second, high specification, whether of both goods and services, requires a degree of 'diversified quality production' ensuring rapid response to changes in demand. It implies that skills have to be relevant to a range of tasks and also to an extent can be redundant (not all skills will be employed on all jobs). It makes a great deal of sense in economic and pedagogic terms to ensure that skills are cognate, so that the occupation makes use of generic and related skills organized in hierarchies or looser families. Third, modern production techniques make use of applied theoretical knowledge, integrated into and thus part of the skills employed. This, because of its relative generality (as opposed to particular factual knowledge), also provides conceptual unity to the skills employed. An HSE and strong occupational identities within well-established industrial structures tend to belong together.

This is the case with Germany, where an occupation (*Beruf*) not only provides a significant degree of social identity, but also a legal status that recognizes a social consensus about the importance of the recognition of *Berufe* and the associated processes of knowledge specification, training and labour market recognition. This can be seen, for example, in the definition of *Beruf* or occupation in Germany, in which the bringing together of theoretical and practical knowledge, together with social identity, is made explicit, which is:

> a body of systematically related theoretical knowledge [*wissen*] and a set of practical skills [*können*], as well as the social identity of the person who has acquired these. Achievement of such an identity is certified by a diploma upon passing an examination and is on this basis recognised without question by all employers.
>
> (Streeck 1996: 145)

France runs a VET system which is much more state-directed than the German one. Nevertheless, the existence of occupational categories within an industrial context is an important part of the economic scene there. The qualification and the place it has in a classificatory scheme of occupations, nested within industrial classifications, is important:

> It expresses the articulation between credential (certificate, diploma or degree), job and wage. This articulation, which exists to varying degrees, is linked in particular to the existence of 'classification grids' (*grilles de classification*), which are societal realities essential to the functioning of the labour market.
>
> (Shore 2004: 22–3)

When occupations are more than contingent groupings of workers and employers with cognate knowledge and skills, they have an institutional presence in the form of employer federations, trade associations and trade unions. Employers have an interest in maintaining a pool of skills, employees in maintaining the skilled status of their occupations, and clients and the public in quality assurance and continuing innovation.

This confluence of interests leads to a common interest in occupational formation, of new workers and the preservation, updating and extension of skills. Occupations also have an interest in maintaining a face of integrity to their clients and the general public, implying a concern with professional ethical standards. This in turn implies that occupational formation will attempt to provide prospective employees with knowledge of and commitment to the aims, values and history of the occupation in order to develop an occupational *esprit de corps*.

What are the implications of the occupational model of an HSE? First, VET will involve a significant 'front-loading' element. Task and job skills, if learnt in the course of performance or immediately prior to it, cannot by themselves provide knowledge of a structure or family of skills, nor can they provide the social aspect of skill. On the other hand, prior education or training is a very good indicator for subsequent take-up of training, suggesting that initial vocational education has strong benefits for the continuing upgrading of skills (HM Treasury 2002: 115). Neither, finally, does job-based learning provide the 'outward looking' attitudes and skills needed for the promotion and maintenance of occupational identity. This does not mean that there need be no job training after initial occupational formation. In fact, one implication of work-eudaemonism is that post-initial vocational education should not merely build on the initial element, but should enhance not only workers' skills but their satisfaction in the workplace.

Even in the non-occupational model, such as in Japan, high levels of initial general education are considered important to enterprise-specific skill development. Initial vocational education should enable workers to plan independently and to work in teams without excessive managerial supervision and it is difficult to see how these 'key skills' can be learnt effectively outside some occupational context (Brown *et al.* 2001: 211–27). On the other hand, these have to be learned partly at the interface between occupations within an overall industrial structure that articulates the relationships between occupations.

Much knowledge required in high-skill work is abstract, that is relatively general in content and closely linked to theoretical knowledge. It is, at the same time, neither as general nor as theoretical as expert knowledge in the non-applied sector of the subject with which the theory deals (for example, the physics underlying electrical engineering). Such knowledge, when integrated with relevant practical abilities, becomes applied theoretical knowledge which is of its nature difficult to acquire completely in either a practicum or a workplace context. The classroom is often best for learning the theoretical background underpinning practical knowledge and so this aspect of initial VET needs to be classroom based.

Use of this knowledge has a number of features:

- recognition of which situations are relevant to the deployment of appropriate theoretical knowledge. These will often be situations that are different in important respects from those previously encountered;

- assessment of which component of that knowledge is required to achieve the desired outcome;
- the application of these principles to the situation in hand, integrating them with practical techniques;
- an assessment of the appropriateness and efficacy of the knowledge and skill used.

Such complex procedures rarely involve the straightforward transfer of college-acquired knowledge into complex and varied workplace situations. This complexity and variety, because it is related to changes in specification and changing workplace conditions, is difficult to describe fully in the classroom. Even if one could, this would not of itself provide skill in the application of theoretical knowledge to a practical problem. Perhaps a practicum associated with the classroom could take account of at least some of these complexities by simulating the situations in which they are likely to occur. And so it could, up to a point. However, that the workplace situation is 'for real' means that mistakes made matter beyond the assessment of the student. Products and services may be compromised if techniques are practised badly or if the wrong attitudes are deployed. The time criticality of procedures makes for a sense of urgency and reduces margins of error. The safety of workmates and the confidence of clients may be compromised by poor or ill-judged execution of procedures. That it really matters can only really be brought home to one in situations where it really does matter.

That is why controlled practice in the workplace is important for a complete occupational formation. It performs an integrative function in realistic conditions and provides a sense of moral immediacy to the pressures under which tasks are carried out. Obviously it is important to make a good product or deliver a good service; a mistake made in the workplace has bad consequences for the economics of the operation and the confidence of clients. But poorly executed procedures make it difficult for colleagues to work well, since they are to some extent dependent on other individuals doing their part well. The moral imperative of thinking about the welfare of one's colleagues becomes important. Finally, in many cases practice of the occupation involves not just the practice in the studio, workshop, site or classroom but interactions with workers in related occupations within the industry, clients and public officials. Applied knowledge related to the impact of the occupation on clients and the wider society comes into play, together with the social knowledge and moral sensibility necessary to negotiate such situations with integrity and concern for others' interests.

Induction into an occupation, when carried out properly, is then a total experience involving theoretical, practical and moral knowledge and understanding in a way that engages and develops individuals' personalities. It is a preparation for a significant and demanding aspect of life and, as such, fully entitled to be called an educational experience. An HSE, when it requires strong occupational categories, requires occupational formation of a significant and systematic kind.

ECONOMIC AIMS, WORK-EUDAEMONISM AND VOCATIONAL EDUCATION

How are politics and vocational education related? A decision to opt for an HSE is frequently political, since co-ordination problems cannot often be optimally solved by rational individual actors. Provision of adequate initial forms of vocational education is part of the solution. But, since this deals only with the supply side, it cannot of itself provide an answer to the employer aspect of the demand side, which is why co-ordinated action is required. But what are the connections between work-eudaemonism and the other aims of economic activity?

Work-eudaemonism in contemporary economic conditions, maintained via a HSE, has the following consequences. It is compatible neither with Aristotelian self-sufficiency nor with a Millian or Rawlsian steady state, where economic output reaches a more or less permanent plateau. A sectoral HSE needs to maintain competitive advantage through the continual development and improvement of high-specification goods and services. Both the means of production in Marx's sense and the productive powers in List's undergo constant renewal. It is also arguable that the forces of production (in Marx's sense, the social technique of production) go through a transformation towards greater worker autonomy (Hodgson 1999: 211–27). This entails, on the demand side, consumers who wish for ever-higher specification goods and services. Maintenance of an HSE is therefore bound up with consumptionism rather than self-sufficiency or a steady-state as a central economic aim. Stasis is not an option.

On the other hand, the maintenance of an HSE requires that productive powers are highly developed, that is a workforce not only with managerial and administrative capacities but with very substantial craft and technician level qualifications, not to mention more than adequate levels of general education (Prais 1995). This in turn requires high levels of basic education, initial vocational education for professional, managerial, technical and craft operatives and the capacity of the workforce to engage in career-long self-improvement. One would expect to find, in a country oriented towards an HSE, some inclination towards what Mill called higher pleasures (Mill 1968). Indeed, one would expect the capacity to find spiritual satisfaction at work to be enhanced in such a situation, through the release of the individual's active powers, through their independence of judgment, through inter-reliance on workmates and social interaction in the workplace.[4]

CONCLUSION

All economic activity has some eudaemonic goal, even if this is just consumption. An Aristotelian form of eudaemonism regards self-sufficiency adequate for a leisured life of contemplation and enjoyment of friendship as the material condition of well-being.

Implicit in the Aristotelian account, however, is the view that such a condition is only available to a small section of the population. This form of eudaemonism, appropriate to an aristocracy, recognizes that well-being requires a broader range of satisfactions than consumption: leisure, friendship and an appropriate balance in life (Aristotle 1924).

Work-eudaemonism recognizes the importance of these satisfactions but claims that they are not sufficient in large-scale democratic societies where all feel entitled to a worthwhile life and practically all are dependent on their own labour. Inevitably much if not most economic activity occurs in the commercial sector and is concerned with the production of goods and services for consumption. It occurs in rapidly changing commercial environments in which the international division of labour means that societies that enjoy high levels of material wealth and education find it advantageous to concentrate on the production of high-specification goods and services requiring high levels of skill. Such societies, dependent on the state, on intermediate institutions of civil society or on family structures for the sustaining of their productive powers, also need ways of balancing their activities between production and the renewal of productive powers.

Work in these circumstances has to provide many of the constituents of well-being. Such societies tend to need a large non-trading sector, part of whose role will be maintaining the conditions for successful commercial activity. In this sector, too, work may contribute to well-being. Because the commercial economic activity of such societies assumes that citizens are more than self-sufficient, leisure involving consumption is important. Recognition that the workplace is a source of self-worth and intrinsic satisfaction, even for those not currently in paid employment, has important educational implications. If we are serious about following a high-skill route which requires more workers with intermediate level qualifications, we should pay much more attention to the development of Level 3 qualifications in tandem with a regulatory framework that addresses the 'double demand' problem. Demand from employers and potential employees has to be encouraged through the imposition of costs for not training, either in the form of a levy or licensed labour market entry, although this solution does not seem to be favoured in current British government thinking (HM Treasury 2002: 18–20, 2.21–2.33). From employees it has to come through the much-enhanced provision of school-based pre-vocational education, together with an improved apprenticeship system with block release to properly develop the general educational and applied theoretical components of the craft and technician occupations skill base. One cannot expect a high demand for a facility that is under-resourced and of low prestige as well as being of dubious economic value. Appropriate levels of qualification might need to be made the condition of labour market entry. Finally, level 3 qualifications need to be made 'permeable' or accreditable for further study to levels 4, 5 and beyond.

To answer our original question, a case can be made in both traditional economic and in eudaemonic terms for high-skill economic development. If this is right, then vocational education must have a very significant liberal element.

NOTES

1 When utilities are measured in goods, they are naturally seen as being of instrumental value. When considered in terms of functionings, they have potential intrinsic value.
2 Marshall makes the point that prosperity engenders a concern with beauty and hence with demand for artisanal production. Hence changing conceptions of well-being for sections of the population affect the demand for products and services with high-skill inputs (Marshall 1890: 113).
3 Occupations may have cognate skills and knowledge, which allow individual occupational flexibility by building on common or similar skills. Mechatronics, for example, combines elements of electronic and mechanical engineering.
4 The German vocational philosopher, Kerchensteiner, for example, saw vocational education as in part a process of spiritual formation.

REFERENCES

Aristotle (1924) *Nichomachean Ethics*, London: Dent.
Ashton, D. and Green, F. (1996) *Education, Training and the Global Economy*, Cheltenham: Edward Elgar,
Brown, P., Green, A. and Lauder, H. (2001) *High Skills: Globalization, Competitiveness, and Skill Formation*, Oxford: Oxford University Press.
HM Treasury (2002) *Developing Workforce Skills: Piloting a New Approach*, April, London.
Hodgson, G. (1999) *Economics and Utopia: Why the Learning Society is Not the End of History*, London: Routledge.
Kerschensteiner, G. (1964) [1901] *Staatsbürgerliche Erziehung für der deutschen Jugend in Ausgewählte Pädagogische Texte*, Band 1, Paderborn: Ferdinand Schöningh.
Keynes, J.M. (1973) *The General Theory of Employment, Money and Interest*, London: Macmillan.
List, F. (1991) [1841] *The National System of Political Economy*, New Jersey: Augustus Kelley.
Marshall, A. (1890) *The Principles of Economics*, London: Macmillan.
Marx, K. (1970) [1887] *Capital*, London: Lawrence and Wishart.
Mill, J.S. (1968) [1861] *Utilitarianism, Liberty and Representative Government*, London: Dent.
Mill, J.S. (1994) [1848] *The Principles of Political Economy*, Oxford: Oxford University Press.
Prais, S. (1995) *Productivity, Education and Training*, Cambridge: Cambridge University Press.
Rawls, J. (1971) *A Theory of Justice*, Oxford: Oxford University Press.
Raz, J. (1988) *The Morality of Freedom*, Oxford: Clarendon.
Shore, M. (2004) 'Questions of Terminology', in Bernadette Clasquin, Nathalie Moncel, Mark Harvey and Bernard Friot (eds), *Wage and Welfare: New Perspectives on Employment and Social Rights in Europe*, Brussels: P.-I.-E.-Peter Lang.
Smith, A. (1981) [1776] *The Wealth of Nations*, Indianapolis: Liberty Press.
Streeck, W. (1996) 'Lean Production in the German Automobile Industry: A Test Case

for Convergence Theory', in S. Berger and R. Dore (eds), *National Diversity and Global Capitalism*, New York: Cornell University Press.

Verdon, M. (1996) *Keynes and the Classics*, London: Routledge.

White, J. (1997) *Education and the End of Work*, London: Kogan Page.

Chapter 11

Social justice and vocational education

John Halliday

INTRODUCTION

The English Department for Education and Skills (DfES) puts the relationship between social justice and vocational education to the fore in its recent consideration of the economic benefits of what it calls 'high quality learning': 'High quality learning is strongly linked with higher earnings, lower chances of becoming unemployed, better health and reduced crime' (DfES 2003: 4).

Social justice appears to require everyone to have equal access to such learning, but what is it and how could governments ensure equal access? For the department, high quality learning appears to mean the development of skills for employment – what is commonly termed a vocational education. 'By developing the skills of the current and future workforce, the Department's policies are helping to create both a more prosperous society and a more equal one' (DfES 2003: 8)

Yet this chapter presents compelling evidence that in the UK high quality learning and its associated benefits are best ensured through types of what is commonly termed a formal academic education. What is termed a vocational education comes a poor second and in some cases shares third place with those who appear to have benefited little from the many millions that are put into the provision of formal educational opportunities of any kind (DfES 2003: 13, 17, 19; Sianesi 2003: 1–2).

It therefore appears entirely reasonable for governments to want to move as many people as possible from third and second positions to first but there are at least two problems associated with such an attempt. First, it seems highly unlikely that national economic prosperity would result if everyone became academically engaged. Second, social justice involves not only the principle of equality but also two other principles which may be summarized as truth and just desert. It is argued that these three principles are always in some degree of tension and that it is simply not possible to resolve the tension once and for all. Rather, it is argued that the principles are held in some degree of balance through the notion of myth which governments necessarily draw upon in order to sustain any sense that they are working towards a socially just society. One central myth concerns the very distinction between academic and vocational to which attention has already been drawn. Others are explored in the course of the chapter.

High quality learning is intended by DfES to occur within schools and other publicly funded educational institutions. It is widely accepted that such learning can lead to at least three sorts of educational good (Chapman and Aspin 1997: 27) although the DfES (2003) stresses only one sort. First, education is seen to improve the ability of citizens to choose rationally among a range of competing perspectives on the basis of a presumed expansion of cognitive and practical capability. In this sense educational activities encourage personal fulfilment. Second, educational activities are seen to enable greater social cohesion. For example, an initiation into a common curriculum is seen to be a prerequisite for effective communication between citizens and a means of providing sufficient common ground for them to resolve any differences they might individually have. In this way it enables people collectively to determine those things that are in their interests and to live together in some degree of harmony. Third, education is seen to enable individual prosperity and national economic growth through enhancing the ability to perform paid work. It is seen to be vocational and it is this third sort of good that forms the focus of DfES (2003) concern.

This third sort of good is somewhat different from the other two in that its distribution can more easily be measured. Hence the justice of its distribution can be more transparently ascertained. So while all educational courses of study can lead to the achievement of all three kinds of goods, those that are specifically labelled as 'vocational' are most readily considered in relation to social justice. All should have access to such courses and those who put time, money and effort into completing them are entitled to expect that they will be proportionately rewarded through the work that they enable. Increasingly however, research into the rates of return of different courses of vocational education challenges this expectation (Applebaum *et al.* 2004; Ashton and Green 1996; Berg 1973; Brown and Hesketh 2004; Conlon 2002; Dearden *et al.* 2004; Keep 2003; Lafer 2002; Robinson 1997b; Sianesi 2003; Wolf 2002).

In her summary of research in the British context Sianesi notes that:

> The most robust findings to date are that . . . academic qualifications generally earn higher rewards. . . . Qualifications which on the other hand seem to fail to generate any wage premium for males or females are . . . vocational qualifications, RSA [Royal Society for the Encouragements of Arts], BTEC [Business and Technology Education Council], apprenticeship and most notably NVQ [National Vocational Qualification] level 2 and below.
>
> (Sianesi 2003: 1–2)

Great variety now exists in vocational education courses. The motivations of those who undertake them are not necessarily or at all concerned with social justice. For

150

example, many students might be attracted to the different styles of teaching that such courses offer or the opportunity to do practical work of a particular kind that does not involve so much 'essay writing' (Halliday 1996). Moreover, the goods of personal fulfilment and social cohesion might be much better realized from courses labelled 'vocational' than those that are not. Similarly, vocational goods might be much better realized from courses that are commonly labelled as 'academic'.

Indeed in the view of many commentators including this author, it would be preferable to attempt to drop the academic/vocational distinction altogether and to argue that all forms of publicly funded educational institutions should pay due regard to all three kinds of benefit. By concentrating exclusively on the economic benefits of education, government through DFES (2003) makes its concern for greater social justice all the more difficult to realize.

No one imagines that there could ever be equal rewards given for different types of work. Indeed it would be hard to know the basis on which equality in reward was to be decided. It does not help considerations of social justice however when the fundamental principle of truth is violated by ignoring the evidence for the relative returns on academic and vocational qualifications. In summary, academic learning which might appear in historical context to be least instrumental seems in many cases most effective in actually securing a good rate of return. The opposite is the case for what is called a vocational education. It would better, as I have argued elsewhere, to encourage different forms of practical activity involving tools other than pens and paper (what might be presumed to be academic tools) in the search for worthwhile educational activities (Halliday 1996).

A main problem in not doing this is that courses leading to such worthwhile practices as plumbing, building and social care turn out all too often to be courses in writing about these practices through the process known as academic drift. As I argue (Halliday 1996), such drift – however well-intentioned – can only hinder the development of courses designed for those who prefer to work with tools other than academic tools. Moreover, customers are not interested so much in whether, for example, a plumber can write an essay. Rather, they want their bathroom installed properly. A qualification which is based on writing about practice is of little interest to students, potential customers or those concerned to ensure greater social justice through the promissory exchange value of a qualification to which all should have access. This further exacerbates the problem government has in trying to persuade people to take intermediate-level qualifications in such practical areas as the above: 'Economic performance has also been held back by a shortage of intermediate-level qualifications' (DFES 2003: 14).

Quite apart from the problem of academic drift, it is hardly surprising that there is such a shortage because according to the logic embedded in DFES (2003), students will seek courses with the highest rates of return which are not at intermediate level: 'The returns to holding a degree have generally remained high' (DFES 2003: 30) and

'The demand for higher level qualifications, especially at degree level, is set to increase further in the future' (DFES 2003: 39).

So by framing the relationship between social justice and vocational education in instrumental terms, the shortage of people qualified practically at intermediate level seems likely to get worse. Moreover, it seems unlikely that higher level qualifications will maintain their promissory exchange value leading to increased levels of disappointment and potentially even greater levels of social injustice. That is because those who have invested in their education as government encourages them to do and who have acquired huge debts as a result, may find themselves even poorer than they would have been without such investment.

SOCIAL JUSTICE

There is a long tradition of enquiry through Aristotle to Rawls that takes the view of justice as fairness. Socrates puts forward the view in Republic 1 that justice is 'to speak the truth and to pay your debts' (Buchanan 1977: 287). He goes on to problematize this view. Nevertheless, the requirements of fairness plainly involve the notion of truth. For example, if some courses of study are distinguished specifically as vocational then the requirement of truth demands that at least some people undertaking them have as a result secured at least one employment and perform better in employment. Fairness seems to require that the reward secured as a result of taking a course of vocational education is proportionate to the effort and resources put into it. Fairness also seems to require that no group in society is systematically excluded, either from certain forms of vocational education or from the rewards that such an education normally brings for the members of other groups. Justice therefore presupposes principles of truth, equality and just desert. These three principles are often in conflict and there is no 'view from nowhere' or super principle that enables any society to determine once and for all how they should be combined (Taylor 1994: 38).

Rather, the priority in the way that these principles are applied is contextually specific and in many contexts their application conflicts. For example, our current use of the term 'social justice' tends to prioritize equality and truth rather than just desert. Prioritizing just desert tends to work against equality. It is much easier to disguise such conflict if the principle of truth is not given priority and so on. Yet such disguise is essential because, as Bernard Williams put it:

> The ultimate concern is that we, a 'we' that extends into the future, can go on telling a truthful enough story that will not leave everyone with despair . . . [because] . . . there are very compelling true accounts of the world that could lead anyone to despair who did not hate humanity.
>
> (Williams 2002: 268)

152

On this account the stories that members of society tell about the contexts they find themselves in should be truthful enough to keep the principles of equality and just desert in some degree of acceptable balance. For example, it is obvious that despair would arise if it came to be accepted that education in general was little other than a gamble hopelessly weighted in favour of those who have more wealth and property. An emphasis on the vocational in education forms the basis of a truthful enough story that social mobility is possible through educational effort. Yet, as evidence mounts that many courses labelled vocational to which Sianesi (2003) draws our attention, which are taken precisely because it is reasonable to presume that they lead to worthwhile employment or increased earnings in employment, do no such thing, then other hopeful, truthful enough stories must emerge. In short, the story that emphasizes the vocational in education becomes no longer truthful enough.

STRUCTURE AND MYTH

These stories cannot make explicit what is presumed to be a common good, for the precise detail of such a good is always contestable as the balance between principles of justice shifts. Rather, stories touch on such presumptions in a way that resonates with people's concerns and avoids direct confrontation with the contested nature of common goods. The stories take the form of myth, of 'depoliticised speech' as Roland Barthes puts it. Myth gives things 'a natural and eternal justification . . . it gives them a clarity which is not that of an explanation but that of a statement of fact' (Barthes 1993: 132).

Myths provide some hope that in the end human relations are not so politicized that they depend exclusively on relations of power. Without such hope no settled or any sense of justice is possible. On this account myths are truthful enough stories that suggest that there is a value-neutral basis to the structures and policies that are set up to regulate human and social relations. It is not that those working within such structures are somehow being duped. Nor is it that policy-makers are intent on deception. Rather, it is that myth is necessary to maintain a sense of social justice and it is attractive and hopeful to claim that:

> good education can also help to break the inter-generational cycle of under achievement and deprivation. There is a clear link, for instance between parents' qualifications and the GCSE attainment of their children.
>
> (DFES 2003: 18)

It is much less attractive and hopeful to realize that the cycle is not going to be broken through good education alone, however. Using information from the National Child Development Study, Conlon (2002) concludes:

153

> There is a strong implication . . . that the earnings potential of an individual is determined by the type of qualification undertaken, which in turn is determined not by ability but 'even less fair' factors such as region of residence and parental social class.

(Conlon 2002: 3)

As Ashton and Green report, the evidence of education links to economic growth is thin and there is no evidence whatsoever of a link between education and the profitability of enterprises (Ashton and Green 1996: 65). Even if there were such evidence, we cannot be sure whether any perceived correlation between amounts spent on vocational education and the economic returns of such education are really correlations between some measure of natural ability or personal values and economic returns rather than between qualifications and economic returns. The human capital model offers good explanatory and predictive power in understanding the individual rates of return on different programmes of vocational education, but it seems that the amount of human capital is largely determined more by circumstances at birth than any educational intervention. In essence there is much evidence to suggest that those who start out succeeding in education continue by and large to do so and that without structural changes to society, educational policy alone is unlikely to have much effect on this (Adonis and Pollard 1997).

CHANGING MYTHS

Ashton and Green (1996), Winch (2002) and others distinguish between a high skills equilibrium (HSE) and a low skills equilibrium (LSE). They make the point that nations exhibit the characteristics of an HSE and an LSE in differing degrees. While there is no room here to outline all these characteristics, it is important to note that within an HSE, vocational qualifications may be seen as a kind of property because the state regulates employment through such qualifications. Germany would be an example here. In a real sense a vocational qualification and courses leading to the award of such qualifications enable participants and holders to reach a degree of financial security and prosperity. Thus they enable more people to have a stake in the society of which they are a part than might be possible if attempts were made to distribute land and real estate more equitably. They may thus serve as a form of goods to be distributed on the basis of their promissory exchange value. Plainly the justice of their distribution depends upon the extent to which their promise can be realized and that depends not only upon the supply of people with such qualifications and the quality of the education that led to those qualifications, but also upon demand. Moreover, it probably depends on some regulation of all three, which is something that British and American governments have tended to resist, and such lack of regulation is related to the characteristics of an LSE. Nevertheless, it is easy to see why any government might wish to attempt to sustain the view that a vocational qualification is property worth having.

On this view some courses of vocational education may be seen as a means to ensure greater social justice. Something like a status quo of employment opportunities and a settled sense of what is just in terms of the rewards afforded by different types of work may be maintained. At the same time more difficult distributive concerns with land and property may be avoided. This is not to suggest some sort of conspiracy thesis. It is simply to acknowledge that the three principles outlined earlier are bound to be in constant tension. Those who feel they have worked hard to maintain their land and property are hardly likely to favour the principle of equality in access to their land and property, for example.

In contrast to countries in which the labour market is regulated, deregulated markets in the UK and the USA lead to a proliferation of changing structures all of which may be seen as attempts to sustain the idea that a vocational qualification has promissory exchange value. Acronyms proliferate that are based on government departments, qualifications authorities and special funding bodies set up to support research and practice in the area of vocational education (Keep 2003; Lafer 2002; Wolf 2002). Often these are unashamedly short term in their aims and methods (Felstead 1993). This should not surprise us. Such structures are bound to need to change, as myths develop and shift to sustain a sense of what is socially just. The shifts are likely to be more rapid within countries where there is little or no regulation of the labour market, because in those countries it will more easily become obvious that particular vocational courses have little exchange value. New ones will therefore be invented to support the idea that there is nothing wrong with vocational education per se; rather, the previous manifestation of such education is blamed and replaced.

An analogy with Thomas Kuhn's account of natural science and the theory dependence of observation statements may help to illustrate this (Kuhn 1962). When an observation runs counter to what might be expected according to a dominant and accepted theory, it is not clear whether the theory or the observation should be rejected. Kuhn argues that in order for science to be seen to progress, some theories have to be assumed to be correct to enable laboratory and other structures to be set up in order for the scientific community to experiment in a systematic way. When the number of observations that run counter to the expectations predicted by a theory reach a certain level, doubt begins to creep in about the veracity of the theory itself.

In a similar way we may imagine a central myth concerned with vocationalism in general supported by a number of smaller myths concerned with qualifications frameworks, job availability, skill shortages and so on. These myths are in turn supported by structures that are based on predictions of the outcomes of types of government expenditure. In time, as those predictions fail to be realized through the observations of those on the various schemes of vocational education and research that attempt to determine correlations between outcome and expenditure, the myths themselves come to be called into question and new myths emerge supported by new structures and so on. It is not that myth is destroyed by direct confrontation with truth. After all, it can never be clear which should be abandoned – observation or myth – and the numbers of those caught up in what turn out to be temporary structures always give a degree of permanence to the structures and the myths they support. Moreover, it is always possible to appear to change structures in the light of new myths in order to make the myths truthful enough.

MYTH AND TRUTH

Barthes suggests that myth is 'stolen language' (Barthes 1993: 118). By this he means that myth always robs language of its primary meaning in order to suggest something naturalized and depoliticized. He gives some examples of standard forms of myth, which are developed below in the context of current emphasis on the vocational in education. For example, suppose attention was concentrated upon inequalities in access to different programmes of vocational education for people of different ethnic background, gender and class, what Barthes calls inoculation might prevent consideration of a more widespread injustice that results from the false dualism of the academic and the vocational. Inoculation might prevent consideration of the view that many programmes of so-called 'vocational' education are largely irrelevant in securing access to rewarding work (Conlon 2002; Dearden *et al.* 2002; Keep 2003; Lafer 2002; Wolf 2002).

Inoculation might also prevent consideration of the idea of an education for consumption. At the very least it seems impossible to implement high quality forms of vocational education unless students are taught to consume high quality goods. There seems little point focusing so much attention on a vocational education without at the same time educating people to consume whatever is produced or offered as a result. Yet we tend to balk at this prospect. Myth inoculates us against the full implications of an obsession with the economic aims of education. It suggests we may neglect all those forms of social capital that give value to objects in addition to their monetary value. The cost of sustaining this myth is to reduce social capital through increasing privatization, to render public spaces unattractive and to damage the very traditions that might have encouraged social cohesion and highly skilled work. We can be invited to forget that some of the finest creations were brought about long before anyone began to talk about such a system. In these ways myth deprives vocationalism of its history.

The related myth, that there should be an overarching vocational qualifications framework, presents justice as a weighing operation, which suggests that, unless similar objects are put on the scales, justice cannot be properly considered. Hence all people must be assumed to have the same motivations, desires, fears, etc. The same acquisitiveness that drives some business people might be assumed to be the correct moral direction for everyone. All are assumed to put similar weightings on the things they value. Both investments and returns are supposed to be similarly commodified.

156

What Barthes refers to as the quantification of quality challenges the very idea that there could be a multiplicity of meanings of quality in work, from personal relationships to the ways that a product or service contributes to social and political capital in the longer term. In this way intelligence is economized.

Myth suggests that education and economic success are like fresh air and fun – obvious good things to be maximized! It is hardly surprising then that an increasing proportion of 16 to 21 year olds are undertaking formal education programmes. While so doing an increasing proportion of these students in the UK support themselves in part-time work (DfES 2001). It is estimated that at the end of 2000 58 per cent of 16 to 18 year olds in England and Wales were in employment. This illustrates that the type of education they received pre-16 was a very good vocational education for them. This should not surprise us for, as Braverman and others, for example Robinson, have argued, a large number of jobs do not seem even to require much pre-16 formal education of any sort for successful completion (Braverman 1976; Robinson 1997 a, 1997b, 1997c).

It might appear strange then that the main area of expansion has come in post–18 vocational education. According to Wolf the huge growth in the number of vocational qualifications awarded in further and higher education at the higher levels is the result not so much of increased demand for higher level skills (Wolf 2002: ch. 6). Rather, 'the tyranny of numbers' simply racks up the stakes in attempting to secure for employers the best new employees and for prospective employees the best employment. That means that, whatever government or individuals do, the requirement for equality can never be achieved. It also means that the requirement for proportionate reward can also never be achieved because there is bound to be a polarization that has nothing to do with effort between those who form the bottom part of a normal distribution and those at the top.

The recognition of a hierarchy of educational institutions surely follows. As Archer et al. report, 'All respondents were aware of some sort of hierarchy between higher education institutions . . . respondents described the "worst" institutions as the "sad", "concrete" "inner city" universities, "without trees" and catering for "working class" and minority ethnic student populations' (Archer et al. 2003: 128). They go on: 'Many respondents recognised that employers were also aware of the hierarchy of universities, as publicised through league tables, and argued that going to a lower ranking institution would compromise the value of a degree' (Archer et al. 2003: 130).

Such recognition and awareness works against considerations of social justice. It is not just that the principle of equality seems to be violated; the principle of just desert is violated too. For it seems that once a student's position in the hierarchy is established, then they soon come to recognize that no amount of hard work is going to change that position much. For a fuller account of this relationship between myth and truth, see Halliday (2004).

157

CONCLUSION

Three principles of social justice are always in some kind of tension and myths intertwined with truths serve to maintain a settled balance between them. Some of those myths that support increased attention to the vocational in education appear increasingly implausible in the light of research. A requirement that the stories are truthful enough is often violated, because in so many cases what purports to be most vocational in education turns out to be least vocational. The requirement for just desert is also always likely to be violated. In the case of public sector occupations, the rates of return on vocational qualifications are always subject to government views on what is economically and politically possible at any particular time. In the case of private sector occupations, the rates of return available from certain types of vocational education are always going to depend in part on the numbers of other people who choose to take the same type. Finally, the requirement of equality is violated because certain social, ethnic, gender and class groups tend to be excluded from the benefits that education can bring to some other groups (Conlon 2002).

The account of the relationship between justice, myth, truth and structure presented here may be seen as political theory with some explanatory and predictive power. It has been used to explain how a reasonably settled sense of justice may be maintained within a liberal democracy and how myths and structures concerned with vocational education within deregulated labour markets are more likely to shift than those in regulated markets. It predicts that myths surrounding vocationalism are now beginning to come to the end of their useful lives and that some new legitimation will emerge to justify the notion that people should invest in their and society's future prosperity through education.

Wood suggests that government might be coming to accept responsibility for enabling:

> every citizen . . . meaningful access to a minimal range of basic goods, necessary for a freely chosen life. When these conditions are met, citizens must be expected to bear the costs of the free choices they make . . . inclusion rather than equality is the primary goal.
>
> (Wood 1999: 2)

In this way, the principle of equality comes to be replaced by guaranteed baseline provision of fundamental goods. Above this baseline, calculated gambling comes to replace the principle of just desert. Hopeful myth replaces depressing truth to complete newly formulated principles of social inclusion. In the light of this shift, we may not be surprised to find not only a proliferation of changing structures but also a proliferation of television, newspaper and other game shows to provide the basic metaphors upon which a new myth of social inclusion is founded. Whether such a myth is sufficiently rich to enable social cohesion or whether other myths will emerge to support it remains to be seen. The remnant meaning of the term vocational might be to denote practical courses of study or types of teaching that are significantly different from those on offer in most schools at present. It might come to be accepted that such courses are no more related to employment opportunities or to the economy than other types of course. In all cases, education comes to take the form of a gamble, which, as Giddens points out, may well continue to be heavily weighted in favour of those who have significant wealth and property (Giddens 1973: 264). Such weighting cannot become hopeless, however.

REFERENCES

Adonis, A. and Pollard, S. (1997) *A Class Act: the myth of Britain's classless society,* London: Hamish Hamilton.

Applebaum, E., Bernhardt, A. and Murnane, R.J. (eds) (2004) *Low-wage America: how employers are reshaping opportunity in the workplace,* New York: Russell Sage Foundation.

Archer, L., Hutchings, M. and Ross, A. (2003) *Higher Education and Social Class: issues of exclusion and inclusion,* London: Routledge/Falmer.

Ashton, D. and Green, F. (1996) *Education, Training and the Global Economy,* Cheltenham: Edward Elgar.

Barthes, R. (1993) 'Myth Today', in S. Sontag (ed.), *A Roland Barthes Reader,* London: Vintage.

Berg, I. (1973) *The Great Training Robbery,* Harmondsworth: Penguin.

Braverman, H. (1976) 'Labor and Monopoly Capital: the degradation of work in the twentieth century', New York: Monthly Review Press.

Brown, P. and Hesketh, A. (2004) *The Mismanagement of Talent: employability, competition and careers in the knowledge driven economy,* Oxford: Oxford University Press.

Buchanan, S. (ed.) (1977) *The Portable Plato,* London: Penguin.

Chapman, J. and Aspin, D. (1997) *The School, the Community and Lifelong Learning,* London: Cassell.

Conlon, G. (2002) 'Determinants of Undertaking Academic and Vocational Qualifications in the UK', London: Centre for Economics in Education. Accessed from http://cee.lse.ac.uk/cee%20dps/CEEDP20.pdf

Dearden, L., McIntosh, S., Myck, M. and Vignoles, A. (2002) 'The Returns to Academic, Vocational and Basic Skills in Britain', *Bulletin of Economic Research,* 54(3), 249–273.

Department for Education and Skills (DfES) (2001) 'Participation in Education, Training and Employment by 16–18 Year Olds in England: 1999 and 2000'. Accessed from hyperlink http://www.dfes.gov.uk/statistics/DB/SFR/

Department for Education and Skills (DfES) (2003) *Education and Skills: the economic benefit,* London: Department for Education and Skills.

Felstead, A. (1993) 'Funding Government Training Schemes: mechanisms and consequences', CLMS Working Paper no. 2. Accessed from hyperlink http://www.clms.le.ac.uk

Giddens, A. (1973) *The Class Structure of the Advanced Societies,* London: Hutchinson.

Halliday, J.S. (1996) 'Values and Further Education', *British Journal of Educational Studies*, 44(1), 66–81.

Halliday, J.S. (2004) 'Distributive Justice and Vocational Education', *British Journal of Educational Studies*, 22(4), 151–165.

Keep, E. (2003) 'The State and Power: an elephant and a snake in the telephone box of English VET Policy', paper presented at the University of Greenwich 27 November (University of Warwick: ESRC Centre on Skills, Knowledge and Organisational Performance).

Kuhn, T.S. (1962) *The Structure of Scientific Revolutions*, Chicago: University of Chicago Press.

Lafer, G. (2002) *The Job Training Charade*, New York: Cornell University Press.

Mill, J.S. (1972) *Utilitarianism*, London: Dent.

Robinson, P. (1997a) *Water under the Bridge: changes in employment in Britain and the OECD*, London: London School of Economics, Centre for Economic Performance.

Robinson, P. (1997b) *The Myth of Parity of Esteem: earnings and qualification*, London: London School of Economics, Centre for Economic Performance.

Robinson, P. (1997c) *Literacy, Numeracy and Economic Performance*, London: London School of Economics, Centre for Economic Performance.

Sianesi, B. (2003) *Returns to Education: a non-technical summary of CEE work and policy discussion*, London: Institute for Fiscal Studies and Centre for the Economics of Education.

Taylor, C. (1994) 'Justice after Virtue', in J. Horton and S. Mendus, *After MacIntyre*, Cambridge: Polity Press.

Williams, B. (2002) *Truth and Truthfulness: an essay in genealogy*, Princeton: Princeton University Press.

Winch, C. (2002) 'The Economic Aims of Education', *Journal of Philosophy of Education*, 36(1), 101–19.

Wolf, A. (2002) *Does Education Matter? Myths about education and economic growth*, London: Penguin.

Wood, S. (1999) 'Education, Training and the British Third Way', Skope Policy Paper no. 1, Warwick: University of Warwick.

Chapter 12

The multiple paradoxes of state power in the English education and training system

Ewart Keep

INTRODUCTION

This chapter explores three issues. First, what are the main reasons why national government has become so dominant in English education and training (E&T) policy formation? Second, why is the English E&T system perhaps the most statist in Europe? Third and finally, what factors underlie the apparently strong continuity in the broad thrust of E&T policy since the 1980s? In seeking answers, the chapter points to the peculiarities of the English state in eschewing social partnership and tripartist E&T structures (of the type generally found elsewhere in Europe), and underlines the importance of government's pursuit of a 'unipartist' strategy whereby it designs, funds and controls more and more E&T activity. In particular, this account stresses the central paradox, that because of a laissez faire attitude towards governmental responsibility for employer behaviour, the state has been forced to act as a substitute for employer effort.

The chapter draws upon extant accounts of the evolution of policy, the extensive policy analysis literature and the author's experiences as an occasional participant (if peripheral) observer within the policy process. In the space available only general developments can be described. Where appropriate, attention is pointed towards more detailed accounts of developments.

CENTRAL GOVERNMENT POWER: EVER ONWARD AND UPWARD

The dominant trend within English E&T since the early 1980s has been the increasing power of central government to design, control and implement policy at every level across an increasing range of topics. The strength with which this has occurred has waxed and waned over time. For detailed descriptions of some of the ways that circumstances have shaped the speed of tendencies towards centralization of state power, see Ainley 2001; Ainley and Corney 1990; Evans 1992; King 1993; Jenkins 1995; Jones 1999.

These often complex fluctuations notwithstanding, since the 1980s it is clear that the power of central government has increased markedly and that, particularly since 1987, the pace and scale of change has been rapid (Jenkins 1995). In 1981 the role of the central state in E&T was limited and peripheral (Ashton and Keep 2007). Today, central government and its agencies are the prime movers in the system, with the other stakeholders acting in subordinate, usually minor positions. The resulting shift has been characterized by a process of delocalization, centralization and nationalization, whereby the English education system moved over a period of 15 years from being the least to the most centrally controlled system in the world (Bash and Coulby 1989: 17; Bassey 2003: 28).

As a result, the state now possesses the legal power and administrative capacity to intervene in detail in what gets taught to whom and at what level and type of certification, and to direct how this learning process is funded, conducted, monitored, inspected and managed. The overall effect has been to greatly increase the importance and spending power of the Department for Education and Skills (DfES). The heightened profile of E&T as a political issue has meant that other central government departments, most notably the Department for Trade and Industry (DTI) and the Treasury, have acquired an interest in this field. At the same time, through the abandonment of any meaningful notions of tripartism and the abolition of those institutional arrangements that gave it force (such as the National Economic Development Council and the Manpower Services Commission), the ability of the social partners to exert serious influence on policy has also been sharply diminished.

As Gamble (1994), Jenkins (1995) and others have noted, these developments paradoxically commenced under a Conservative administration ostensibly committed to reducing the role of the state and encouraging neo-liberal, market-based solutions to public policy problems. These trends have continued unabated under New Labour – indeed it has acquired new means to intervene within education and has proved at least as ruthless as its Conservative predecessor in re-shaping the institutional landscape of E&T (Wood 1999: 13).

Independent entities or arms of government?

One criticism of the account given above is that it omits the myriad of bodies that exist and that, it might be argued, mediate between central government and individual schools, colleges and training providers. The problem is that these bodies – for example, the Learning and Skills Council (LSC) and the 47 Local Learning and Skills Councils (LLSCs) – are themselves the creatures of government. They are financed by central government, with governing bodies or councils appointed by and solely responsible to the Secretary of State for Education and Skills. Their chief function is to carry out the wishes of ministers and civil servants and to meet central government's targets. For instance, the LSC – the largest quango in Europe in spending terms – claims that it exists to deliver policy not to make it (House of Commons 2004: 5). Far from acting as a bulwark against the intervention of Westminster and Whitehall, these bodies are arms of the central state and enforcers of its will.

Even those groupings that are nominally designated as representing employer interests exist only by ministerial sufferance and when this is withdrawn the illusion of their independence is exposed. Despite being termed employer bodies and employer-led, neither the Training and Enterprise Councils (TECs), nor a succession of sectoral training bodies, escaped abolition by central government once their usefulness to ministers had been exhausted (see Jones 1999 for the story of the TECs).

It is unclear whether the latest set of sectoral organizations – the Sector Skills Councils (SSCs) – mark any real break with this tradition. Although the government has invested them with an apparently key role in developing a new, more demand-led and employer-led E&T system, they remain state-licensed entities, receiving their core funding from government and expected to deliver national programmes and targets the design and setting of which they have played no role in whatsoever (DfES/ DTI/HMT/DWP 2005).

England versus Europe

The centralization of English E&T runs counter to trends elsewhere in Europe. Since the 1990s in many other European Union (EU) countries, such as the Netherlands, Italy, Sweden and Finland, E&T policy has been devolved to local social partnership arrangements, wherein the governmental role is taken up by elected local authorities or municipalities. In Germany, the *Lander* have a key role in determining how E&T is conducted. In the USA, the role of the federal government is very limited and E&T interventions are generally dealt with at the level of the individual state and below. In England, while elected local government's role has continued to diminish, the only element of devolution has been to the unelected, centrally sponsored, government funded Regional Development Agencies (RDAs), which are supposed to help plan E&T provision.

Moreover, as suggested at the outset, under Conservative administrations between 1979 and 1997 the UK as a whole abolished tripartite E&T structures and moved away from any commitment to European-style social partnership arrangements. Since 1997 the New Labour government has done little to reverse this fundamental rift between practice in the four UK countries and the general pattern of E&T governance found elsewhere in Europe.

E&T in a broader context

It is important to stress that the developments within E&T outlined above reflect a general trend within the English polity towards ever-greater centralization of political power, a marked decline in the role and influence of locally elected government and the rise of central government-controlled agencies as a substitute for locally accountable institutions. Other areas where such developments have been broadly co-terminous have included the police service and the National Health Service (Glennerster *et al.* 1991; Jenkins 1995).

THE DRIVERS OF STATE INTERVENTION AND POWER

Why has central government, under both Conservative and New Labour administrations, found itself becoming more and more closely involved in dictating and implementing all aspects of E&T policy? At one level, explanations can be sought within the complex interplay between the political and economic circumstances facing politicians; attempts to restrain public expenditure; ideological imperatives; inter-agency turf wars and battles for political space, influence and budgetary clout; and the personal agendas and ambitions of powerful ministers and senior civil servants (see, for example, Ainley 2001; Ainley and Corney 1990; Jenkins 1995; Jones 1999). This chapter adopts a more distant perspective, seeking to identify some of the underlying forces and processes that have served to drive policy developments in the general direction of greater state power in England since the 1980s.

The dynamics of intervention

The key process, it will be argued, has been the development of a cycle of state intervention that has witnessed central government (and its agencies) drawn into undertaking more and more E&T activity, and then being forced to intervene further in order to shore up earlier interventions, targets and policy goals. This process in turn has driven a continuous reproduction and strengthening of state power within the E&T system. In relation to training the cycle goes thus:

1 The state ascribes a centrality to upskilling that is not shared by many employers. Without much in the way of meaningful consultation with other actors, it defines E&T policy goals aimed at social and/or economic agendas. These can take the form of expected levels of investment or patterns of participation and achievement, sometimes expressed as national targets.
2 It becomes clear that other actors in the E&T system – usually employers, but sometimes individuals or institutions that deliver E&T – cannot or will not deliver these aspirations.

164

3 The state, constrained by its long-standing commitment to a de-regulated labour market and voluntarism in training, combined with the absence of strong pressure on employers to train, has limited options for securing its objectives. In many cases it can only step in, either through subsidy for employer training activity or through expanding education as an alternative source of skill supply.

4 The state justifies this through recourse to arguments about market failure. The evidence to support assertions of widespread market failure is, in reality, very thin (Keep 2006).

5 Because central government is in charge of the resultant intervention, both matters of principle and detail are within the political arena (Jenkins 1995: 246). This dictates the need for political accountability for this stream of public expenditure (which means that its disbursement tends to be managed through relatively high levels of bureaucracy and low levels of trust) and for the results of such expenditure to generate simple, measurable outcomes (generally either levels of participation or the achievement of whole qualifications).

6 Employers come to realize that no sanctions will befall them if they fail to deliver more skills or to co-operate with government on achieving targets, and also that the state is willing to offer subsidy for some forms of training or will expand the education system (at taxpayers' expense) to fill the perceived gap. If these are the fruits of market failure, it makes sense to ensure that the market keeps on failing.

7 The state continues to see skills as key to economic success and aspires to new, more demanding policy goals. The cycle begins again.

A broadly similar process operates in education more generally, whereby central government is repeatedly sucked into further detailed intervention in order to help ensure the delivery of earlier objectives, strategies, promises or targets for which it now finds itself directly accountable. For example, having detailed what should be taught within the National Curriculum, the state soon found a need also to define how key elements of it (for example, literacy and numeracy) should be taught.

Alongside this cycle of intervention have been two subordinate but supportive developments. The first is a growing belief among policy makers in the efficacy of centrally imposed planning regimes, particularly what used to be termed 'manpower planning'. This is an area that appears to experience long wave fluctuations in its appeal. In the late 1970s it seemed to hold promise. It went sharply out of fashion in the era of Thatcherism and mass unemployment, and instead the concept of the training market took hold. Under New Labour a technocratic approach to planning by central government and its agencies is back in fashion. Besides the work of the LSC and LLSCs (Keep 2002), there are now national policy commitments to inter-meshing levels of national, regional, local and sectoral planning systems that will better match skill supply with demand (both from individuals and employers). The result is something that looks suspiciously like the old Soviet bloc's GOSPLAN system for economic planning.

The second factor has been the persistent belief among civil servants that they are masters of institutional design. The desire to abolish old institutional structures and substitute new ones within the E&T system has been matched by a self-belief in the capacity of central government to rise to the challenge of designing complex organizational forms (and the relationship structures between them) at a high level of detail. For a fascinating account of this belief in action in respect of the TECs see Jones (1999). Much the same has been true of government's perceptions of its capacity to oversee qualification and curriculum design and to create training programmes and interventions (Raggatt and Williams 1999).

This faith has remained undimmed despite the unhappy histories of much of this activity – witness Curriculum 2000, National Vocational Qualifications (NVQs) and the National Council for Vocational Qualifications (NCVQ), TECs, the succession of sectoral training bodies, youth training interventions from the Youth Training Scheme (YTS) through to Modern Apprenticeship (Chapman and Tooze 1987; Coffield 1992; Jones 1999; Fuller and Unwin 2003; Lee *et al.* 1990; Raggatt and Williams 1999; Hodgson and Spours 2003; Unwin *et al.* 2004). In part, the persistence of confidence may reflect a capacity on the part of the system's architects to distance themselves from any unintended or unwanted consequences that arise from flaws in their designs. Thus, in the White Paper on the Skills Strategy, its authors observe, presumably without any hint of irony, that:

> Our best colleges and training providers already show abundant creativity and commitment in meeting local needs. But too often 'the system' gets in their way – the framework for planning, funding, monitoring, qualifications and student support does not give incentives or clear signals to support active, effective reach-out to meet needs.
>
> (DfES/HMT/DTI/DWP 2003: 22)

Furthermore, this cycle of intervention takes place at a pace and tempo dictated by the internal dynamics of the political process. The extremely short time horizons that ministers have within which to make their mark on any given field of policy mean that the institutions, programmes and initiatives that arise as the result of government intervention have but a short time to prove themselves (Jenkins 1995; Rose 1991; Ryan 2005). The disjuncture between the time it may take in the real world for changes to be introduced, bed down and start to deliver results and the time that policy makers may give them to achieve this has led to endless problems and incoherence, of which the debacle that followed the overly hurried introduction of the Curriculum 2000 reforms in secondary education is a classic example (Hodgson and Spours 2003; Coffield 2002).

THE STATE AS BOTH STRONG AND WEAK PLAYER

The tendencies outlined above are born out of a paradoxical mixture of strength and weakness. On the one hand the state's power to intervene in and control the publicly funded VET system has become ever greater. There are few checks on this within a constitutional settlement that allots massive power to the Executive. Subject only to review by the legal system, the government can enact whatever measures its parliamentary majority enable it to pass, and the influence of those outside central government over either policy process or outcome is generally limited (Blackstone *et al.* 1992: 39–43).

The only non-governmental player that has been able to exercise any real influence has been the national employers' confederation – the Confederation of British Industry (CBI). As Wolf suggests, the CBI has sometimes been successful in floating ideas for new E&T interventions that the state might make (and finance) (Wolf 1998). It has, however, had little impact on how the state then manages and delivers these. Nor has the CBI been able to exert real leverage over the training decisions of its member firms (Gleeson and Keep 2004).

The state as actor of first and last resort

The weakness of the other stakeholders within the E&T system creates yet another paradox. On the one hand, it gives the state great latitude in what it does, as few are in a position to mount any effective challenge to its dictates and desires. On the other, the weakness of other actors, particularly trade unions and bodies that might represent the collective interests of employers, means that much that in other countries is done through and by the social partners has here to be undertaken by the state (Scharpf 1997: 203).

Although government has recently taken to talking in terms of social partnership in relation to the governance of E&T, there is little substance to this. The main focus for such claims revolves around the Skills Alliance, established in 2003 to superintend the delivery of the government's new Skills Strategy (DfES/HMT/DTI/DWP 2003). This body, which covers the central government departments with an interest in skills, some delivery agencies, the Confederation of British Industry, the Small Business Council (but not any of the SSCs) and the Trades Union Congress (TUC), meets about four times a year to discuss and co-ordinate policy. It does not create policy itself, sets no budgets or targets and does not appear to be asked to approve new policy developments. It has little real power and represents social partnership in its weakest form. Moreover, the social partnership within the Skills Alliance is not replicated anywhere else in the system. None of the other bodies involved, such as the LSC, LLSCs, Regional Development Agencies (RDAs) and SSCs, could realistically be characterized as a social partnership organization.

As a result of this situation, trade unions have only very limited formal input into national policy deliberations. Nor are they able to exert much influence on firms' competitive strategies by extracting wages that block off low cost, low quality routes to competitive advantage in the way that their counterparts in northern Europe have often been able to (Streeck 1989).

The role of employers in helping design and manage the national E&T system is also limited. Although the notion of employer leadership in E&T has been a recurrent element in government rhetoric since the 1980s, it is unclear what influence employers actually can exert over policy. Most often, their expected role within the national system appears to be a subordinate, supportive one as recipients of public subsidy and delivery agents for an ever-growing list of schemes the government has designed for them (Huddleston *et al.* 2005).

In part, this situation reflects the dismantling of tripartite structures that afforded employer interests a formalized role in national policy formation. It also mirrors the structural problems that confront attempts at building up institutions that can concert, represent and mobilize employer interests around skills. Such attempts have taken place against the unhelpful backdrop of a de-regulated product and labour market and an atomized system of collective bargaining that deprives the UK of the type of relatively strong employer collectivities seen in other EU countries where national and sectoral level bargaining exists (Culpepper and Finegold 1999; Porter and Ketels 2003; Soskice 1993). In these circumstances the design and maintenance of employer institutions that can deliver the types of collective incentives to train, that Streeck suggests are a vital part of the underpinning infrastructure of an effective E&T system, are extremely difficult (Streeck 1989; Wood, 1999). UK-wide policies have tried to appeal to the enlightened self-interest of employers on an individual basis, without real acceptance of Streeck's argument that the sum of individual short–term interests on the part of employers may not add up to the long-term societal interest.

In the absence of attempts by employers themselves to create viable institutional frameworks, the state has stepped in but has undercut its own efforts by a short-termist, stop–go approach that has failed to allow institutions to mature. Thus, since the end of tripartism we have witnessed the creation of a succession of state-sponsored attempts to provide employers with a vehicle for participation (on the state's terms) in the governance and funding of E&T. These have included the TECs, the LSC (touted as being a vehicle for a strong employer voice when first established (Hook 2000)) and now the SSCs.

Unfortunately, the state has been unwilling to cede real power to any of these bodies. In 2002, in an internal document, the DfES noted that in terms of strengthening the department's relationship with employers:

> the key to real improvement will be early and sustained employer input to the strategic development of policy – and a recognition across the Department that

employers have an important role in shaping, not determining, the full range of DfES policy.

(DfES 2002: 4)

Despite the subsequent deployment of a language of employer engagement and employer leadership, the substantive reality of policy formation has yet to be transformed, with the state continuing to formulate and promulgate policy at a considerable level of detail without any meaningful prior input from employers or their representatives (DfES/DTI/HMT/DWP 2005).

Furthermore, most employer bodies have as yet proved unable to exert significant leverage over the training decisions of individual employers and instead have tended to become delivery agents for government schemes (Gospel and Foreman 2006). All hopes now appear to rest on the SSCs and their ability, via the creation of sector skills agreements (SSAs), to link the state's E&T expenditure with complementary efforts by employers to bring about significant upskilling.

The state is thus faced with the problem that both employers and, much less importantly, other actors within the E&T system are weak and cannot be depended upon to deliver the public policy goals it espouses. It has sought to disguise these difficulties through use of a rhetoric that has revolved around the concepts of employer leadership and partnership. As suggested above, to date employer leadership has been a fairly empty concept.

The primacy of E&T as a reflection of weakness

State intervention in and funding of E&T are also borne out of weakness, in that they act as substitutes for other measures that might impact on employers but that are deemed politically and ideologically unacceptable. The English state's long-standing commitment to free market neo-liberalism and relative de-regulationist tenets renders unavailable a host of potential policy interventions used in other countries – for example, training levies, strong trade unions and statutory rights to collective bargaining on skills, strong forms of social partnership arrangement, regulated labour and product markets (such as extensive licence to practise requirements) or an industrial policy that might favour higher skill sectors. In other words, the political space within which E&T policy can be constructed and manoeuvred is delineated by higher order decisions concerning labour market regulation and models of economic management.

This was neatly encapsulated in a survey of employers' current and future skill needs in Scotland, which also examined the relative importance of skills issues to employers vis-à-vis other challenges and pressures, such as changing market structures and growing competition within Scotland. The survey concluded: 'Skills are . . . a middle ranking challenge for Scotland's employers, but they are the highest ranking challenge over which the public sector could act' (Futureskills Scotland 2002:15).

E&T policy is thus largely subordinate to and determined by these prior choices

169

about what it is and is not legitimate for the government to intervene in. Because the state has ruled itself unwilling to exert direct leverage through regulation upon employers' skill demand and usage, it is forced to act as a substitute through skill supply initiatives (Keep 1999).

This situation produces a final paradox. On the one hand, choices in other, more dominant policy domains circumscribe the subordinate political space available for E&T policy. Because the range of policy moves is tightly bounded by ideological no-go zones that are absent in many other developed countries, English E&T policy-makers find themselves with very limited political space for policy development or experimentation. The labour market must remain highly de-regulated, and the firm has to be treated more or less as a 'black box'. This makes problematic attempts to secure change in competitive strategy, product or service specification, work organization and job design (Keep 2002). As the author and others have argued, such an approach is unlikely, on its own, to address deep-seated problems about the demand for and productive utilization of skills (Keep and Mayhew 1998; Keep and Mayhew 1999; Lloyd and Payne 2002; Wilson and Hogarth, 2003). Because policy is lopsided and can only address skill supply instead of skill demand and supply together, this in turn produces a situation where the skills 'problem' is not solved and further intervention is then deemed necessary.

Given this situation, over time the policy process has more or less consumed all the available options in this area. Policy development therefore tends to represent variations on previous themes and 'more of the same' – usually exhortation, the dissemination of examples of good practice, attempts to produce evidence that 'skills pay', and skills supply schemes of one sort or another.

On the other hand, the high level ideological constraints that bind E&T policy to a laissez faire approach with regard to regulating employers' behaviour, simultaneously invest E&T policy and activity generally with greater importance, since they render it one of the primary points for legitimate government intervention in the economic sphere. As the Prime Minister put it:

> This is simply the most important national purpose for us, in the first few years of the 21st century: to raise our education standards significantly . . . If we don't have a first-class well-educated workforce, then we can't compete. It is the single biggest driver of increased productivity. There is no way we can compete with low-wage economies in the developing world. But we can compete on the basis of skill and aptitude and knowledge. I don't personally believe we've yet really understood the importance of education. We're at the beginning of understanding it.
>
> (Blair, quoted in St John-Brooks 2000: 4)

Policy makers are often trapped by their own rhetorical devices. If skills are so important to the national interest, the state cannot afford to be seen to leave their delivery to others, particularly when some of these others, such as employers, appear unable or unwilling to deliver what it is alleged is required.

IDEOLOGICAL CONTINUITY

Given the foregoing, it is apparent that the main reason why the broad thrust of E&T policy under New Labour has exhibited many elements of continuity with the policy trajectory developed by previous Conservative administrations is because the underlying ideological assumptions have also remained constant. The main intellectual underpinnings have remained constant in the shape of de-contextualized forecasts of universal upwards trends in demand for skill and simple readings of human capital theory and market failure. The main change has been the willingness of New Labour to load additional social inclusion and social equity expectations onto E&T. Given limited development in the underlying directions of policy intervention, these have simply increased the need for the state to intervene to supply or subsidize what is required – witness Educational Maintenance Allowances (EMAs), the Employer Training Pilots (ETPs) and now the National Employer Training Programme (NETP).

PATH DEPENDENCY AND THE FUTURE

This chapter has argued that there exists a high degree of path dependency in the general conduct of E&T policy in England and that one of the key trends within this policy trajectory has been a growing dominance by the state (in the shape of central government) in the design, management, and funding of E&T. As suggested at the outset, the monolithic and heavily 'imprinted' nature of this meta-level policy discourse has to a large extent been disguised by the massive amount of government induced meso- and micro-level instability and change in ministerial personnel, institutional arrangements and programmes and by fluctuations in the need for E&T policy to address not just a skills agenda but also problems of unemployment (Lee *et al.* 1990; Jones 1999; Mansfield 2000; Rose 1991; Ryan 2005).

National policy is now locked into a cycle whereby the state finds it necessary to intervene frequently and in detail in order to secure its objectives and to safeguard the expected fruits of earlier rounds of intervention. The state's endless need to do more and more, and to intervene more heavily, coupled with its subsequent requirement to finance, manage and account for this activity, has produced strong stability in the underlying form and direction of E&T policy. This encompasses the process of state policy formation, the underlying dispensations of power and control, and the main thrusts of policy direction (see Coopers and Lybrand (1985) for the blueprint of most subsequent English E&T policy development).

In making these interventions the state is relatively untrammelled by any perceived need to involve other stakeholders in meaningful prior consultation about the shape or direction of the next wave of reform. The other 'partners', as the state terms them, are too weak to be of much moment in the generation of national policy.

In addition, although the range of E&T interventions is constrained by a series of long-held ideological positions about what forms of intervention are acceptable, the importance of E&T within economic and social policy has grown. Supplying more skill is one of the few things that government believes it can do to help ensure competitiveness and social justice. It is hard to envisage how the process of policy formation or its outputs can be disrupted or moved to embrace any new paradigm as long as these ideological underpinnings remain in place.

From state-led to employer-led: dream or delusion?

One of the very few forces that served to disrupt the smooth flow of policy since the 1980s was the Cabinet Office Performance and Innovation Unit's (PIU) project on workforce development. This made the case for moving towards an E&T system that was much more demand-led, with a stronger role for employers and a greater emphasis in state policy on seeking to stimulate the demand for skill rather than simply trying to increase the supply of qualified labour (Cabinet Office 2001, 2002). The PIU project generated the outlines for a radically different approach to policy and one that has, at least on the surface, been absorbed into the rhetoric of government policy pronouncements. The underlying ideological constraints, which forbid real social partnership, an industrial policy or significant regulation of the product or labour markets, nevertheless remain firmly in place.

The state thus now finds itself hankering after a shift whereby employers (and to a much lesser extent other partners like trade unions) will of their own volition do more to deliver public policy goals within a framework set by the state (DfES 2004; DfES/HMT/DTI/DWP 2003; DfES/DTI/HMT/DWP 2005). In the short term the government's hopes rest with the SSCs; with attempts to make the E&T system more responsive to employer demand; and with a programme of public subsidy for task-specific adult training (the NETP) which it is anticipated will bring about a 'once and for all change in the training market', act as a lever to enable the state to secure greater investment in training by employer themselves, and, through employers' decisions about spending this subsidy, make the E&T system more demand-led (DfES/DTI/HMT/DWP 2005; HM Treasury 2002: 15). In the longer term, the stress is on the work of SSCs and the development of business support services and regional economic strategies that can begin to shift the competitive strategies of more firms into higher value-added sectors that demand a more skilled and qualified workforce to deliver them.

The success of these moves depends, to some extent at least, on the willingness for the state to come to terms with what a more demand- and employer-led system might look like. Here the prognosis does not look particularly encouraging. As argued above, the government has made little real progress in consulting with or involving other stakeholders in the design of public policy developments. Nor has it shifted in its belief that it should act as the sole architect of the E&T system, directing the actions of the other stakeholders (DfES 2004: 102). However, as this chapter has indicated, unless and until the state manages to allow this, it finds itself trapped in a situation where it has to do more and more, leaving less and less opportunity or motive for others to play a more active role in the E&T system and develop their capacity to act as strong partners.

REFERENCES

Ainley, P. (2001) From a National System Locally Administered to a National System Nationally Administered: The New Leviathan in Education and Training in England, *Journal of Social Policy*, 30(3), 457–476.

Ainley, P. and Corney, M. (1990) *Training for the Future: The Rise and Fall of the Manpower Services Commission*, London: Cassell.

Ashton, D. and Keep, E. (2007) The State, in Keep, E., Mayhew, K., Payne, J., and Stasz, C. (eds), *Education, Skills and the Economy: The Politics of Vocational Education and Training*, Cheltenham: Edward Elgar.

Bash, L. and Coulby, D. (eds) (1989) *The Education Reform Act: Competition and Control*, London: Cassell.

Bassey, M. (2003) More Advocacy: Give Autonomy Back to Teachers, *BERA Newsletter*, no. 84, July, 26–30.

Blackstone, T., Cornford, J., Hewitt, P. and Miliband, D. (1992) *Next Left: An agenda for the 1990s*, London: Institute of Public Policy Research.

Cabinet Office (2001) *In Demand: Adult Skills in the 21st Century: Part 1*, London: Cabinet Office PIU.

Cabinet Office. (2002) *In Demand: Adult Skills in the 21st Century: Part 2*, London: Cabinet Office Strategy Unit.

Chapman, P. G. and Tooze, M. J. (1987) *The Youth Training Scheme in the United Kingdom*, Aldershot: Gower.

Coffield, F. (1992) Training and Enterprise Councils: The Last Throw of Voluntarism?, *Policy Studies*, 13(4), 11–51.

Coffield, F. (2002) *A New Strategy for Learning and Skills: Beyond 101 Initiatives*, Newcastle: University of Newcastle, Department of Education.

Coopers and Lybrand Associates (1985) *A Challenge to Complacency: Changing Attitudes to Training*, Sheffield: Manpower Services Commission/National Economic Development Office.

Culpepper, P. D. and Finegold, D. (eds) (1999) *The German Skills Machine, Sustaining Comparative Advantage in a Global Economy*, Oxford: Berghahn Books.

Department for Education and Skills (2002) Building a Stronger Relationship Between the Department and Employers, DfES Strategy and Innovation Unit Project Report, London: DfES (mimeo).

Department for Education and Skills (2004) *Department for Education and Skills: Five Year Strategy for Children and Learners*, Cm 6272, London: HMSO.

Department for Education and Skills/HM Treasury/Department for Trade and Industry/

Department for Work and Pensions (2003) *21st Century Skills – Realising Our Potential – Individuals, Employers, Nation,* Cm 5810, London: Stationery Office.

Department for Education and Skills/Department of Trade and Industry/HM Treasury/ Department for Work and Pensions (2005) *Skills: Getting on in Business, Getting on in Work,* Cm 6483, London: Stationery Office.

Evans, B. J. (1992) *The Politics of the Training Market: From Manpower Services Commission to Training and Enterprise Councils,* London: Routledge.

Fuller, A. and Unwin, L. (2003) Creating a 'Modern Apprenticeship': A Critique of the UK's Multi-sector, Social Inclusion Approach, *Journal of Education and Work,* 6(1), 5–15.

Futureskills Sotland (2002) *Skills in Scotland 2002: The Employers' View,* Glasgow: Futureskills Scotland.

Gamble, A. (1994) *The Free Economy and the Strong State,* London: Macmillan.

Gleeson, D. and Keep, E. (2004) Voice without Accountability: The Changing Relationship between Employers, the State and Education in England, *Oxford Review of Education,* 30(1), 37–63.

Glennerster, H., Power, A. and Travers, T. (1991) A New Era for Social Policy: A New Enlightenment or a New Leviathan?, *Journal of Social Policy,* 20(3), 389–414.

Gospel, H. and Foreman, J. (2006) Inter-firm Training Coordination in Britain, *British Journal of Industrial Relations,* 44(2), 191–214.

HM Treasury (2002) *Developing Workforce Skills: Piloting a New Approach,* London: HMT.

Hodgson, A. and Spours, K. (2003) *Beyond A Levels: Curriculum 2000 and the Reform of 14–19 Qualifications,* London: Kogan Page.

Hook, S. (2000) 'No Excuses' for Strong Business Voice, *Times Educational Supplement, FE Focus,* 17 November, 33.

House of Commons (2004) Uncorrected transcript of oral evidence taken before the Education and Skills Committee, Monday 17 May, Mr Bryan Sanderson and Mr Mark Haysom, London: House of Commons (available from: www.publications.parliament.uk/pa/cm200304/cmselect/cmeduski/uc197-xii/uc19702).

Huddleston, P., Keep, E. and Unwin, L. (2005) What Might the Tomlinson and White Paper Proposals Mean for Vocational Education and Work-based Learning?, *Nuffield Review Discussion Paper,* no. 33, Oxford: Oxford University, Department of Educational Studies, Nuffield 14–19 Review.

Jenkins, S. (1995) *Accountable to None,* London: Hamish Hamilton.

Jones, M. (1999) *New Institutional Spaces: TECs and the Remaking of Economic Governance,* Regional Policy and Development Series 20, London: Jessica Kingsley/ Regional Studies Association.

Keep, E. (1999) The UK's VET Policy and the 'Third Way': Following a High Skills Trajectory or Running up a Dead End Street?, *Journal of Education and Work,* 12(3), 323–346.

Keep, E. (2002) The English Vocational Education and Training Debate – Fragile 'Technologies' or Opening the 'Black Box': Two Competing Visions of Where we Go Next, *Journal of Education and Work,* 15(4), 457–479.

Keep, E. (2006) Market failure in skills, *SSDA Catalyst,* issue 1, Wath-upon-Dearne Sector Skills Development Agency.

Keep, E. and Mayhew, K. (1998) Was Ratner right? Product Market and Competitive Strategies and Their Link with Skills and Knowledge, *Employment Policy Institute Economic Report,* 12(3), 1–14.

Keep, E. and Mayhew, K. (1999) The Assessment: Knowledge, Skills and Competitiveness, *Oxford Review of Economic Policy*, 15(1), 1–15.

King, D. S. (1993) The Conservatives and Training Policy 1979–1992: From a Tripartite to a Neo-liberal Regime, *Policy Studies*, 41, 214–235.

Lee, D., Marsden, D., Rickman, P. and Duncombe, J. (1990) *Scheming for Youth: A Study of YTS in the Enterprise Culture*, Milton Keynes: Open University Press.

Lloyd, C. and Payne, J. (2002) On 'the Political Economy of Skill': Assessing the Possibilities for a Viable High Skills Project in the UK, *New Political Economy*, 7(3), 367–395.

Mansfield, R. (2000) Past Imperfect?, Harrogate: PRIME Research and Development Ltd (mimeo).

Porter, M. and Ketels, C. H. M. (2003) UK Competitiveness: Moving to the Next Stage, *DTI Economics Paper*, no. 3, London: Department of Trade and Industry.

Raggatt, P. and Williams, S. (1999) *Government, Markets and Vocational Qualifications: An Anatomy of Policy*, London: Falmer.

Rose, R. (1991) Too Much Reshuffling of the Cabinet Pack?, *Institute of Economic Affairs Inquiry*, no. 27, September, London: IEA.

Ryan, A. (2005) The DfES Seems to Be a Transit Lounge . . ., *Times Higher*, 20 May, 15.

St John-Brooks, C. (2000) Education Is Still My Number One Priority, *Times Educational Supplement*, 21 January, 4–5.

Scharpf, F. W. (1997) *Games Real Actors Play: Actor-centered Institutionalism in Policy Research*, Oxford: Westview Press.

Soskice, D. (1993) Social Skills from Mass Higher Education: Rethinking the Company-based Initial Training Paradigm, *Oxford Review of Economic Policy*, 9(3), 101–113.

Streeck, W. (1989) Skills and the Limits of Neo-liberalism: The Enterprise of the Future as a Place of Learning, *Work, Employment and Society*, 3(1), 89–104.

Unwin, L., Fuller, A., Turbin, J. and Young, M. (2004) What Determines the Impact of Vocational Qualifications? A Literature Review, *DfES Research Report*, no. 522, Nottingham: DfES.

Wilson, R. and Hogarth, T. (2003) *Tackling the Low Skills Equilibrium: A Review of Issues and Some New Evidence*, November, London: DTI.

Wolf, A. (1998) Politicians and Economic Panic, *History of Education*, 27(3), 219–234.

Wood, S. (1999) Education, Training and the Third Way, *SKOPE Policy Paper*, no. 1, Coventry: University of Warwick, SKOPE.

Chapter 13

New developments in continuing vocational education and training reform in France

Philippe Méhaut

(Translated by Janet Fraser)

The early 2000s have seen a transformation under way in France's system of continuing vocational education and training (*formation continue*). Legislation on accreditation of experiential learning (*validation des acquis de l'expérience*, known as *VAE*) was underpinned by a national collective agreement signed in September 2003 by employer and trade union representatives. Further legislation was passed to translate the key measures contained in this agreement into provisions in the French Labour Code, making them binding on all private sector enterprises, and they were then fleshed out at lower levels in sector- and company-level agreements (Méhaut 2005).

In most respects, this trend has followed the traditional process of 'negotiated agreement' on legislation in this area: as Luttringer (2004) points out, the French system of continuing vocational education and training incorporated this as long ago as 1970/71, and the process is central to the 'lifelong learning' initiatives prompted in particular by major international organizations and the European Union. It is also part of a wider trend in the reform of social and employment policy, which is often at odds with the logic of individual risk and individual development (Ramaux 2003).

The 2003 agreements and 2004 legislation also integrate earlier stages in thinking, such as the emergence of accreditation of prior experiential learning (introduced by legislation in 2002) or joint qualifications, introduced at sector level and concerning primarily the young unemployed and those undergoing continuing vocational education and training.

While these trends are in keeping with the 1970/71 framework (Géhin, this volume, Chapter 3), they have also, in certain respects, marked a potential departure from former ideas and practices, although it is still very difficult to assess their real impact. This chapter therefore aims to interpret the current reforms and to identify a number of hypotheses concerning the shifts that they may introduce into France's model of continuing vocational education and training. The first part will consider the general framework within which these reforms are taking place, particularly from the perspective of the debate about employment 'risk'. The chapter will then move on to an outline of the letter and spirit of the 2003 national agreement and the 2004 legislation and of the main institutional changes that preceded them. The third part of the chapter will analyse the shifts that the new framework has imposed on the concept of continuing vocational education and training, concluding with an outline of different scenarios for future development.

THE GENERAL CONTEXT

Notions of risk and emerging concepts of individual responsibility

The notion of risk was central to the design of some aspects of social protection in France, such as the risk of industrial injury. It is used extensively in other areas of social protection, for example in discussions of 'family risk' or 'pension risk'. Social security coverage through contributions made by employer and employee, which typifies the French system and is reproduced in its continuing vocational education and training system,[1] probably explains this, coupled with the concept of social insurance. Unemployment used to be the risk on which employment and vocational training discourse focused, but the term is now used increasingly to refer to a situation in which all employment is more precarious than in the past.

Beck, Ewald and Kessler: a generalized risk society?

The work of Beck (2001), along with that of Giddens, has had a major influence on thinking, especially among liberal employers who now stress the notion of a 'generalised risk society'. Kessler (2001), for example, was one of those whose ideas influenced the thinking of Medef (France's main employer organization, Mouvement des entreprises de France) and opened the negotiations on 'Refondation Sociale'[2] with his ideas on the growth of risk in modern societies. Like Beck, Kessler defines these risks extensively, including not only major collective risk (that is, risk from natural or environmental disaster etc.) and 'traditional' employment risk (industrial injury, sickness and retirement pensions, for example) but also 'new' risks (that is, unemployment and social exclusion). Risk has changed not only in nature but also in frequency (unemployment, for example). Kessler also hypothesizes both growing individual awareness of risk and greater individual risk aversion, suggesting that we will see individual behaviour becoming more prevention-oriented and more reliant on insurance and depending less on a welfare state that is itself in crisis. He argues that such behaviour becomes more evident the more 'endogenous' the risk is to the individual: for example, risky behaviour in health terms is generating a growing proportion of 'preventable' and, hence, insurable risk. Moreover, what is true for health will also, according to Kessler's analysis, apply in employment: the concept of employability is an individual attribute in the same way as unemployment is linked at least in part to individual behaviour. This makes it easier to allocate risk and cost between enterprise and individual. On this point, however, Kessler differs significantly from Beck, who prefers to see 'diffuse', multi-causal risk that is increasingly difficult to attribute to a single individual or organization.

This analysis prompted Kessler and Medef to challenge the principles of the French welfare state which, they argue, was built on risk categories that are now considered obsolete. They also challenge the decline of the family as a risk prevention institution and argue that the market is a modern – and stable – means of protection through the growth in private insurance schemes.

Transitional markets and social security at work

The debate has, however, also been influenced by other, very different, concepts of labour market development and industrial relations. What the majority of these concepts have in common is recognition of growing uncertainty on the labour market, potential growth in mobility and the greater risk of unemployment, even where the core workforce still appears to enjoy a high level of employment stability (Auer and Cases 2000; L'Horty 2004). They also recognize that individual lifestyles and expectations are changing, which in particular requires greater flexibility in allocating time to work, training and family.

The French system of social protection (and the continuing vocational education and training system in particular) is fundamentally unsuited to such transitions: there is a sharp distinction between initial and continuing vocational education and training, which restricts individuals' opportunities to engage in long-term continuing training; entitlement to continuing vocational education and training is based on permanent employment and is centred on the enterprise and hence dependent on the employer; and schemes are strictly demarcated between those in employment, the unemployed and other groups.

Supiot's (1999) work and that on 'transitional markets' (Schmidt and Gazier 2002; Gazier 2003) aim, therefore, to create a base of what might be described as 'drawing rights', specific to the individual and usable in any employment situation, including also unemployment, training or temporary withdrawal from the labour market. These rights would be both a safety net and a benefit, designed to cover individuals whatever transitions they may choose or have imposed upon them.

Such ideas are, for example, to be found in work done by the CGT (Confédération générale du travail) trade union confederation on proposals for a new vocational social security system (Le Duigou 2005). They were also evident between the lines of other texts from 2000 onwards (e.g. Thibault 2005), constituting alternatives to employers' analysis of risk and unquestionably influencing trade union negotiators when the 2003 agreement was being negotiated. They are reflected in the spirit of the legislation on accreditation of experiential learning.

THE LIMITS OF THE FORMER SYSTEM

At national level, negotiators and the government were faced with an old system that was largely exhausted and obsolete (Méhaut 1995, 2005; Géhin, this volume); indeed, a series of reports throughout the 1990s had underscored this time and time again (Gauron 2000; Pery 1999).

An initial level of 'internal' criticism focused on a number of aspects: the major inequality of access to continuing vocational education and training, in particular between enterprises of differing sizes and between sectors; the limited room for manoeuvre that individuals had, given that training policy was generally based on a virtually unilateral decision by the employer; the narrow concept of 'training', which was often limited to short-duration courses; and, finally, the short-term vision of such courses, which were usually aimed solely at equipping individuals to cope with the (changed) requirements of their post.

The second level, 'external' criticism, related to the fact that the system was ill-suited to an environment that was widely acknowledged to be changing. Access by employees to continuing vocational education and training was based on contributions by enterprises and relied on approval by the employer and, hence, was not reflecting the greater mobility that typified changing labour markets. The policies of individual enterprises were, moreover, unable to anticipate demographic trends, and so over the next few years, the French labour market is likely to have to confront a number of pinch-points, including increasing recruitment problems linked with major distortion of the supply of labour as large numbers of workers retire and smaller cohorts join the workforce. The working population is also ageing and tending to retire later, creating problems with outdated skills and requiring more active training policies for older workers (Fournier 2004). More broadly, frequent reference (even if controversial) to the 'knowledge society' assumes a growing need for both knowledge and skills and more efficient management of all types of skills acquisition (Méhaut 2005).

This was the backdrop against which the social partners embarked, in 2001, on a first round of (unsuccessful) negotiations and, in 2003, on a second, to produce a national agreement and legislation, which were then fleshed out at sector level to reflect individual circumstances. This was also the background to the legislation adopted in 2002 on accreditation of prior experiential learning.

THE NEW FRAMEWORK

Individual training entitlement

The individual training entitlement (Droit Individuel de Formation, DIF in French) is probably the 'beacon' provision and the most innovative aspect of the national agreement. Prior to this agreement, workers' main access to training was via the enterprise's training plan, which was adopted and financed by the employer with most courses taking place during working hours.[3] A further provision, for individual training leave, enabled individual workers to make applications for leave for a lengthy period of training during which their contract of employment was suspended on full or partial pay. Such individual leave, however, was used primarily for long-term training, often leading to academic qualifications, and related to only a tiny minority of workers (of the order of 20,000 a year).

After having experimented in their 2001 negotiations with individual 'training accounts', pots of cash funded by the employer, the social partners shifted their attention in 2003 to a different system that would, nevertheless, give all workers an individual right to training. This was for each individual to have an annual 'theoretical' DIF of 20 hours, with each year's entitlement capable of being carried over for up to five years. Workers are required to negotiate with their employer concerning their aims for training and the organization of courses, which must be aimed at improving their skills and not just at re-training them for their current job. Courses awarding formal qualifications are included, and employers pay fees and related expenses, such as travel. Courses may be attended during working time or in the employee's own time (or both), and where workers attend a course outside their normal hours of work, they are paid a lump sum of about 50 per cent of net pay. On completion of courses, enterprises must also reflect workers' new skills, for example by changing job specifications or offering promotion.

This innovation, combined with previous arrangements, is reshaping the boundary between enterprises' training plans (largely enterprises' own initiative) and individual training leave, which is, by contrast, at the initiative of the individual worker.

Contrats de professionnalisation and *périodes de professionnalisation*[4]

The national agreement provides for *contrats de professionnalisation* and *périodes de professionnalisation* to be set up. The former are contracts targeted primarily, and as a matter of priority, at young unskilled workers and/or the unemployed. They include periods of training either in or outside enterprises, for which the trainees receive payment based on a specific percentage of France's statutory minimum wage. The contracts also integrate, into a single system, existing arrangements for getting these groups into work. Combining employment and training, they are primarily a way of

180

giving training to the unemployed and untrained young people, to get them into employment.

The latter are more recent and target those workers 'threatened' by changes in their posts, such as those facing radical technological change, those whose posts are undergoing restructuring and older workers. Workers alternate between work and training and aim at a specific qualification at the end of the training period. Accreditation of prior experiential vocational learning can also form part of the arrangements. This is clearly a pre-emptive measure, designed to anticipate 'employment risk'. The operation of the scheme is subject to sector-level negotiation, which defines the categories of worker covered, and funding is provided by a collective insurance scheme run through mutual funds.

Broader responsibilities under law and collective agreement

Two key aspects of the 2003 agreement and the legislation helped standardize the regulatory framework. Pre-negotiation discussions had highlighted the extent of inequality of practice, particularly between enterprises of different sizes (Lichtenberger and Méhaut 2001). The structural differences between SMEs (small and medium-sized enterprises) and large enterprises are more marked in France than in other European countries (Géhin and Méhaut 1993), and one of the issues raised with the negotiators was the extent to which the gap could be narrowed. The two sides failed to agree, with employers raising particular objections, and so, when bargaining began in 2001, the organization representing SMEs in France, CGPME (Confédération Générale des Petites et Moyennes Entreprises), published the findings of a survey carried out among SMEs. Its commentary, whose title translates into English as 'Why change?', pointed to high levels of satisfaction with regard to the existing system, thereby highlighting a tension within the employers' side.

The 2003 agreement made two important changes in this area. The first was a significant increase in mandatory spending by enterprises with fewer than ten workers, which more than tripled[5] and helped narrow the gap between very small enterprises (VSEs) and SMEs without requiring the VSEs to contribute on the scale of enterprises with more than ten workers. This provision helped to maintain fair labour market competition at a level above that of the individual enterprise. There may be a question mark over the effectiveness of such a measure in terms of training policy: work on SMEs by Verdier (2001) and on VSEs by Bentabet, Michun and Trouvé (1999) highlights the extent to which mandatory contributions alone would help significantly to reshape training policies, particularly in conceptual and accounting frameworks that frequently differed radically. Nonetheless, the increase has been a major factor in reducing inequality.

The second was the DIF, an individual and standard entitlement for all workers, regardless of size of enterprise (although subject to some variation according to type of contract). A notional entitlement to 20 hours' training a year may make a big difference in small organizations that have previously offered little, if any training. (For comparison, in 2002, 7 per cent of workers in a VSE (10–20 workers) had access to training as against 50 per cent in enterprises with more than 2000 workers (CÉREQ 2004).

This broadening of the regulatory framework therefore has different implications, depending on whether the sector concerned has a high proportion of VSEs and SMEs and only rudimentary training policies or has a more developed approach to training.

Development of joint qualifications

Alongside what are known as 'public' qualifications, which are regulated and awarded by the state (although some may also be studied for in private institutions), France has seen a growing number of 'joint' qualifications, so called because they have been devised at sector level. These vocational qualifications, known in French as *certificats de qualification professionnelle* or CQPs (literally, 'vocational skills certificates'), are growing rapidly, although the numbers studying for them are still fairly low. They form part of a strategy devised by employers' organizations and trade unions to strengthen their influence on certificated learning in the vocational field. The CQPs target primarily young unemployed people who are engaged on schemes that combine training with employment and/or adults undergoing continuing vocational education and training. In the longer term, however, CQPs could constitute an alternative to some 'public' qualifications. They are administered jointly at sector level and are designed in some cases along similar lines to more traditional qualifications, identifying a target occupation and setting benchmarks for skills and training but often within a more specialized framework. CQPs can, therefore, be seen as a specialist 'top-up' to a traditional 'public' qualification, as a means of acquiring training in an area not covered by existing 'public' qualifications, or as a direct rival to such qualifications (Veneau *et al.* 1999). Jointly validated CQPs are considered to be directly equivalent to some traditional qualifications, and so the arrival of competition could in the long term cause a shift in the balance of France's system of qualifications, particularly as far as the links between initial training and continuing vocational education and training are concerned.

Accreditation of prior experiential learning

This further change marks a significant departure from the wholly training-based model of qualifications. It brings into a single framework existing but little-publicised provisions to offer any individual with substantial experience in their occupation or other social roles to apply to have this experiential learning validated towards a qualification. The applicant compiles a dossier that narrates and analyses his or her occupational experience and sets it alongside the benchmark skills of a traditional qualification; this serves as the basis on which a board decides to accredit part or all of his or her experiential learning towards that qualification. Teachers, trainers and training providers are, however, frequently reluctant to explore this option on the grounds that it marks a departure from traditional pedagogical principles and risks deterring trainees from undergoing traditional training and/or devaluing existing qualifications. In an attempt to force training providers to open up the scheme, therefore, any qualification its provider wants included in the national directory of qualifications[6] must include provision for such accreditation. Incentives to individuals are also included for the same reason, in particular under the new arrangements for DIF.

It is too early to assess how widely the change will be taken up, in terms both of supply and of demand, but initial indicators are that the number of workers taking advantage is growing, with almost 15,000 applicants for national qualifications – three times the numbers in 2001. Some 6,000 have so far obtained their full qualification (Ancel 2004). A number of large enterprises are setting up schemes within their training plans to encourage staff to take part, but most significantly, this system (known by its French abbreviation, VAE) marks a significant departure from the traditional French model of vocational education and training in that it acknowledges and puts on a formal footing the training potential of working situations and other social situations. To that extent, it forms part of the potential development of an entirely new model, although it also helps to strengthen the hegemony of the formal qualification. It may also be that a combination of DIF and VAE will strengthen access to award-bearing continuing vocational education and training. And in the long term, the success of VAE may well reduce the concentration in initial training on academic qualifications and help achieve better co-ordination between initial training and continuing education and training.[7]

IMPACT ON MODELS OF TRAINING?

The new provisions described above, along with other provisions in the various pieces of legislation, all point to the way the concept of continuing vocational education and training is changing and how it is orienting itself to the labour market. There is, of course, strong continuity, particularly in the use of the training levy and in the shared involvement of employers' organisations and trade unions, and the reforms described here form part of a series of incremental changes. Nevertheless, the changes also herald further reforms of both the institutional framework within which training takes place and its conceptual framework.

A broader concept of training and its relationship to occupational situations

The traditional shape of continuing vocational education and training in France has been that of training by means of short courses (in French, *stages*). In the 1970s, this was broadly in keeping with the model of initial training in which *stages* predominated and where there was no acknowledgement of the training value of situational learning. This has, however, gradually changed with the re-development of apprenticeships (see Géhin, this volume, Chapter 3) and with the increased frequency of schemes combining work and training. In continuing vocational education and training, however, French enterprises clearly privilege the *stage* (Nestler and Kailis 2002), particularly because of the need to justify their spending and hence to be able to account for clearly identified training hours.

The 2003 agreement between the social partners marked the acknowledgement of a multiplicity of training situations and environments. Alongside the *stage*, on-the-job training (in particular for *contrats de professionnalisation* and *périodes de professionnalisation*) and autonomous training (with or without e-learning technology) were recognized, supported by VAE schemes, which marked a major conceptual shift as experiential learning was recognized as being of equal value with other modes of learning. The greater diversity of training modes and, in particular, the new focus on work as a source of training gave a new complexion to a concept of knowledge acquisition that had previously been dominated by the academic model and based on formal transmission of knowledge.

Individualization and personalization

In the system that developed from the 1971 legislation, the main power and initiative, as well as the bulk of the costs, lay with the employer, despite the individual training leave provisions (which were not very extensive at the time). Enterprises' training plans were adopted on an individual basis and took the form of 'collective' management of training, centred on groups or categories of workers who were sent for training by the employer.

Against this backdrop, greater individualization was one of the major issues tacked in the new agreement in various guises, including the concept of the worker assuming individual responsibility for his or her own training (Maggi Germain 2004; Berton *et al.* 2004). This reflected the slow progress of ideas raised in previous discussions and agreements from the late 1980s, which had, albeit only in general terms, laid important foundations for shifts in the way training was considered and discussed. A number of themes emerge:

■ Lifelong learning needs to be integrated into changes in the employer/ employee relationship which, in turn, it helps to shape. This covers such aspects as the individualized management of careers and skills and development of a logic of 'contractualisation' with the employer by means of DIF and *contrats de professionnalisation* within the framework of collective regulation. Such 'contractualization' introduces 'autonomy in subjection' (Supiot 1999), primarily in the form of DIF, since time spent on DIF on the basis of a bilateral agreement and outside working hours is essentially not subject to normal employer controls (Favennec-Héry 2004) and relies on individual rights, enabling Maggi Germain (2004) to write of 'personalisation' of training rights. At a semantic level, the plan abandoned in 2001 had stressed in its preamble, the worker's own initiative in 'taking responsibility for his or her own vocational skills', citing the risk that skills could become obsolete and referring to workers as engaged in and, with employers, jointly responsible for their own vocational development. Some employer representatives who had also played a part in developing the competence model (Méhaut 2004) preferred, however, to talk about the worker 'constructing his or her own parachute to counter the risk of losing his job' (Ostermann 1999). Most of these terms had vanished by the time the 2003 agreement was signed in favour of more traditional notions of 'rights' and 'entitlements'. These 'rights' formed part of a situation in which occupations were subject to transitions, both within and outside the employment setting, that were framed around the notion of occupational planning. The new framework thus marked a partial departure from the former system and, with the model of internal labour markets, from employment security, 'jobs for life' and organizational careers.

- There is a need for some shift of emphasis in the notion of improvement of workers' knowledge and skills. DIF along with some aspects of the training plan could, under certain circumstances, be moved outside working time, with the worker concerned bearing part of the cost by sacrificing leisure time. This would mark a shift in the stance of the trade unions, who have traditionally emphasized the need for training to take place during working hours, but is consistent with the emphasis on giving the individual greater bargaining power: the concept of training taking place completely within working hours and completely at the cost of enterprise had, paradoxically, strengthened the employer's hegemony.

- The individual needs to be given the skills to move from notional rights to being able to manage actively the two aspects outlined above, including mandatory individual vocational guidance, employee information and involvement, skills profiling, training passports and so on.

- Finally, training packages need to be individualized and better adapted to the assumed needs of the individual rather than depending on standardized training courses.

A new concept of occupational mobility?

The 2003 agreement noted the changes under way both in work organization and in mobility and so emphasized the need for workers' career development. The very first article of the agreement stresses the need for workers to devise a career plan, which may be discussed with the employer and must be accompanied by a skills assessment and by careers guidance. It provides for an 'education and training passport' to be created and used as individuals choose. The passport summarizes the individual's education and training activities (both initial training and continuing education and training, certificated or uncertificated) as well as work experience and competences. It could include European Union proposals and could be used as the worker concerned moved around his own country or took up employment abroad.

Considering occupational mobility alongside VAE or skills management in some enterprises shows that the landscape of 'internal labour markets' is changing: there is less reliance on training levels with regard to entry into these markets and more stress on the accreditation of experiential learning and/or continuing vocational education and training in securing 'lifelong' mobility. The workplace is recognized as a training ground but there is also acknowledgement that such training has its place in the award of formal qualifications.

Shifting the balance between initial and continuing training?

France's training model differs from the Anglo-Saxon model and, to a lesser extent, from that adopted by countries with a 'dual' vocational training system: in France, there has traditionally been a sharp distinction between initial training and continuing education and training. Indeed, the terms differ to such an extent that the notion of 'lifelong learning' is often understood in France as relating almost exclusively to continuing vocational education and training. The role of the various players and the funding arrangements for the two sub-systems differ substantially. France has often been described as being dominated by initial training, by formal academic awards achieved early in life and by academic qualifications that regularly involve a long initial period of study. And indeed, the part played by continuing vocational education and training in acquiring such formal qualifications has seemed to be restricted, if not actually diminishing, alongside its significance in individuals' career paths (Beret *et al.* 1997). DIF opens up new scope for access to continuing vocational education and training that may be combined with VAE to signal the end of this separation. And although the broader theoretical scope for access to qualifications in continuing vocational education and training underlines the dominant role of the formal qualifica- tion in the French model, it also opens up the potential for continuity between these two forms of education and training. A stronger link between continuing education and training and individuals' careers, the new ways being developed by enterprises of managing their workforce and, in particular, skills management, all look set, then, to weaken the 'dictatorship' of formal initial training. Shifts in practice could then emerge if continuing vocational education and training take the form of real alternatives to initial training.

FUTURE SCENARIOS?

A distinction must be made between the short term and the medium or longer term. In the short term, it is highly likely that the reforms will have little impact because of the lead-time for their implementation at enterprise level and the time both workers and employers will take to adjust to and make use of the new system. Experience of the 1970 agreement and the 1971 legislation showed that it took around ten years for their provisions to change the environment.

Several medium- and/or longer-term scenarios are possible and may well differ from sector to sector or from economic area to economic area. The first scenario is that of 'absorption'. The changes contained in the 2003 national agreement, the 2004 legislation, VAE and sector-level agreements offer continuity with the existing framework, with social trends and with short-term interests, particularly where the procedures set down by agreement or by law are loose enough to be interpreted in a variety of ways. Employers are resisting DIF and VAE and/or are integrating them with their existing training policies. Educators and the training system are resisting VAE, which, they argue, is at odds with the French tradition of acquiring knowledge solely through formal means. Workers make few demands, either because of ignorance or because of fear. *Contrats de professionnalisation* are recreating the practices of the past, with a lack of targeting and a continued focus on long initial training programmes, which is in the interests both of some employers and of some training organizations. And, in a climate of continued high unemployment, *périodes de profesionnalisation* remain largely a dead letter, with enterprises still preferring to make some workers redundant and take on new ones, in some cases with the blessing of government agencies.

The second scenario is that of 'partial implementation', based on what happened after the 1971 agreement. Some sectors and some enterprises see it as being in their interests to draw on the resources generated by the new institutional framework, not least because these resources may sit comfortably alongside their own situation in terms of labour markets or human resource mangement. 'Controlled' individualization goes hand in hand with skills management, and the challenge of making the individual worker responsible for his or her own training is in line with new forms of work organisation. A proportion of the workforce (most probably those individuals who have the best initial training and are best integrated in skills-based organizations) make full use of the new system and individual initiative dovetails with the employer's interests, most frequently where 'internal labour markets' formerly dominated. Formal qualification by VAE becomes more important, including in internal mobility, but evolves in a very restricted way, constrained by the production framework and the structure of the workforce, and reproduces and/or intensifies the inequalities and limitations of the old system.

The third and final scenario is the 'leopard's spots' scenario, which builds on its predecessor (selective, patchy implementation in milieux already shaped to accommodate the new arrangements) but extends beyond its predecessor's boundaries. New milieux, including at international level, open up beyond the most active and institutionalized sectors as a result either of growing pressure on labour markets or of the growing demands of better-trained workers who expect their working conditions and pay to reflect their vocational development. Government intervention may enable these 'spots' to intensify or to extend, by making the new provisions more attractive to both the employer and the individual. The 'spots' are large enough to merge into a system and, through competition and/or imitation, to achieve necessarily circumscribed practice. This scenario represents development towards an occupational-type labour market model in which qualifications gained through initial or continuing education and training continue to play a key role, not only in initial entry to the labour market but also in individual careers. The balance between initial training and continuing education and training shifts in favour of continuing education and training, including in the strategies adopted by families and students. Internal labour markets, based on new principles, take on new life and the French model of education and training undergoes profound changes.

NOTES

1 The employer makes a mandatory contribution, based on payroll and may either use this for training or may pay it in to a mutual fund.

2 This was the title given to the negotiations initiated by employers with the aim of fundamentally reforming social protection.

3 In 2002, 34 per cent of all private-sector workers had access to an average of 30 hours' training.

4 Translator's note: *professionnalisation* in French has a much broader meaning than its obvious English translation, 'professionalisation' as it is not limited to 'the professions' but refers to the process of integrating a particular occupation or employment more generally. These terms will, therefore, be left in French after a brief explanation.

5 Initially (from 1971), mandatory spending on training covered only those enterprises with more than 10 workers. Those with fewer than 10 workers were subsequently required by law to pay but at a rate of 0.15 per cent of their payroll.

6 A national listing set up in 2002, when many countries took similar action.

7 One of the proposals made by the social partners but not yet translated into law was to use public funds to strengthen DIF for those workers who had not reached a minimum level of initial training. See also the chapters on Germany and the United Kingdom in this volume.

REFERENCES

Ancel, F. (2004) La VAE au sein du ministère chargé de l'emploi en 2003, Une rapide montée en charge, Ministry of labour, *Premières synthèses*, 41.1, 1–6.

Auer, P. and Cases, S. (2000) L'emploi durable persiste dans les pays industrialisés, *International Labour review*, 139, 4, 379–408.

Beck, U. (2001) L*a société du risque, Sur la voie d'une autre modernité*, Paris: Aubier.

Bentabet, E., Michun, S. and Trouvé P. (1999) *Gestion des hommes et formation dans les très petites entreprises*, Collection des Etudes, 72, Marseille: Céreq.

Beret, P., Daune-Richard, A.M., Dupray, A. and Verdier, E., (1997) *Valorisation de l'investissement formation sur les marchés du travail français et allemand*, Rapport pour le commissariat au plan, Aix en Provence: LEST-CNRS.

Berton, F., Coreia, M., Lespessailles, C. and Maillebouis, M. (eds) (2004) *Initiative Individuelle et Formation*, Paris: L'harmattan.

CEREQ (2004) La formation professionnelle continue financée par les entreprises, www.cereq.fr

Favennec-Héry, F. (2004) Temps de formation, temps de travail, quelques observations, *Droit Social*, 5, 494–498.

Fournier, C. (2004) Aux origines de l'inégale appétence des salariés pour la formation *BREF-Cereq*, 209, June, 1–4.

Fournier, C., Lambert, M. and Perez, C. (2002) *Les Français et la formation continue, statistiques sur la diversité des pratiques*, Documents, 169, Série Observatoire, novembre, Marseille: Céreq.

Gauron, A. (2000) *Formation tout au long de la vie*, Rapport du Conseil d'Analyse Economique, Paris: La Documentation Française.

Gazier, B. (2003) '*Tous Sublimes'*, vers un nouveau plein emploi, Paris: Flammarion.

Géhin, J.P. and Méhaut, P. (1993) *Apprentissage ou formation continue? Stratégies éducatives des entreprises en France et en Allemagne*, Paris: L'harmattan.

Kessler, D. (2001) L*'avenir de la social protection*, Paris: Medef.

Le Duigou, J. C. (2005) La sécurité sociale professionnelle: une utopie réaliste, *Analyses et documents économiques*, 98, February, 44–49.

L'Horty, Y. (2004) Instabilité de l'emploi: quelles ruptures de tendance? *Les papiers du Cerc*, 2004–01, 1–34.

Lichtenberger, Y. and Méhaut, P. (2001) Les enjeux de la refonte de la formation professionnelle continue – bilan pour un futur, *Liaisons sociales*, March, 1–21.

Luttringer, J. M. (2004) Formation professionnelle tout au long de la vie et négociation sociale, *Droit social*, 2, May, 472–481.

Maggi Germain, N. (2004) La formation professionnelle continue entre individualisation et personnalisation des droits des salariés, Ministry of Labour, paper presented at symposium on trends in continuing vocational education and training.

Méhaut, P. (1995) The French system of training levies and the dynamics of the wage earning relationship. *International Contribution to Labour Studies*, supplement of *Cambridge Economic Journal*, 115–130.

Méhaut, P. (2004) Competencies based management: what consequences for the labour market? *Economia e Lavoro*, 38, 1, 165–180.

Méhaut, P. (2005) Reforming the training system in France, *Industrial Relations Journal*, 36, 4, July, 303–317.

Nestler, K. and Kailis E. (2002) Formation professionnelle continue en entreprise dans l'Union européenne et en Norvège, Eurostat, *Statistiques en bref*, 3, 1–8.

Osterman, P. (1999) *Securing prosperity*, New Jersey: Princeton University Press.

Pery, N. (1999) *La formation professionnelle, diagnostics, défis et enjeux*, Secrétariat d'état aux droits des femmes et à la formation professionnelle, Paris: La Documentation Française.

Ramaux, C. (2003) Comment penser l'état social au-delà du risque et des assurances sociales? Contribution to the Forum de la régulation, Paris, October.

Schmidt, G. and Gazier, B. (eds) (2002) *The dynamics of full employment. Social integration through transitional labour markets*, Cheltenham: Edward Elgar.

Supiot, A. (1999) *Au-delà de l'emploi, transformation du travail et devenir du droit du travail en Europe*, Paris: Flammarion.

Thibault B. (2005) Compétence(s), une notion controversée en quête de « requalification », *Analyses et documents économiques*, 98, February, 61–65.

Veneau P, Charraud, A.M. and Personnaz E. (1999) Les certificats de qualification professionnelle concurrencent-ils les diplômes? *Formation Emploi*, 65, 5–21.

Verdier E. (2001) La France a-t-elle changé de régime d'éducation et de formation? *Formation Emploi*, 76, 11–34.

Chapter 14

Workers' education in the twentieth-century British labour movement

Class, union and role

John Holford

INTRODUCTION

For most of the twentieth century, 'workers' education' was widely considered rather different from vocational education or training. In her doctoral thesis – probably the first on the topic – Margaret Hodgen explained why. 'As a man and a bread-winner,' she wrote, 'the worker seeks knowledge in order to . . . improve his earning power' (Hodgen 1925: 4). The vehicle for this was vocational training; in a few cases, it might enable a worker-student 'to emerge from the constraints of working-class existence'. But it was 'fundamentally different' from workers' education:

> As a unit in a group effort for more complete participation in the common life, the working-man . . . has been frankly sectarian. He has sought information as a member of a social class, a voter or a trade union official . . . [W]orking-men enrolled as students in the [workers' education] movement are committed to some programme of class action, for which special knowledge and a peculiar technique are necessary. In other words, Workers' Education . . . is a discipline for a specific purpose. It concerns itself in teaching the social sciences to men and women who seek to use that knowledge for class, and possibly social, advancement.
>
> (Hodgen 1925: 4–5)

Although always modest in scale – when compared with vocational education, or general adult education, for example – workers' education became widespread and important as labour and trade union movements developed through the twentieth century (Hopkins 1985). The central argument here is that workers' education may be considered as a form of vocational education, where the vocation is inherent in commitment to furthering the collective 'sectarian', class purpose.[1]

WORKING-CLASS EDUCATION AND STATE CONTROL

The terms of debate in British workers' education were defined by an organizational and ideological bifurcation. This underpinned an often vitriolic dispute, whose echoes could be heard as late as the 1980s. The main opposing parties were the Workers' Educational Association (WEA) and the National Council of Labour Colleges (NCLC), though around each spread a network of institutions, some lasting, some transient. The dispute originated during the first decade of the twentieth century; its kernel can be seen in two events in Oxford.

The first was pressure for universities to meet the needs of working people. Founded in 1903 by trade unionists and co-operators, the WEA grew apace, gathering some influential supporters. In response to one of these, R.H. Tawney, and students from his Rochdale WEA class, the University promoted a conference with the WEA in the University's Examination Schools in 1907 (Jennings 1987). At it, John Mactavish, a leading Portsmouth trade unionist and prospective Labour parliamentary candidate, made an impassioned, celebrated and influential speech:

> I am not here as a suppliant for my class. I decline to sit at the rich man's table praying for crumbs. I claim it as a right – wrongfully withheld – wrong not only to us but to Oxford. What is the true function of a University? Is it to obtain the nation's best men, or to sell its gifts to the rich? Instead of recruiting her students from the widest possible area, she has restricted her area of selection to the fortunate few . . . We want workpeople to come to Oxford [and] . . . to come back as missionaries . . . We want her [Oxford] to inspire them not with the idea of getting on, but with the idea of social service.
>
> (Quoted Mooney 1979: 13–14)

This view was common not only to those who built the early Workers' Educational Association (e.g., Jennings 1973: 12–14; Jennings 1976, esp. 5–12; Stocks 1953, esp. 19–36), but also to the founders and many early staff and students of Ruskin College (Fieldhouse 1987; Pollins 1984).

The second was the strike at Ruskin College. To Ruskin's more radical students, one outcome of the 1907 conference – the University's 1908 report, *Oxford and Working Class Education* – seemed 'a bare faced attempt to seize control of the education of working men in the interests of the governing class' (Millar 1979: 6). Founded in 1899 by American philanthropists, Ruskin sought trades union and co-operative movement students, but staff and students had widely divergent conceptions of the function of a 'Labour College'. Dennis Hird, for instance, the first principal, a committed socialist and member of the (Marxist) Social Democratic Federation, wanted the college to provide teaching from a socialist viewpoint, and its students to take leading roles in the struggle against capital. To his deputy, on the other hand, the college was not Socialist: 'All the teaching is carefully impartial, and all its tutors are not socialists' (quoted Griggs 1983: 179). Personal attitudes matched the political. One tutor (and later principal) famously recorded that when first appointed he 'was completely ignorant of Trade Unionism . . . had never read a line of Marx . . . knew very little of the Socialist writers . . . [and] had hardly ever spoken to a working man except gardeners, coachmen, and gamekeepers' (quoted Millar 1979: 9).

More 'traditionalist' staff wanted Ruskin to be respected by the academic establishment. After Labour's advances at the 1906 General Election, the University began to show interest (Pollins 1984: 20–21). Some students began to study for University diplomas. But in 1907 friction arose between students and staff. When students applied for exemption from non-socialist tutors' lectures, they were made compulsory. To these militantly socialist students, the working class should 'independently manage our own educational affairs' just as it had its own unions, party and co-operative movement (*Plebs* 1909: 27, quoted Millar 1979: 8).

The striking students spread the dispute. They formed a rival Central Labour College (CLC); several major unions switched allegiance. Rippling out across the country over the next two decades, two traditions evolved, divided above all by whether workers' education should be funded by the capitalist state. On the one hand, the labour colleges adopted a simple Marxist view: the state was an instrument of the ruling class. On the other, the WEA and Ruskin College adopted a liberal notion of education and were broadly reformist in politics: they saw the state as having a positive duty to finance working-class education (a view endorsed by the 1919 Ministry of Reconstruction report (Cmd 321 1919)). For the labour colleges, the WEA's belief in objectivity and impartiality made it (at best) a dupe of the capitalists: as John Maclean (1978: 125) wrote during the industrial unrest of 1917, 'big attempts will be forthcoming to use the WEA to muddle the minds of the workers'. For the WEA, the labour collegers – blinded by dogma – could neither see the complexity of truth nor distinguish between education and propaganda. This bitter dispute echoed through the twentieth century, underpinning the identities and loyalties of individuals and even, at times, whole trade unions.

POLITICS AND THE TRADES UNIONS

While there was justice in the labour colleges' claim that, in taking money from the state, the WEA compromised its independence (Fieldhouse 1985; 1990), they oversimplified. In practice, engagement with the state involved levels of autonomy, and provided areas of relative autonomy – spaces for worthwhile workers' education. Educators, initially in the WEA, later in the Trades Union Congress (TUC) and elsewhere, explored these spaces: there were problems, but much was achieved (Holford 1994). And to the extent that the labour college critique was a Marxist one, it oversimplified. The labour colleges had their own paymasters – affiliated trade unions – and from the 1920s these drew the colleges away from their revolutionary roots.

Modern workers' education was formed during the first two decades of the twentieth century: a period of unrest when not only the Labour and Communist parties, but the modern trade union movement, were also formed. Workers' education was part of the fabric of the developing labour movement; its trends and disputes mirrored arguments on the left between various strands of Marxism and Labourism. Many across the labour movement saw 'little distinction between the political and the industrial'; workers' education had an 'intimate' relationship with the trade unions, but was not dependent upon them (McIlroy and Spencer 1989: 36).

Social movements of the poor, as Hobsbawm (1984: 293) has observed, 'become a subject rather than an object of history' only through organization. From about 1920, workers' education – like the labour movement in general – embarked on a period of institution-building: 'movement gave way to organisation'. During two decades of 'consolidation and institutionalisation' (McIlroy and Spencer 1989: 36–37), the WEA established the Workers Educational Trade Union Committee (WETUC) to strengthen its trade union links. The network of local labour colleges accepted the need for national co-ordination: the National Council of Labour Colleges was formed in 1922. On the Ruskin model, Newbattle and Coleg Harlech were established as Scottish and Welsh workers' residential colleges.[2]

Despite these new formations – which in no way diminished the bitterness of the great dispute – the central reality for workers' education by the mid-1920s was the growing dominance of the trade unions. 'Whatever may be said . . . in favour of one side of the controversy or the other is not of great importance. The future of Workers' Education belongs to the unions, and the unions are beginning to realize it' (Hodgen 1925: 151). Although the TUC burnt its educational fingers in the 1920s, with the failure of the Easton Lodge scheme (Holford 1994: 31–32), and few trade unions established significant programmes of their own until after 1945, both the TUC and trade unions took an increasingly dominant role in the direction of workers' education.

THE CURRICULUM IN WORKERS' EDUCATION BETWEEN THE WARS

In theory, the dispute over state finance was about the nature of the workers' educational curriculum. State finance implied state control of what was taught; and *ex hypothesi* the state would seek to limit what was taught. In its classic *Final Report*, the Ministry of Reconstruction's Adult Education Committee argued strongly that the state should not seek control:

The State should not, in our opinion, refuse financial support to institutions, colleges and classes, merely on the ground that they have a particular 'atmosphere' or appeal specially to students of this type or that. All that it ought to ask is that they be concerned with serious study . . . [T]he State ought to be willing to help all serious educational work, including the educational work of institutions and organisations which are recruited predominantly from students with, say, a particular religious or political philosophy.

(Cmd 321 1919: 118)

This cut no ice with the labour colleges; with some justification (Fieldhouse 1985). Behind the scenes, the President of the Board of Education was arguing for funding of the WEA as 'about the best police expenditure we could indulge in' (Lord Eustace Percy, quoted Fieldhouse 1987: 46). Yet there is considerable evidence that, despite their ideological differences, often biliously expressed, what inter-war trade union students studied in WEA and labour college classes was remarkably similar (Holford 1994: ch. 3). According to Hodgen, although workers' education 'often' included education in the 'cultural branches', it had

> always included the study of economics, politics and the technique of trade union administration. For a trade union has three functions for which officials and rank and file desire preparation. First, it is a business organization. Its officers are called upon to carry on the complicated work of selling labour to employers; to obtain through organization and legislation an approach to equality of bargaining power. Filing systems and card catalogues must be installed. Correspondence must be carried on. Trade agreements must be drawn up, trends of industry followed, and the internal business organization of a union kept in smooth running order. Second, a trade union functions as a fighting body. It undertakes strikes and boycotts. The strategy of industrial conflict is developed by its leaders. The trade union is finally a unit in the larger scheme of politics. Its officers, experts, and members desire not only to play a part in the regulation of local, state, and national affairs, but are themselves chosen by election. For union and interunion relationships are regulated according to the forms of political democracy.
>
> (Hodgen 1925: 4–5)

While organization is essential for social movements of the poor, it is of course a mixed blessing. Early twentieth-century syndicalists – and there were many in the early labour colleges – developed a strong critique along these lines (Holton 1976). Inevitably, as the organizations of the trade union and the labour movement developed, they looked for what workers' education could offer them. In the labour colleges and the WEA between about 1900 and 1925 a curriculum oriented to the political development of local leaders – economics, politics, history – was seen as highly relevant to the movement, and in step with organizations' goals. But from the mid-1920s, the labour movement became more precise about its objectives and functions. Unions especially – members as well as officials – sought classes which would improve their effectiveness in the business of trade unionism. This implied, in Hodgen's terms, a shift away from the 'cultural branches', and even to some extent from economics and politics, in favour of techniques of trade union administration. This was a shift, rather than a radical disjuncture; and strongly resisted by many – especially in the WEA – for whom the three-year academic evening tutorial class was a 'gold standard' of quality (Corfield 1969: 65–67). But it was real.

FROM MOVEMENT TO ORGANIZATION

To achieve their goals, social movements must organize; it is now a commonplace that organizations comprise – as Tom Burns put it – a 'plurality of social systems' (Burns 1969). Their original goals are typically displaced to some degree as organizations and those who work within them develop or express their own practices and routines. During the first half of the twentieth century the British labour movement insti-tutionalized. In part this meant the growth of 'union bureaucracy': salaried, full-time officials, responsible for processing business, recruitment, and increasingly – at least until the 1980s – negotiation and collective bargaining. In part it meant lay officials – branch officers, and increasingly shop stewards, developing and generalizing forms of doing business: procedures for debating policy, relating to members, ways of handling membership 'dues' and other income, structures and systems of collective bargaining, and so forth. Though it was no straightforward process – with periods of decline as well as growth – by the 1950s the labour movement was in many senses institutionalized (Bauman 1972).

Workers' education was, inevitably, part of this process. On the one hand, its own institutionalization from the 1920s contributed to the growth of specialized agencies of the movement. Many of its classes – as Hodgen's description above indicates – played a part in establishing institutionalized modes of behaviour. This was the era of such works as *The Labour Chairman*, and *ABC of Chairmanship* (Citrine 1921, 1939); WETUC and Labour College courses along similar lines were popular. Between the wars, for instance, the Edinburgh Labour College offered 'Chairmanship of Meet-ings', 'Debating', 'Business Meeting Routine' (Holford 1994: 45). On the other hand, as trade unions become more institutionalized, they found themselves needing to relate to 'members' almost as an externalized 'other'. For many purposes, members were unions' *raison d'être*; and of course, they were the ultimate source of power in any confrontation with employers. Workers' education became by and large education for an elite of the movement – not members in general, but active members, many of whom held, or intended to take up, a position of responsibility in their union (or some other labour movement body); and part of its function was to help those active members provide the bonding which would link members in general to union and movement goals.

Viewed from the perspective of building effective trade union organization, the product of workers' educators' undoubted energy and enthusiasm was modest. Some 60,000 trade unionists – at most – attended some kind of class offered by the NCLC, WEA or WETUC in 1937/38. An unknown number of these were 'double-counted', having attended more than one event; some 20,000 are a (probably generous) esti- mate of WEA students who were trade unionists. Yet there were over 6 million trade union members in 1938, of who over 4.6 million were in TUC-affiliated unions. The classes too varied greatly in duration (some were very short), teaching approach, quality and subject-matter.[3]

During the 1940s, workers' educational organizations and unions rethought their positions. Initially, the WEA sought to 'train adults for democratic leadership' and 'equip the workers themselves to participate in social and political organisations' in a new social order (WEA 1942: 36); it also introduced some novel approaches (Holford 2003). The labour colleges, too, saw the need to shift from 'fostering an anti-capitalist viewpoint' to 'providing a training necessary to the intelligent grappling of the vast and complex problems confronting this country and the world' (quoted Millar 1979: 132). By the late 1940s, however, this was plainly not working: the numbers of trade union students joining WETUC and NCLC classes remained fairly static through the 1950s (Corfield 1969: 249; Millar 1979: 267), while the WEA – to its dismay – was increasingly a vehicle for 'cultural' adult education for middle-class students.

WORKERS' EDUCATION AND APATHY IN THE WELFARE STATE[4]

From 1945 onward the TUC, and a number of individual unions, began to develop their own training programmes. Over the following decades the TUC was to establish a dominant role in trade union education. In the early 1960s both NCLC and WETUC agreed to a transfer of their undertakings to a new TUC Regional Education Service.[5] Although the WEA remained a very substantial provider of adult education in general, and continued to provide trade union courses, it did so largely as a junior partner of the TUC and various unions. Paradoxically, however, it was the WEA which developed the most visionary educational statement, in the Report of its Working Party on Trade Union Education (WEA 1953).

The wartime WEA leadership, keen to strengthen democracy and establish the conditions for a new social order, had found trade unions wanting. The problem, they thought, was 'apathy'. The trade union movement,

like all voluntary movements . . . has its inactive members and its apathetic mass. Its problem, like that of all working class voluntary movements, is to inspire the mass of its membership with a sense of social responsibility.

(WETUC 1944: 4)

197

In unions 'the bulk of the members have no deep sense of loyalty to the organization of which they are members', were 'often ignorant of its fundamental purpose' and 'took no active part in its administration' (Roper 1942: 28). But many thought educational work in the armed forces, civil defence groups and factories, showed the way forward. Working with challenging students – most had left school at 14, and had no previous contact with adult education – they found that classes 'based on occupational groupings', and held in the workplace, could take advantage of an established 'group-consciousness . . . among the students'. In addition, the war provided a 'common focus of interest' and an 'obvious starting point for discussion', so that courses could 'turn upon problems directly relating to the war – its background, causes and issues' (Hodgkin 1941: 143).

By the early 1950s, 'apathy' was again seen as a problem – both for adult and workers' education and for the trade unions. The war no longer provided a common focus of interest, but the new welfare state could. The Working Party recommended an approach which would 'build on the immediate interests and experience of students', moving 'from the particular to the general by starting from common experience' and 'in mutual discussion gradually . . . lay bare the conflicts of motive and principle and the obstinate material factors which are involved in a problem' (WEA 1953: 58). There should be 'active participation'; a group had to 'find its own way, in good measure'. 'Frank expression of opinion and mutual and constructive discussion' were vital (WEA 1953: 63).[6]

The Report's organizational proposals were modest – that the WEA establish a few pilot schemes and a union education bureau (WEA 1953: 79–82) – and had little practical impact. But philosophically it struck at the heart of traditional, rather academic, assumptions about workers' education shared in various forms by the WEA, universities and labour colleges: classes were open to all; the tutor lectured; students listened politely, and perhaps took notes, for an hour or so; then came questions and debate. The Report' authors saw education as linked to trade union students' specific organizational functions; and learning as active, situated, participative and student-led. This approach lent a theoretical basis to the new wave of workers' education, as the TUC and various unions began – initially on a small scale, but growing through the 1950s – to offer their own 'practical' courses for 'officers and active members' (TUC General Council report 1949, quoted Holford 1994: 59).

THE TUC PREDOMINANT

With the TUC's formation of a new regional education service in 1964, the trade unions at last assumed a predominant role – belatedly fulfilling Hodgen's prediction of forty years earlier. Workers' education became for most purposes synonymous with trade union education.[7] For the trade union movement, this meant developing a co-ordinated strategy for the first time. George Woodcock, the TUC's general secretary, announced that 'when we move into this field we must move in with TUC traditions and TUC characteristics' (quoted Holford 1994: 73); and the TUC education service rapidly cast aside some of its predecessors' most cherished traditions. Within five years, lectures to union branch meetings – which provided 56,493 'students' for the NCLC in 1962 – stopped. WETUC and NCLC had, between them, provided 1,134 evening classes in 1962, chiefly on political and economic topics; in 1968/69 the TUC offered only 120. Postal course enrolments fell by two-thirds, and day- and weekend-schools by 40 per cent over the same period. Both NCLC and WETUC had taught their own courses: the TUC now did so in partnership not only with the WEA, but with universities and increasingly with technical colleges. For the NCLC in particular, with its entrenched suspicion of engaging with the capitalist state, this was kicking over the traces.

What lay behind these changes was an emerging – perhaps more ambitious, certainly more single-minded – perspective on what trade unions required from education or training. The aim should be to strengthen trade unions' capacity to represent their members effectively in the workplace. The background to this lay in the industrial politics of the mid-twentieth century, with the rising importance of workplace union organization and the shop steward.[8] More training was required so that shop stewards could obtain 'a broader understanding of their functions and responsibilities' (TUC 1963: 190). This 1963 joint statement with the British Employers' Confederation (BEC) (a forerunner of the Confederation of British Industry) also encouraged BEC members to work with 'employers, unions and educational organisations' to provide more courses 'of an appropriate nature, for attendance at which stewards might be released with pay' (TUC Annual Report 1963: 192).

These two features – training shop stewards in their capacity as union officers, and doing so in employers' time – underpinned TUC educational strategy for the succeeding decades. A legal right to paid time off work for union representatives was secured under the Employment Protection Act 1975; rights to time off for union safety representatives followed. National programmes of courses were required to meet union needs, but unions could not (or would not) finance them. Some employers might contribute to the costs of training 'their' shop stewards, but myriad negotiations, varying and perhaps conflicting agreements, and constant local battles over what was taught was no recipe for a national programme. In 1968 the TUC had come to the conclusion that unions, management and government had 'a common interest in getting a union workplace representative who knows his job' (TUC 1968a: 11), and the General Council sought 'additional public funds' for colleges and the WEA so they could employ more 'full-time tutors qualified to teach in courses of trade union education and training' (TUC 1968b: 232). Six years later the TUC sought direct state support for trade union education from the Labour government in 1974, and under the Labour government (1974–1979) an annual grant of around £1.5 million was made to the TUC. To the surprise of many, this continued – though at declining levels – after 1979. Biting the bullet of public funding meant overturning a deep-rooted labour college principle, but without it growth would have been difficult.

It also implied risks: principally, that government, employers, colleges and tutors would try to dilute union aims. From 1967 the TUC identified a solution: 'standard-ised regional courses' (Holford 1994: 82). Over the following years, beginning with the regional network of educational organizers taken over from the NCLC, the TUC negotiated to ensure facilities – teachers, accommodation, libraries and so forth – were available in providing colleges; ensured that courses were taught by a *cadre* of capable, qualified and sympathetic tutors; and developed curricula. By the late 1970s a Course Development Unit, established at Congress House, was generating packages of learning materials for a spectrum of courses (Holford 1994: 160–182). All this was achieved through a complex series of negotiations involving the government, local education authorities, colleges, universities, WEA districts, employers' organizations and individual employers, tutors and union officers, among many others (Holford 1994: chs. 4 and 5). In the era of incomes policy, the TUC had a difficult course to steer: workplace trade unionism and the role of the shop steward were subject to political turbulence from the 1960s to the 1980s – the Donovan Commission and *In Place of Strife*, the Industrial Relations Act and the Commission on Industrial Relations, the Social Contract and Thatcherism. Through the 1980s, disputes with government showed the labour colleges had a point: now they paid the piper, government tried to call a few tunes (Holford 1994: esp. 170–171, 215–228).

Overall, however, TUC education not only implemented a large national pro-gramme of training courses for shop stewards and (from the 1970s) safety representa-tives, but – by and large – protected this from attempts (especially after 1979) by government and employers to 'share' control. The centrepiece of TUC education was a programme of 10-day courses (typically spread over 10 weeks) at which union workplace representatives worked in small groups using an 'active approach' (Holford 1994: 178–9), guided by a tutor. At its peak in 1978–1979, over 40,000 representa-tives attended these courses; this was impossible to sustain as union membership haemorrhaged through the 1980s, but as late as 1991–1992 the figure remained over 14,000 (Holford 1994: 268–269). The 1990s proved a difficult period, especially after the Conservative government put an end to public funding in 1992[9]; but an enrolment of 14,000 was again achieved in 2004 (TUC 2005).

ROLE EDUCATION: UNION ORGANIZATION AS VOCATION

During the 1950s and 1960s, influenced by the WEA's 1953 report, several university extra-mural departments (whose contribution to post-war workers' education is understated in the above synopsis) developed a notion of 'role education': 'education providing a broad background of knowledge relevant to the performing of specific roles' (University of Oxford 1970: 30). This perspective can be contrasted with the 'Industrial Studies' approach preferred by a number of other university extra-mural tutors. Broadly speaking, role education grew in a close relationship with the nascent 'discipline' of industrial relations, as developed by the 'Oxford school' of industrial relations in which Hugh Clegg and Alan Marsh were prominent. Industrial studies was closer to the extra-mural departments' roots in 'liberal adult education': they were wedded to a curriculum of history, politics and social studies more broadly (Holford 1994: 161–4).

There were many differences between the Oxford school's perspective and the TUC's shop steward education – such as the length and depth of study, and how far divergent union and employer interests required shop stewards and managers to study separately.[10] Nevertheless, the notion that education could focus on a role, and that a curriculum could legitimately be developed based on matters relating to the conduct of that role, was central to union education as developed by the TUC during the second half of the twentieth century.

Education for the effective conduct of a social or occupational role seems, of course, remarkably similar to vocational education. For some, the essential difference is that the worker undertakes vocational education in relation to a role for which he or she is paid; the union representative undertakes the role unpaid, for the betterment of the union and its members. While this argument has some ethical force, Hodgen's (1925: 4–5) distinction between workers' and vocational education based on purpose is more salient. In her view, vocational education – though no doubt enabling a few workers to advance as individuals – is essentially designed to suit the interests of capitalist business; workers' education is designed to achieve 'class advancement', or the advancement of some section of the working class. There is no question that, as far back as the 1920s, the curriculum in workers' education was in many ways a vocational one – but the knowledge and skills it sought to develop related to the vocation of serving labour, rather than capital.

To argue that the curriculum can be seen as a vocational one is not, of course, to imply that it can be abstracted from political debate. The evidence is clearly otherwise. The dispute between the WEA and the labour colleges is testimony from the first half of the twentieth century. During the second half, disputes also abounded. One view, developed in the 1980s chiefly by McIlroy, sees a long-run trend in workers' education in which:

> Trade union leaders have taken a greater interest in education, as an instrument of internal control, contributing to the creation of loyal and efficient functionaries, and as an instrument of external control guaranteeing bargains with governments . . . The growth of state aid has provided government with an element of direct control over union education.
>
> (McIlroy and Spencer 1989: 40)

On this view, during the 1960s and 1970s, the TUC became complicit in a state-led – 'corporatist' – project to reshape workplace trade unionism, and saw shop stewards' courses as useful in achieving this. State funding showed how far the TUC had become a trusted agent of the state, and enabled it to control the curriculum and stifle dissent (McIlroy 1990).

In many respects, this critique mirrors the earlier labour college critique of the WEA. Where the labour colleges argued that by accepting state funding the WEA would become catspaws of capital, 'muddling the minds of the workers', McIlroy argues that 'the TUC has tended to police [educational] provision to ensure that tutors and class stick within the "rules of the game" ' (McIlroy and Spencer 1989: 42). However, this approach distorts the complexities of the relations between the state and the trade union movement (Holford 1994). During the 1960s and 1970s, TUC views on industrial relations often overlapped with state priorities, but they were not identical; TUC and government views on union education varied; neither was monolithic.

Workers' education travelled a rocky road over the twentieth century. Devised and debated by some of labour's most active and creative thinkers – but also some of its most vitriolic orators – it sought initially to develop as a quasi-independent movement. From the beginnings, it was there to serve the labour movement; in effect it educated trade union and political activists in the conduct of their roles. From the 1920s – though somewhat more slowly than Hodgen predicted at the time – trade union aims began to supplant broader political goals. By the 1960s it was focusing more or less exclusively on educating union representatives. Areas of debate remain about the curriculum in such education. In general, workers' educators have emphasized what separates them from vocational education. This chapter has drawn attention to a shared feature: both seek to strengthen people's capacity to perform their roles. While the roles are distinct, and differences of purpose matter, exploring the parallels between workers' education and vocational education may also illuminate.

NOTES

1 Twentieth-century British trade unions provided virtually no education relating to their members' paid employment. The main exception, Unison's 'Return to Learn' programmes, developed only during the 1990s (Caldwell and Roberts 2003).
2 However, the labour college movement's residential college (the Central Labour College), formed by the Ruskin strikers, closed after two decades in 1929.
3 Holford (2003: 156) explains these figures, but erroneously excludes NCLC day- and weekend-school and postal course students, who are included here.
4 The background to this report is discussed more extensively in Holford (2003).
5 The TUC took over Ruskin College's Postal Courses department at the same time.
6 The report is discussed in more detail in Holford 1994: 144–150.
7 This is, of course, a simplification. The WEA continued to regard itself as delivering workers' education in important ways (though this was typically adult education directed at workers, rather than firmly embedded in the labour movement); the

1960s and 1970s saw important experiments with community education in working-class neighbourhoods; and so forth.

8 It was commonly estimated that shop stewards numbered between 100,000 and 200,000 in the 1960s (the latter being the TUC's own estimate) (Holford 1994: 77).

9 Public funds were phased out over a three-year period commencing in 1993 (Holford 1994: 231–232).

10 Indeed, the Oxford Department for External Studies ceased to offer TUC courses after about 1980.

REFERENCES

Bauman, Z. (1972) *Between Class and Élite: The Evolution of the British Labour Movement: A Sociological Study*, Manchester: Manchester University Press.

Burns, T. (1969) On the plurality of social systems, in T. Burns (ed.), *Industrial Man*, Harmondsworth: Penguin (pp. 232–249).

Caldwell, P. and Roberts, S.K. (2003) Workplace education and the WEA after 1964, in S.K. Roberts (ed.), *'A Ministry of Enthusiasm': Centenary Essays on the Workers' Educational Association*, London: Pluto Press.

Citrine, W. M. (1921) *The Labour Chairman and Speaker's Companion. Guide to the Conduct of Trades Unions and Labour Meetings*, London: Labour Publishing Co.

Citrine, W. M. (1939) *A.B.C. of Chairmanship: All About Meetings and Conferences*, London: Co-operative Printing Society.

Clegg, H. and Adams, R. (1959) *Trade Union Education with Special Reference to the Pilot Areas: A Report for the Workers' Educational Association*, London: WEA.

Cmd. [JAKH1] 321 (1919) *Ministry of Reconstruction: Adult Education Committee. Final Report*, London: HMSO.

Corfield, A.J. (1969) *Epoch in Workers' Education: A History of the Workers' Educational Trade Union Committee*, London: WEA.

Fieldhouse, R. (1985) Conformity and contradiction in English Responsible Body Adult Education 1925–1950, *Studies in the Education of Adults*, 17(2), pp. 121–134.

Fieldhouse, R. (1987) The 1908 report: antidote to class struggle?, in S. Harrop (ed.), *Oxford and Working Class Education*, Nottingham: University of Nottingham (pp. 30–47).

Fieldhouse, R. (1990) Bouts of suspicion: political controversies in adult education 1925–1944, in B. Simon (ed.), *The Search for Enlightenment: The Working Class and Adult Education in the Twentieth Century*, London: Lawrence & Wishart (pp. 153–172).

Griggs, C. (1983) *The Trades Union Congress and the Struggle for Education 1868–1925*, Lewes, Falmer Press.

Hobsbawm, E.J. (1984) Should poor people organize?, in E.J. Hobsbawm, *Worlds of Labour: Further Studies in the History of Labour*, London, Weidenfeld & Nicolson (pp. 282–296).

Hodgen, M.T. (1925) *Workers' Education in England and the United States*, London, Kegan Paul, Trench, Trubner & Co.

Hodgkin, T. (1941) Some war-time developments in adult education, *Rewley House Papers*, 2(4).

Holford, J. (1994) *Union Education in Britain: A TUC Activity*, Nottingham, University of Nottingham.

Holford, J. (2003) Unions, adult education and post-war citizenship: the WEA and the construction of trade union education, in S.K. Roberts (ed.), 'A Ministry of Enthusiasm': Centenary Essays on the Workers' Educational Association. London: Pluto Press (pp. 153–175).

Holton, R. (1976) British Syndicalism, 1900–1914: Myths and Realities, London, Pluto Press.

Hopkins, P.G.H. (1985) Workers' Education: An International Perspective, Milton Keynes: Open University Press.

Jennings, B. (1973) Albert Mansbridge, Leeds: Leeds University Press.

Jennings, B. (1976) Albert Mansbridge and English Adult Education, Hull: Hull University Department of Adult Education.

Jennings, B. (1987) The making of the Oxford Report, in S. Harrop (ed.), Oxford and Working Class Education, Nottingham: University of Nottingham (pp. 11–29).

McIlroy, J. (1990) Trade union education for a change, in B. Simon (ed.), The Search for Enlightenment: The Working Class and Adult Education in the Twentieth Century, London: Lawrence & Wishart (pp. 244–275).

McIlroy, J. and Spencer, B. (1989) Waves in British Workers Education, Convergence, 22(2/3), 33–45.

Maclean, J. (1978) In the Rapids of Revolution: Essays, Articles and Letters 1902–23 (ed. N. Milton), London: Allison and Busby.

Millar, J.P.M. (1979) The Labour College Movement, London: NCLC Publishing Society.

Mooney, T. (1979) J.M. Mactavish, General Secretary of the WEA 1916–1927: The Man and His Ideas, Liverpool: WEA Liverpool Branch.

Pollins, H. (1984) The History of Ruskin College, Oxford: Ruskin College Library, Occasional Publications, no. 3.

Roper J.I. (1942) Trade Unionism and the New Social Order, London: Workers' Educational Association.

Stocks, M. (1953) The Workers' Educational Association: The First Fifty Years, London: Allen and Unwin.

Trades Union Congress (TUC) (1963) Report of the 95th Annual Trades Union Congress, London: TUC.

Trades Union Congress (TUC) (1968a) Training Shop Stewards, London: TUC.

Trades Union Congress (TUC) (1968b) Report of the 100th Annual Trades Union Congress, London: TUC.

Trades Union Congress (TUC) (2005) TUC Education Annual Report 2005 http://www.tuc.org.uk/learning/tuc–10781-f0.cfm (Accessed 15 Jan. 2006).

University of Oxford (1970) Report of the Committee on Extra-mural Studies. Supplement no. 3 to the Oxford University Gazette 100, March.

Workers' Educational Association (WEA) (1942) Adult Education after the War, unpublished confidential memorandum to the Board of Education, WEA National Archive, London: London Metropolitan University, WEA/CENTRAL/4/1/2/3.

Workers' Educational Association (WEA) (1944) The W.E.A. and the Working-class Movement, London: WEA.

Workers' Educational Association (WEA) (1953) Trade Union Education: A Report from a Working Party set up by the WEA [and chaired by A. Creech Jones], London, WEA.

Workers' Educational Trades Union Committee (WETUC) (1944) Workers' Education and the Trade Union Movement. A Post-war Policy, report of a special sub-committee, London: WETUC

Index